MW01620807

WILLIAM HAWKINS

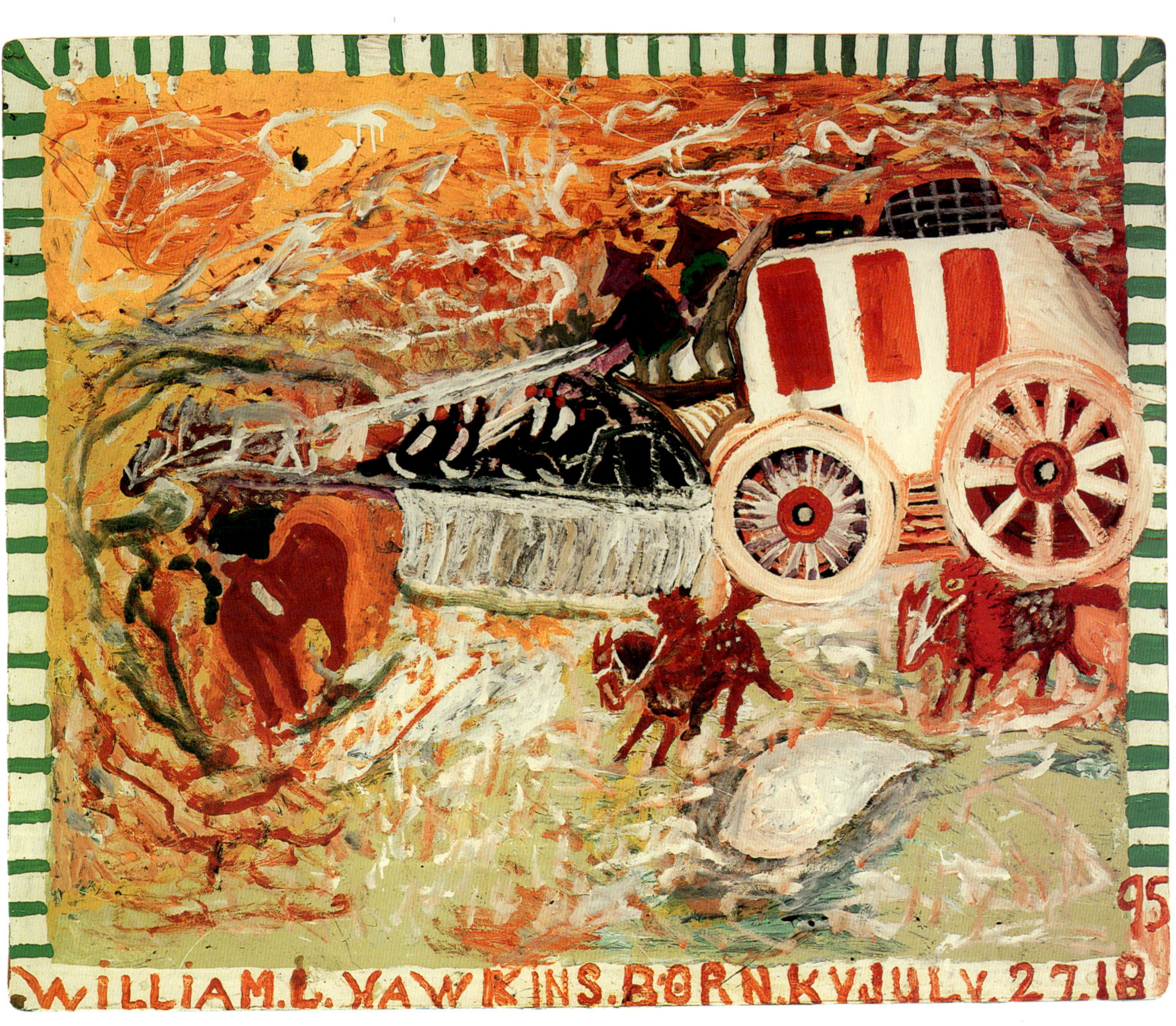

Overland Stagecoach, 1986

Enamel on Masonite, 48″ x 60″

WILLIAM HAWKINS
PAINTINGS

Frank Maresca and Roger Ricco

ALFRED A. KNOPF NEW YORK 1997

Every child born got a gift.

William L. Hawkins

This book is dedicated to all the self-taught and outsider artists that we have known, whose genius, ingenuity, and creative spirit have taught us so much about life.

This Is a Borzoi Book
Published by Alfred A. Knopf, Inc.

 Published in the United States by Alfred A. Knopf, Inc., New York, and simultaneously in Canada by Random House of Canada Limited, Toronto. Distributed by Random House, Inc., New York.

http://www.randomhouse.com/

ISBN 0-679-45075-0
LC 97-73824

Manufactured in Hong Kong

First Edition

This book was planned, prepared, and produced by Constance Sullivan Editions.

"YOU WANT TO SEE SOMETHIN' PRETTY?"

When I first walked into the small gallery in Columbus, Ohio, in 1984, I didn't much like what I saw of William Hawkins' painting. But this aversion was to be the root of revelation.

Lee Garrett and Roger McLane, two Columbus artists, had mounted an exhibition of work by two black Ohio artists, Morris Newman and William Hawkins. Thanks to Garrett and McLane, people were already buying Hawkins' work. I wanted to see for myself. As an artist and a teacher, I had experienced a sort of conversion to self-taught art when I saw the Hemphill Collection in Omaha the year before, but I was not prepared for what confronted me here. "Confronted" is the right word. The paintings were executed on what seemed to be downright ugly surfaces—shabby plywood and Masonite packing-crate panels, pieces of sheet metal, an old door, a tabletop. All were thickly and, to my eye, carelessly painted. The colors were explosive. I wanted to run away.

But the pictures wouldn't leave me alone, and a few months later, as I was planning an exhibition in Columbus, Lee Garrett took me to meet William Hawkins in his apartment above the Manhattan Barber Shop. It was a dark and dusty labyrinth, cluttered with old furniture and objects foraged from the streets. On a makeshift table near the window was an unfinished painting. It glowed in the dismal light. The completed ones that stood nearby were incandescent. They dwarfed the space of their origin, miraculously incongruous. After that, I saw the artist repeatedly, and in 1987 I began documenting his life and work. I recorded hundreds of hours of conversation and took thousands of photographs, including many of him at work on his paintings. In a sense, I became his Boswell until he died in 1990, at the age of ninety-four. It never seemed like a strange way to spend my time. Hawkins was the most entertaining raconteur I've ever met, but more than that, he was a remarkable human being—an unstoppable creative force and a person whose life represented essential patterns of American experience. It's a life worth thinking about.

It seems to me that three aspects of Hawkins' life put us in touch with the sources of his art. The first is Hawkins' energy. The second is his childhood in the hill country of Kentucky. The third is Columbus, Ohio, where he lived for almost seventy years, but always in a kind of exile.

The paintings should have tipped me off about the energy. When I met him, Hawkins was living in a section of Columbus called, for gentrification purposes, Old Town East. In fact, it was a ghetto where the struggle to make a living was punctuated by crime and frustration. The fact that he had reached the age of ninety testified to his resiliency. He was only five feet four, white haired and toothless; I called him "Grandpa." He could still do heavy manual labor, and it dawned on me how physically powerful and assertive he was. He reminded me of Picasso. He never hesitated when he worked and never stopped painting until the day of the stroke that finally took his life. He considered his virility a badge of honor and claimed to have fathered at least thirty-two children.

After he had made enough money from his painting to buy his own house in Old Town East in 1985, he would often set up on his porch and work outside. One day he called out to a young passerby, "You want to see somethin' pretty, come up here, son. I want you to be an artist. Come up here so you learn." In a tough neighborhood, assertiveness is a survival skill, but Hawkins had felt he was special from the time he was growing up. If there were horses to be broken, he broke the toughest, and he was the best trapper in the county. When he played baseball, his pitches were so fast they couldn't be seen. When he daydreamed, he predicted the Wright brothers' flight, and when he played the mouth harp, he could make it talk.

Perhaps this sense of being special came from the strength of his maternal grandmother, who raised him, or perhaps from his experience of nearly being struck by lightning as a teenager and living to tell about it. Or perhaps, as Hawkins always maintained, his gifts came from being racially "crossed up"—a mixture of black, white, and Native American. In any event, a sense of destiny was there in his art's certainty. And it was there in his dealings with everyone. "There are a million artists out there," he said, "and I try to be the greatest of them all."

William Hawkins was born in the rolling hills of Kentucky on July 27, 1895, as he tells you on virtually every painting. His brother, Vertia, was born two years later, and when their mother died soon after, the boys' father took them to Union City to live with their twice-widowed maternal grandmother, Mary Mason Runyon Scudder. Her prosperous farm was the legacy of her father, Frank Scudder, a white landowner who felt responsible for his illegitimate child, born to his black housekeeper. Mary Mason Runyon Scudder was the most important person in William Hawkins' life. She lived by some accounts to be 105, and she took over raising the two young boys at age 69. Her word was law, and if the boys didn't do as expected, "Grandmother would tear you up." Yet what she really gave the artist was an imaginative geography. It centered around the farmhouse.

For a country homestead, the house was opulent, with thick rugs, framed pictures and fine furniture, mirrors, ornamental fans, oil lamps, and a foot-pump organ. It was also a place of strong sensations and deep impressions. Here Mary Mason Runyon Scudder spun the yarn she used for sewing quilts, which she assembled from her vast collection of neckties. Upstairs, she dried sweet potatoes on racks. In the kitchen she commanded a large and elaborate stove, which the young William learned to tend. Hawkins could recall all this as if he were standing in the parlor, and I can imagine him as a boy immersed in the vivid intensity of the place. Unlike many folk artists, he rarely painted so-called memory pictures. I think he had the essential memories of color, of the look and feel of things, deep within him, and they shaped everything he made.

Animals may have drawn him into making art, as they have done since prehistory In good times, farms like the Scudder homestead could be gardens of Eden, where all manner of man (black and white), bird, and beast lived together. This homestead also played an important role in the local breeding of Peavine horses, and William and Vertia became equine experts early on. Hawkins also spent what time he had to himself hunting and trapping. Once I visited him at his house in Columbus and noticed he had built a small structure that looked like a birdhouse in the backyard. In fact, it was a squirrel house. "Some of them squirrels have no place to go," he told me.

Animals were among the first things he drew, according to Vertia—especially horses. Even though he worked from photographs and, when he was young, from other renderings, he invested his felt knowledge in his creations. In *Buffalo #6* (page 45), Hawkins intuits the mass of the creature; in the *Red Dog Running* paintings (page 21), the creature's speed and motion. In many paintings he captures the sentient otherness of animals. He would use any means to get the effect he wanted, to "do something wonderful." In the astonishing *Dragon Snake* (page 52), flexible tubing creates the creature, lifting it out of the picture and into life.

At nineteen, Hawkins began a two-year affair with a young neighbor that resulted in her pregnancy. The family took council, and his aunt Lillian was so suspicious of interlopers trying to work their way into the family that she ruled out marriage and ordered William to go north to relatives in Ohio. According to Hawkins, she used a loaded shotgun as a persuader. I don't want to push the biblical parallel too far, but from the day he arrived in Columbus in 1916, Hawkins lived the truth of that phrase about earning one's living "from the sweat of thy brow." His third-grade education hadn't taught him to read, and he had no experience of a large city, especially its prejudice, poverty, and crime. What he had was enormous confidence.

Until Hawkins began to sell his paintings for serious money in the mid-1980s, he followed the simple philosophy of doing whatever he could to make a living. He worked twice for the Buckeye Steel Casting Company and served in the army in World War I. He was married in 1916 and divorced in 1923, and, much later, ran numbers and operated a brothel. He was a truck driver until well into his eighties. From this experience, he developed a fund of local anecdotes and a feeling for architectural drama. Midwestern state capitals have an imposing public face, and Hawkins loved the grandeur of Columbus. He tried to match it in his work. "Don't draw those old junk houses," he once advised another artist, "draw something no other man would think about—them big fine temples and things."

He also worked for a time in his thirties or forties as a "photographer," with a cheap box camera, and never lost his awe of the camera's ability to capture reality. Almost all his paintings originated with photographs or illustrations, usually culled from magazines and newspapers. He collected them over decades, storing them in a precious suitcase. "Research," he called the culling. He did it for hours on end, looking for an image to strike a chord, to give him a gift, to provoke him to "improve" it. He also went through his suitcase over and over, as if it were a vast theater of memory. It was the silent forge of his imagination.

He'd known as early as the 1930s that he could make money from drawing pictures, since most people couldn't afford photographs or studio portraits. But he probably started painting only much later, perhaps as a consequence of collecting cast-off items, including old house paint and boards. He never stopped collecting, even when he didn't need to, because old habits die hard. "You're steppin' over money if you don't pick them up," he admonished me, and his house was a wonderland of motors, wheels, sheet metal, pipes, and appliances he might be able to fix. "Shit, I'm nothing but a junk man," he once remarked.

Of course he wasn't. Lee Garrett was having his hair cut in the Manhattan Barber Shop in 1981 when he heard about the artist who lived upstairs. Hawkins' apartment was crammed with paintings. Garrett entered one of these paintings in the amateur division of the 1982 Ohio State Fair. It won top prize. Garrett did everything he could to get Hawkins better materials and to give the world a chance to see his work. He mounted exhibitions and took slides to New York in 1983. Success was just a matter of time—until enough people began to have the experience that we had been having in Columbus.

People around Hawkins stole from him and extorted money through one ruse or another—often just by appealing to his generosity. Despite his gallery contract, he sold paintings to whomever wanted to buy them. This drove to distraction all of us who wanted to see him get what he deserved. He didn't care. He just kept working, trying new techniques, growing. He said, "There's nothing to do but sit around and get better."

Gary Schwindler

THE ARTIST REMEMBERED

William Hawkins was the first self-taught artist our gallery represented, and he changed our lives profoundly. A brilliant painter, he was the catalyst for a whole new focus in the world of folk art. In the nine years that we knew him, he drew us—none too gently—into his world, challenging our capacity for surprise and joy. We don't believe that Hawkins ever really knew our names. He referred to us simply as "the boys with the museum in New York."

Every major movement in art has a few key linchpin artists who are instrumental in defining it. When one meets such an artist, one knows that things will never be the same again. Hawkins was that artist for us. The power and clarity of his art helped us to discover exactly what we were all about.

As dealers, collectors, and lovers of the impossible, we had, in the early phase of our partnership, focused our attention on what has come to be considered traditional (but certainly not conservative) folk art. We favored an edgy aesthetic that is difficult to define, falling for rare works that combined a strong sense of magic, mystery, and design. Hawkins' paintings had all of those things; we recognized that the minute we saw them piled up against the wall of his cluttered Columbus apartment in 1983. He made us realize that the same classic qualities we had come to value in art from an earlier time might be found in work by a contemporary artist. This was a revelation, but also an intimidating challenge.

Like the other great self-taught artists—such as William Edmondson and Bill Traylor, whose work was recognized somewhat earlier—Hawkins has proved that great art can emerge in the most unlikely circumstances. Yet unlike that elite group of folk "masters," Hawkins responded to a modern, media-driven environment. While he was connected, if only by his age, to an earlier craft tradition, he was in fact most inspired by the vernacular of popular culture and the reproductions of great art that he came across in discarded magazines fished out of Dumpsters. Although he was completely removed from the intellectual milieu of art history, he was engaged in a joyful battle with it. Outdated myths of folk purity aside, we firmly believe that these cultural circumstances which influenced his work by no means compromised his status as a true master.

As our relationship with Hawkins developed, and as his work became increasingly appreciated within the art community, we found ourselves visiting him in Columbus several times each year. Hawkins kept us busy indeed; with nine decades of living under his belt, he had an amazing ability to level sage advice on any given topic. Hawkins was a master storyteller. Any time he had an audience, he had a story to tell. The notion of chronological time was irrelevant to him. He would typically jump from telling stories about his youth in Kentucky to reminiscing about a painting he'd worked on to providing a thoroughly detailed description of the previous day's storm that would capture the way the snow had fallen and the animated character of the wind.

Witnessing Hawkins at work in his dark, cluttered home was an amazing experience. He would begin by laying a four-foot-square board flat on a table or on his bed, and then unhesitatingly pour paint onto the surface, proceeding to push and prod the paint until it covered the entire surface. He used only one brush, gripped firmly in his left hand, to create his brilliantly polychromatic paintings. Referring to his friend and fellow artist Lee Garrett, he once said, "My manager bought me a whole set of brushes—but I don't need but one! I just wipe it off, don't need to wash it or nothing—just wipe it off and keep painting!" This one brush, worn right down to the metal rim, had only a few crumpled bristles remaining; it was nothing short of a miracle to watch him conjure the sturdy figure of a rhino, or a horse, or the Columbus State House, with such unlikely tools.

Walking down the street with him was to take a journey through his eyes. Often he would be oblivious to our presence and become lost in talking to himself while scanning the ground for interesting debris: a scrap of paper, a button, a piece of wire. A trash container would inevitably provide endless treasures: rejected cans of house paint, a stained magazine photo (which would later resurface in one of his paintings), or a heavy rusted valve from an old pump. Each object was worthy of at least fifteen minutes of thorough historical and technical description, his curiosity matched evenly by his impulse to instruct.

Hawkins often enticed us with what we might hope to expect, should we be so smart as to sustain a working relationship with him: "The children will come into your museum and when they see my painting they won't believe that such an old man could make such pictures.... Every time you get my paintings at your museum you will never expect what you are going to see. You're always going to be surprised by what you get." True to his word, every six to eight weeks a new group of paintings would arrive at the gallery in New York. These were some of the most exciting moments in all our years of dealing art. After stripping off the plastic wrapping, we would be confronted with rhinos, horses, buildings, and snakes, each one more brilliant than the next.

Several years after Hawkins' death, his prediction again rang true when we brought a group of teenagers from the Harlem Horizon School to see a Hawkins show at the gallery. They had just begun to discover the possibilities that art had to offer, and had recently begun painting. They reacted to Hawkins' paintings with wonder; their confidence in their own abilities soared when they realized that an old black man had created these works hanging in a SoHo gallery. One young man laughed, exclaiming: "If that old man can paint this stuff and sell it, then I'm going to be a millionaire!" Several years later, a physically handicapped boy working in this program entitled one of his paintings *Homage to William Hawkins.* This remarkable influence on a younger, emerging generation of artists is one of Hawkins' lasting legacies.

Hawkins greatly enjoyed the attention and praise that he received for his artistic merits. He knew that his talent made him unique, setting him apart from his peers, and this made him proud. Yet his sense of artistic prowess was challenged the day we realized that he lived not far from the barbershop of Elijah Pierce, the well-respected self-taught artist active in Columbus at the same time. Although the two lived within walking distance of one another, they had never met.

Pierce was a barber by trade, and his shop had become somewhat famous as a "museum" for his biblical wood carvings. One day we suggested a visit to Pierce's museum, and Hawkins readily agreed.

When we reached Pierce's shop, the two politely shook hands. The contrast in physical type was dramatic. Pierce was a tall, elegant gentleman in his nineties. Having been a barber most of his life, he displayed an impeccable sense of style, wearing a suit vest and tie, and sporting a gold watch chain and neatly groomed nails. His demeanor was one of virtue, confidence, and refinement.

Hawkins, only two years younger and nearly a foot shorter, was a gnarled junkyard dog by comparison. Small and stocky, with a shock of wild gray hair and thick black glasses, he had covered the front of his tuxedo shirt with tie tacks. His plaid pants, held up with bright red suspenders, were splattered with paint.

Hawkins proceeded to move quickly from carving to carving, stopping to look at the framed awards and certificates that Pierce had received in recognition of his work and mounted on his wall. There were several photographs of Pierce with various presidents and dignitaries, as well as framed articles published in national newspapers. Although Hawkins could not read these documents, he quickly recognized their importance.

"What you doin' these things for?" Hawkins demanded of Pierce. "I could make five paintings in the time it took you to carve one of these things!" Pierce listened patiently, gazing down at his colleague with a look one might give an alien, should an alien attempt communication. After a few moments of awkward silence, we suggested to Hawkins that it might be a good idea to leave. The moment we reached the street he took off ahead of us, and we asked him where he was going. The answer came back: "To paint ... I can beat that old man!"

Roger Ricco with Laura K. Wiley

WILLIAM HAWKINS

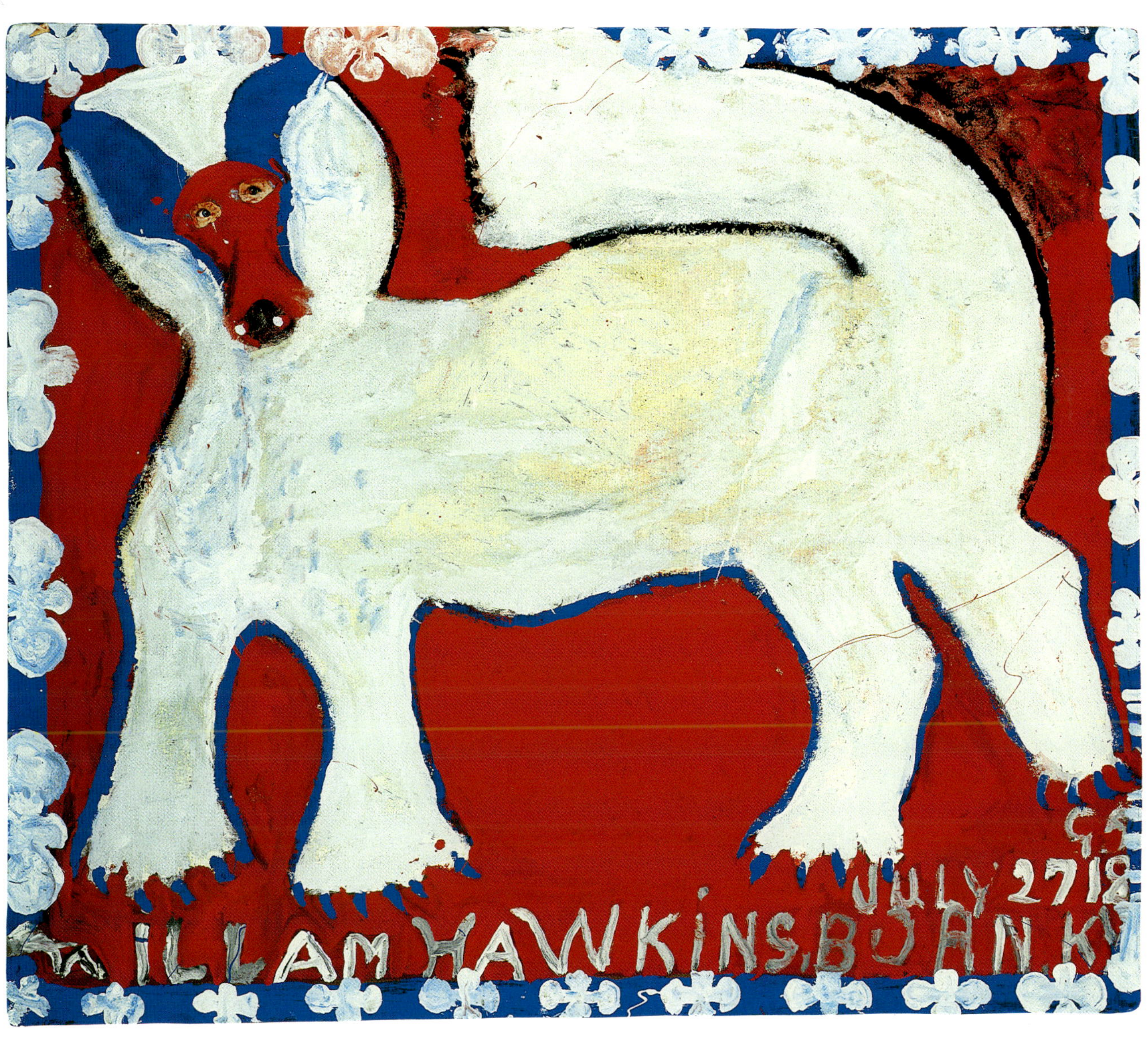

White Dog, 1985

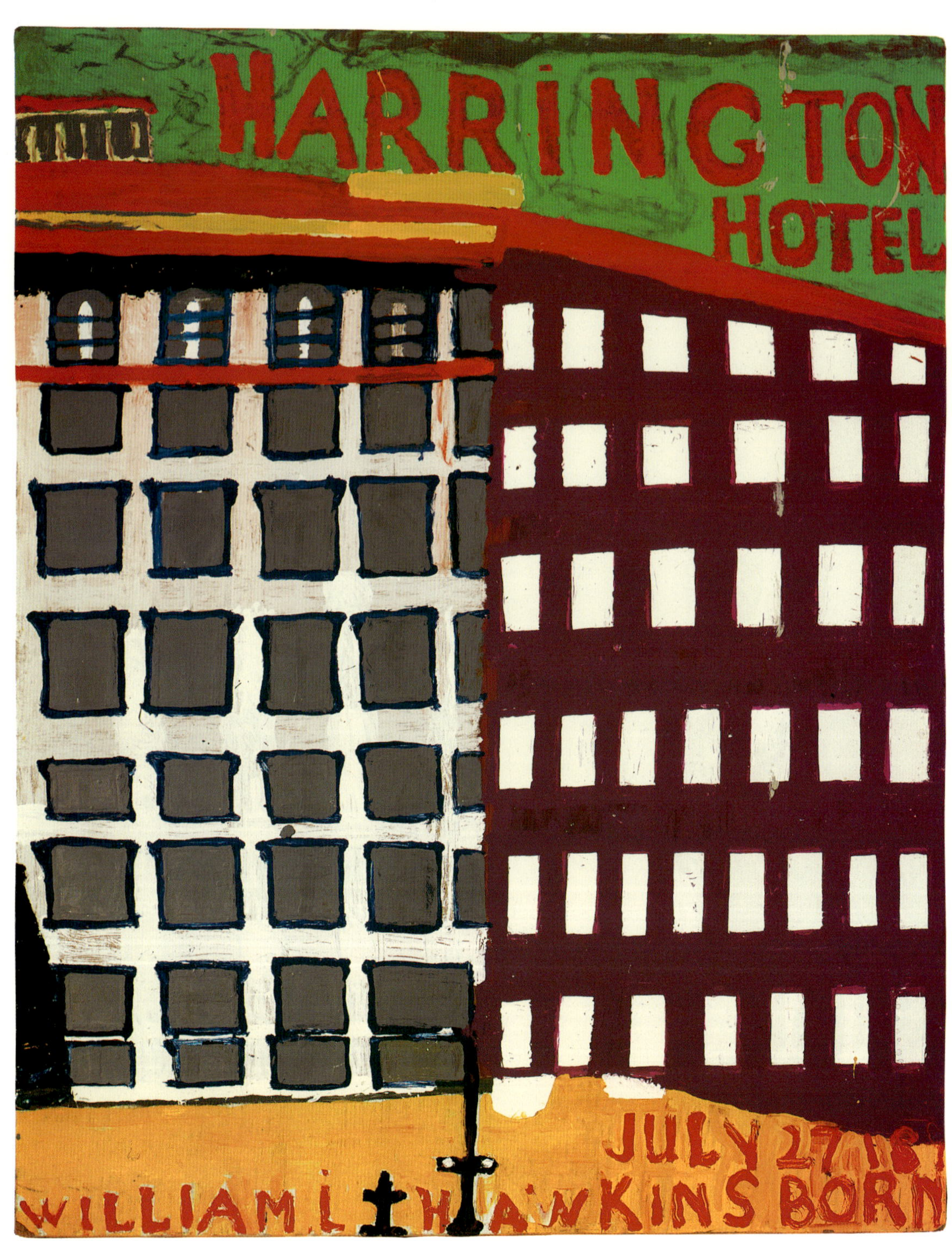

Harrington Hotel, 1987

Enamel on Masonite, 58″ x 46½″

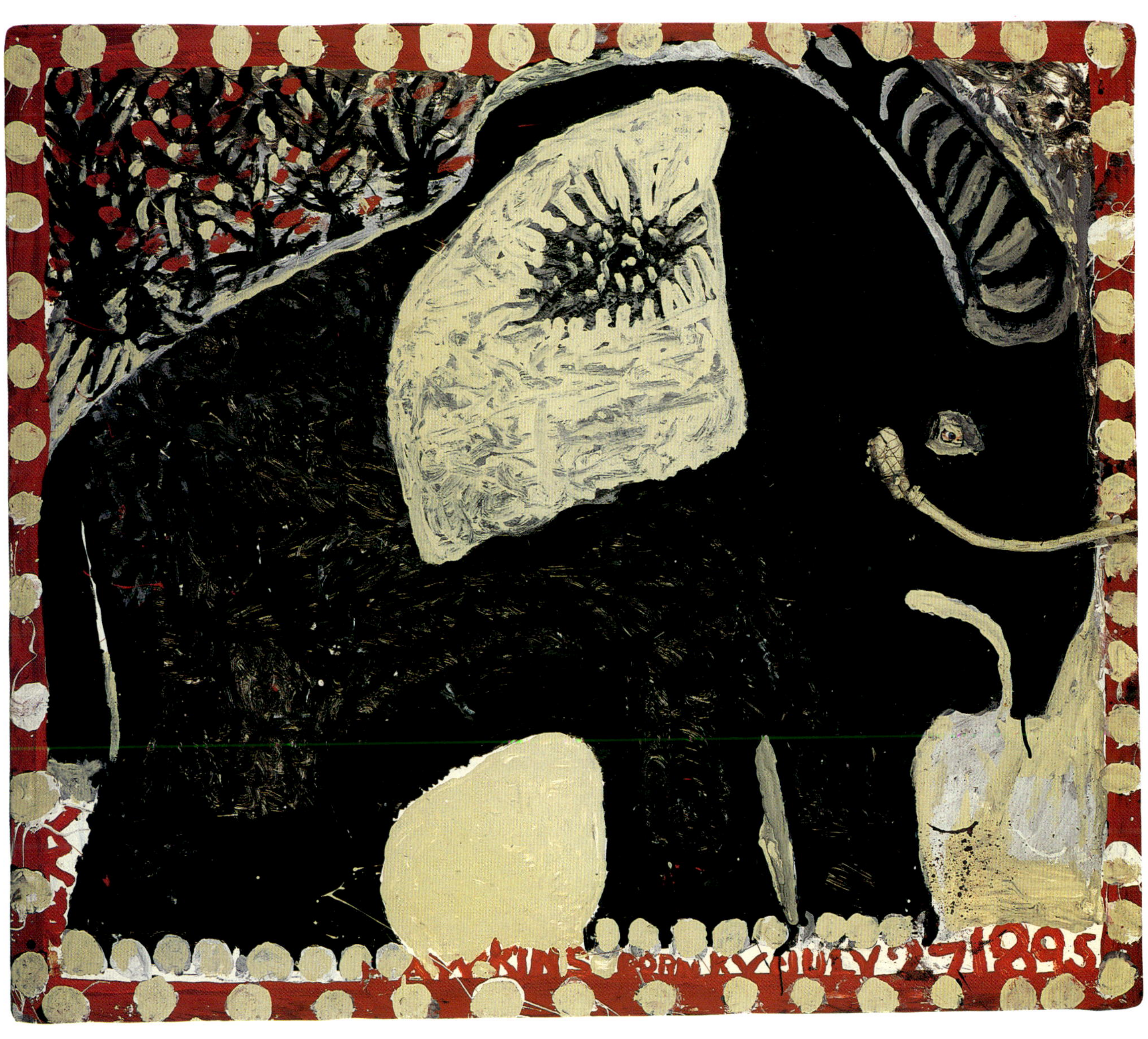

Jumbo Elephant #3, 1989

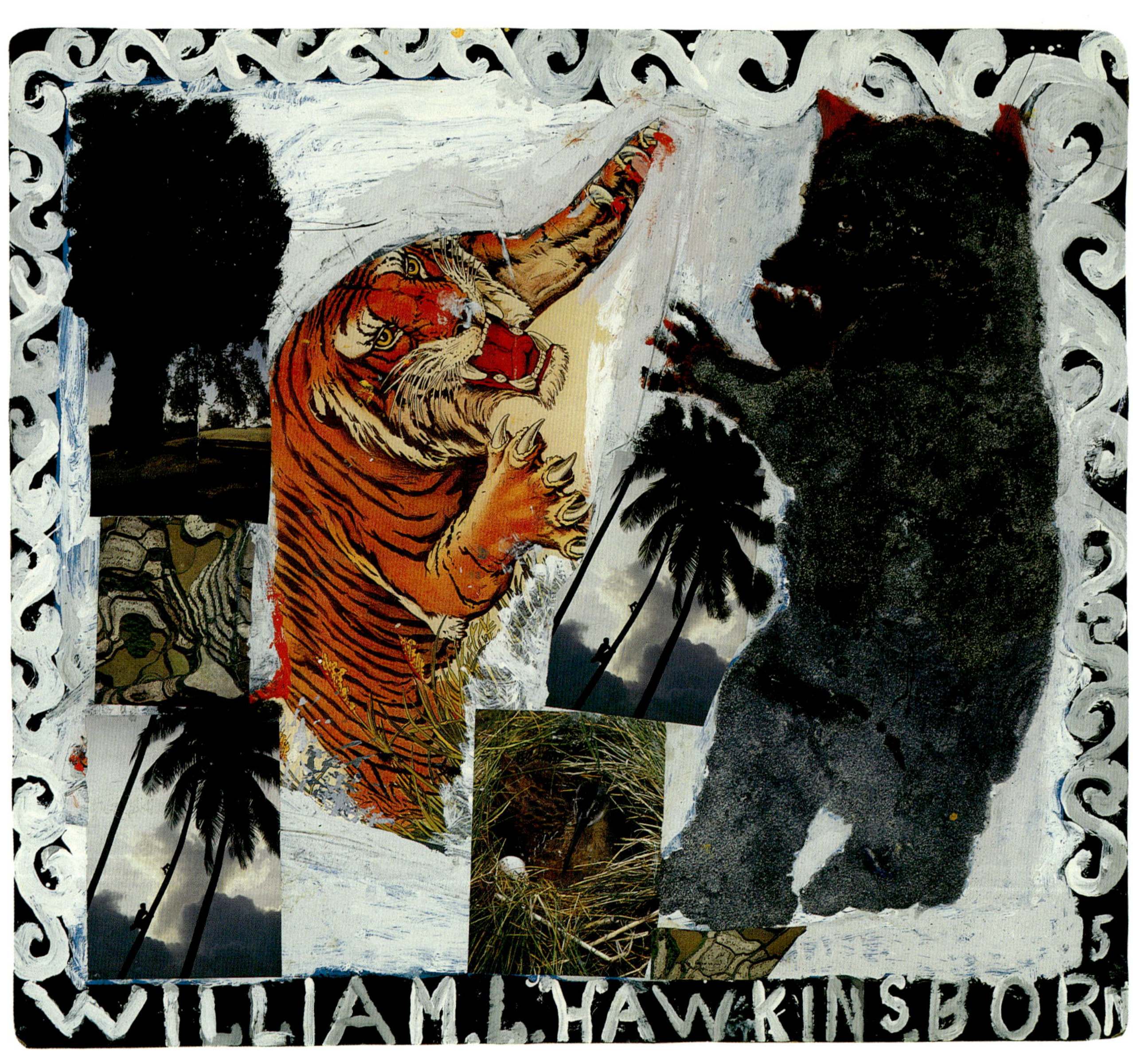

Tiger and Bear, 1989

Enamel, collage, and mixed media on Masonite, 42″ x 48″

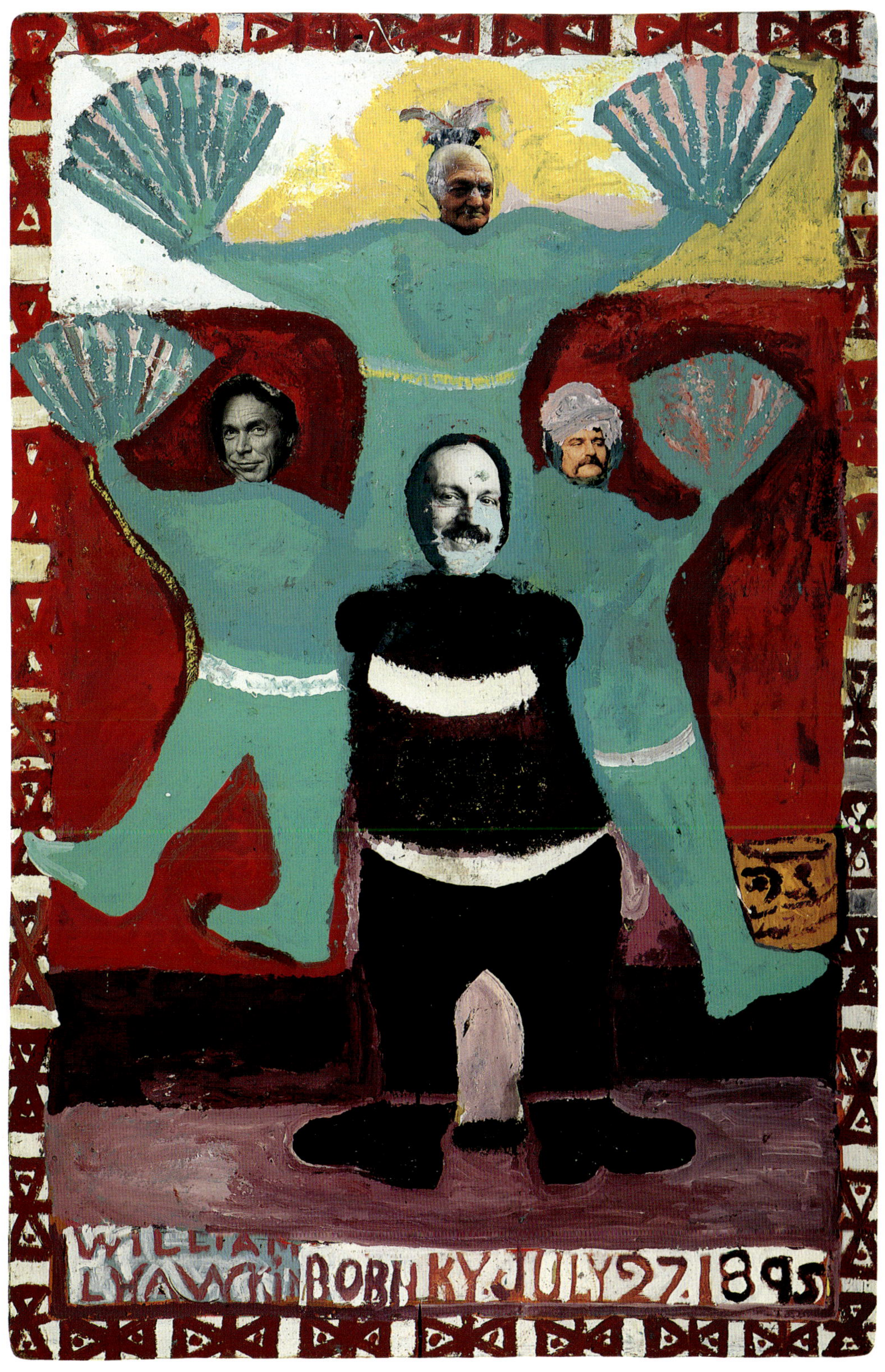

Acrobats, 1988

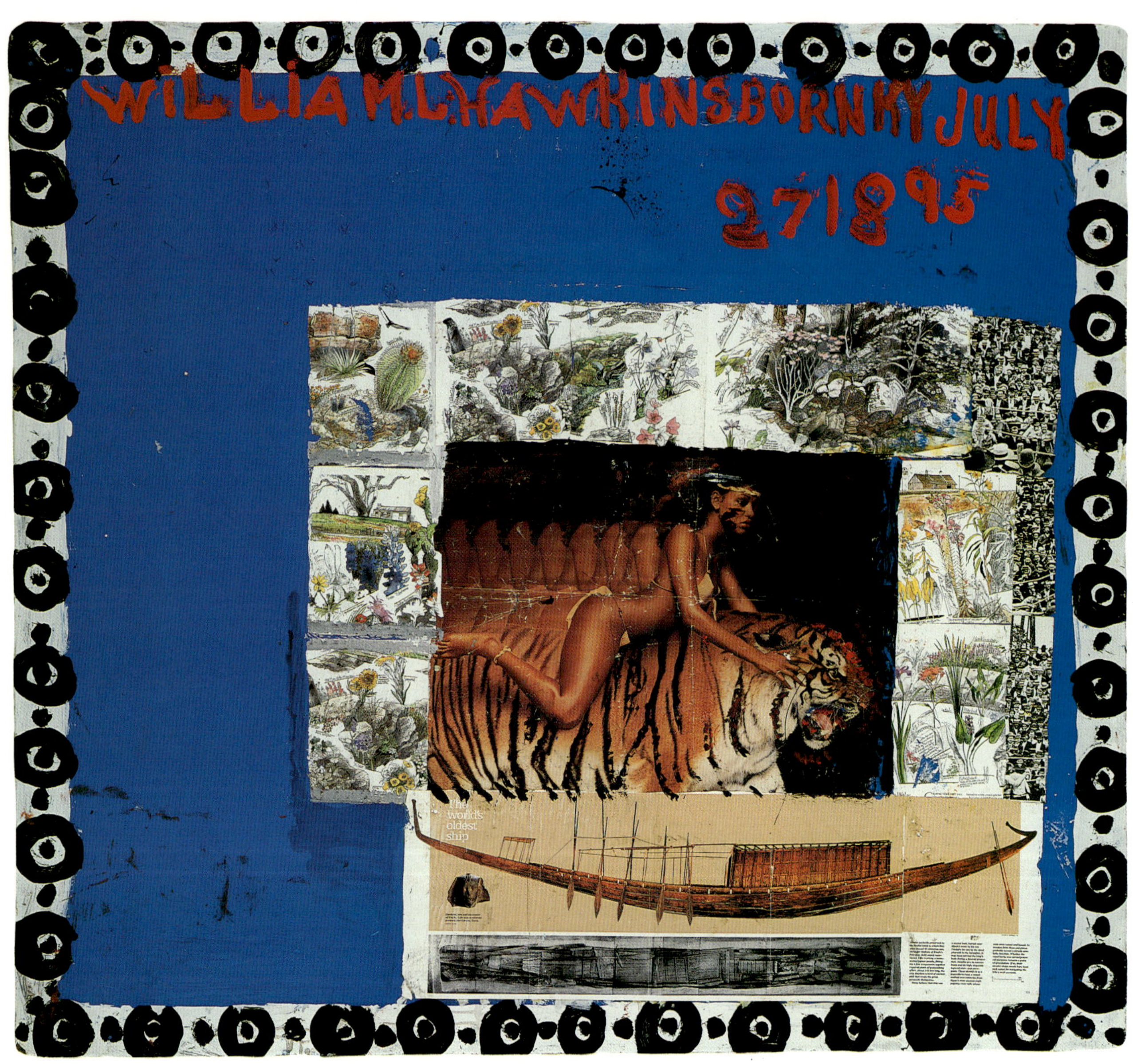

Woman on Tiger Collage, 1989

Enamel and collage on Masonite, 48″ x 54″

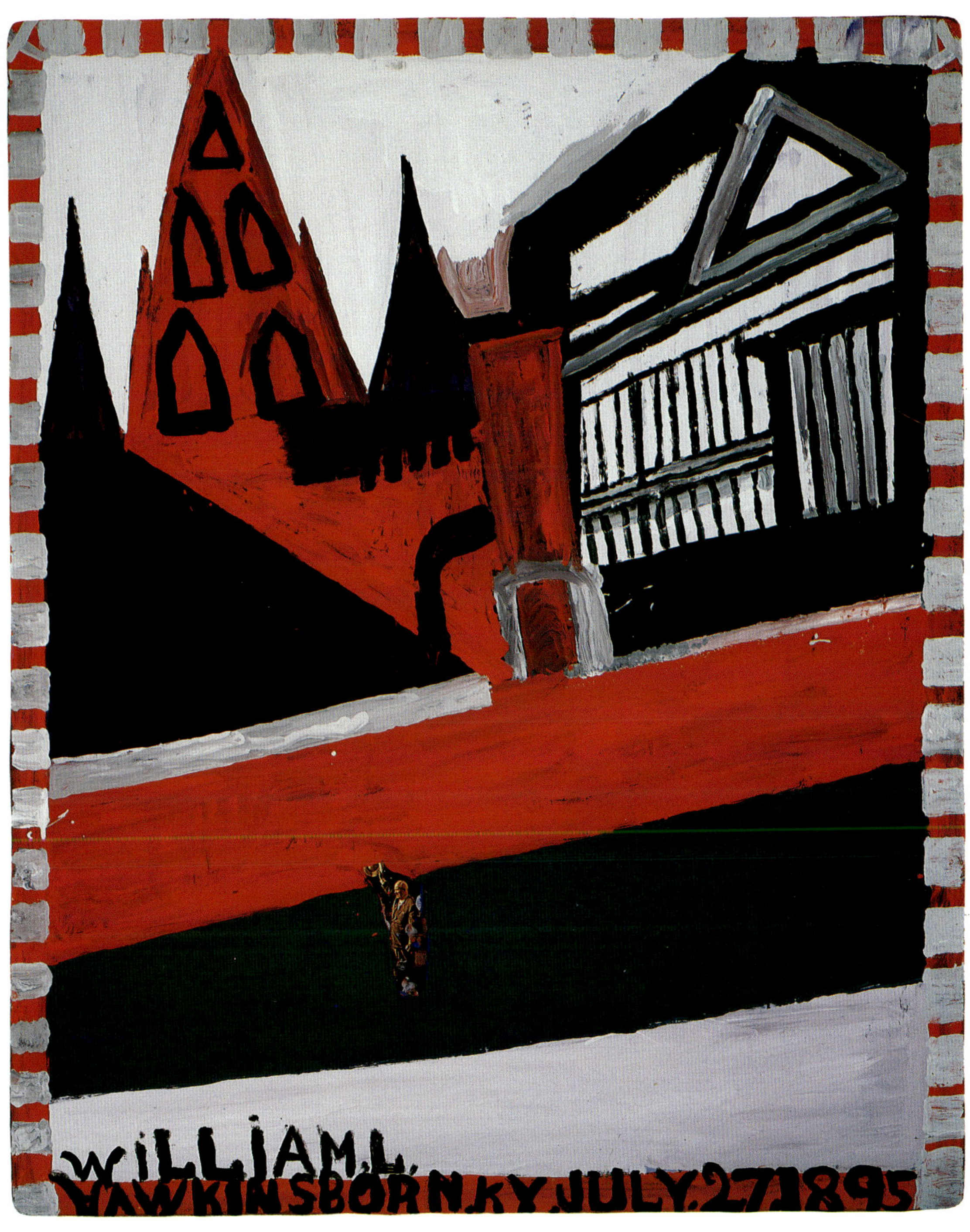

Krushchev Collage, 1989

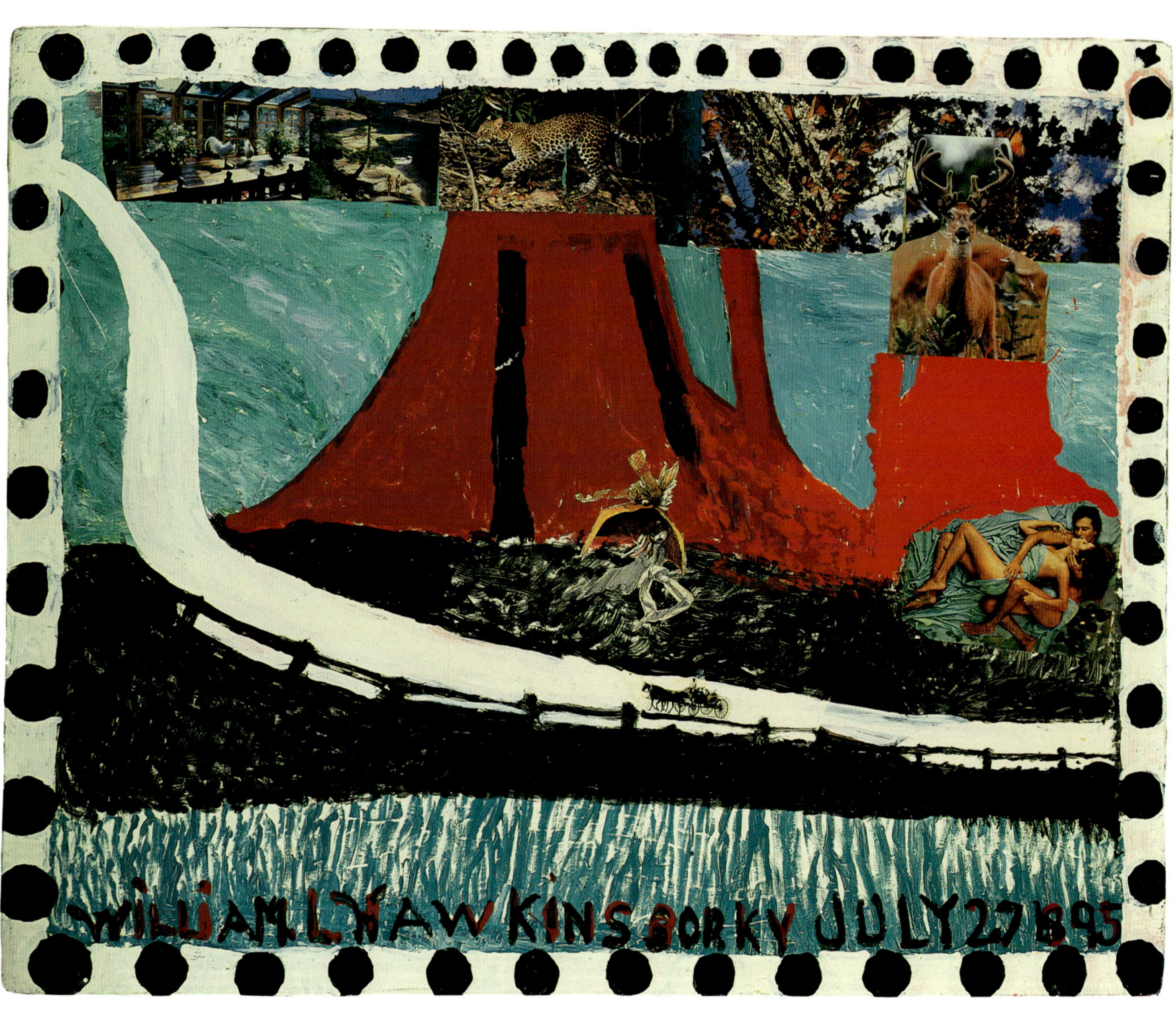

Monument Valley Collage, 1987

Enamel and collage on Masonite, 48″ x 60″

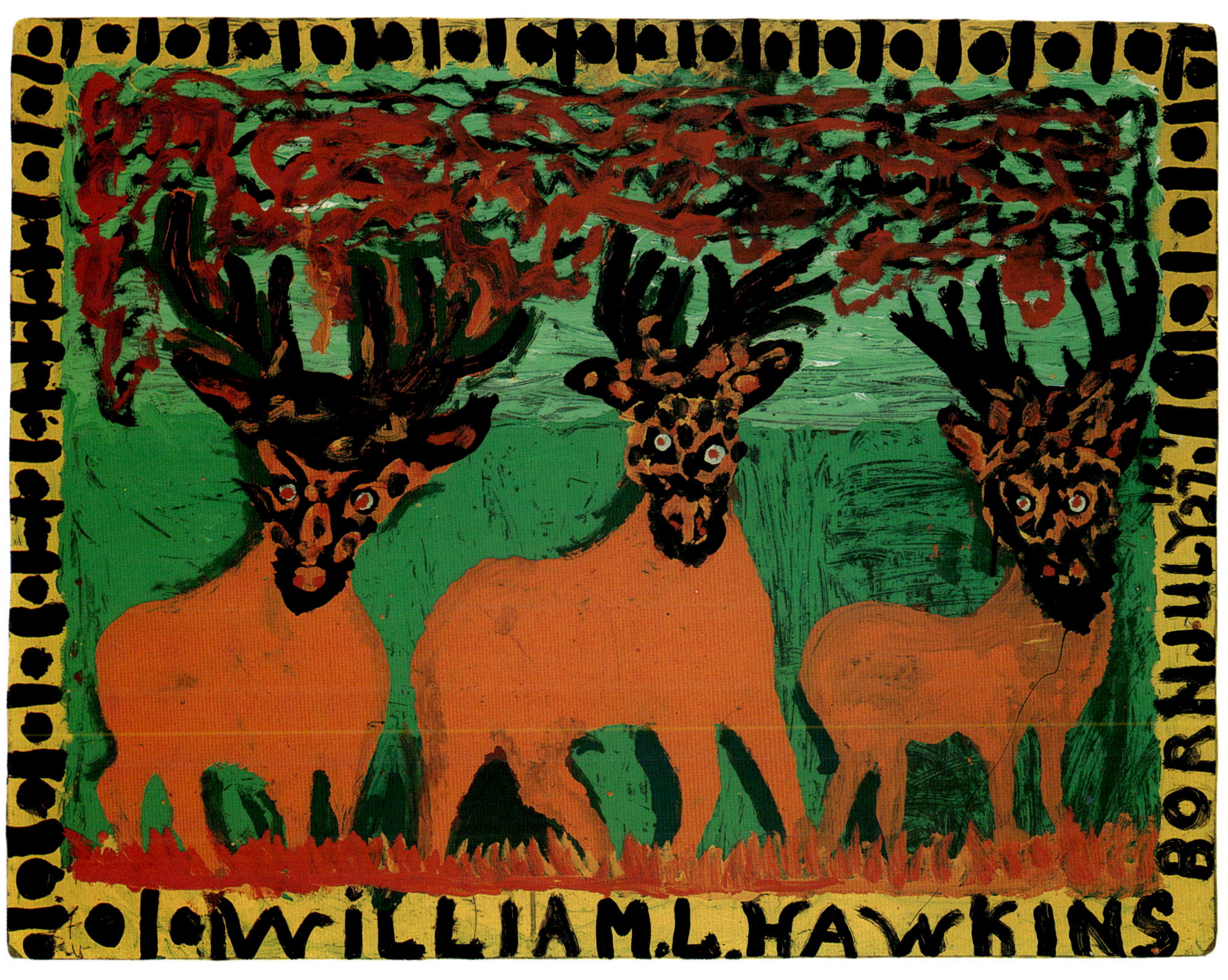

Three Deer, 1988

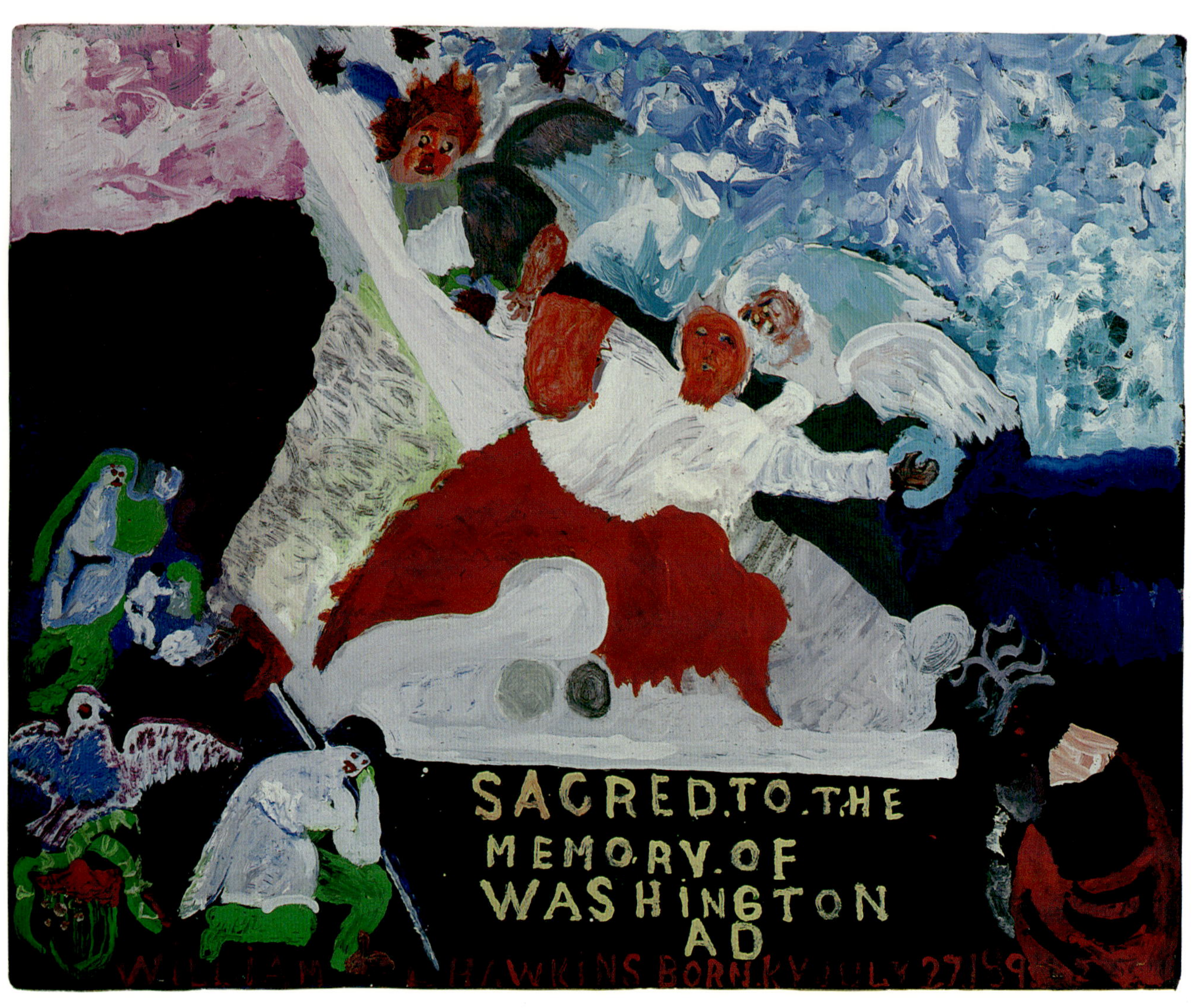

Apotheosis of Washington, 1985

Enamel on Masonite, 38″ x 48″

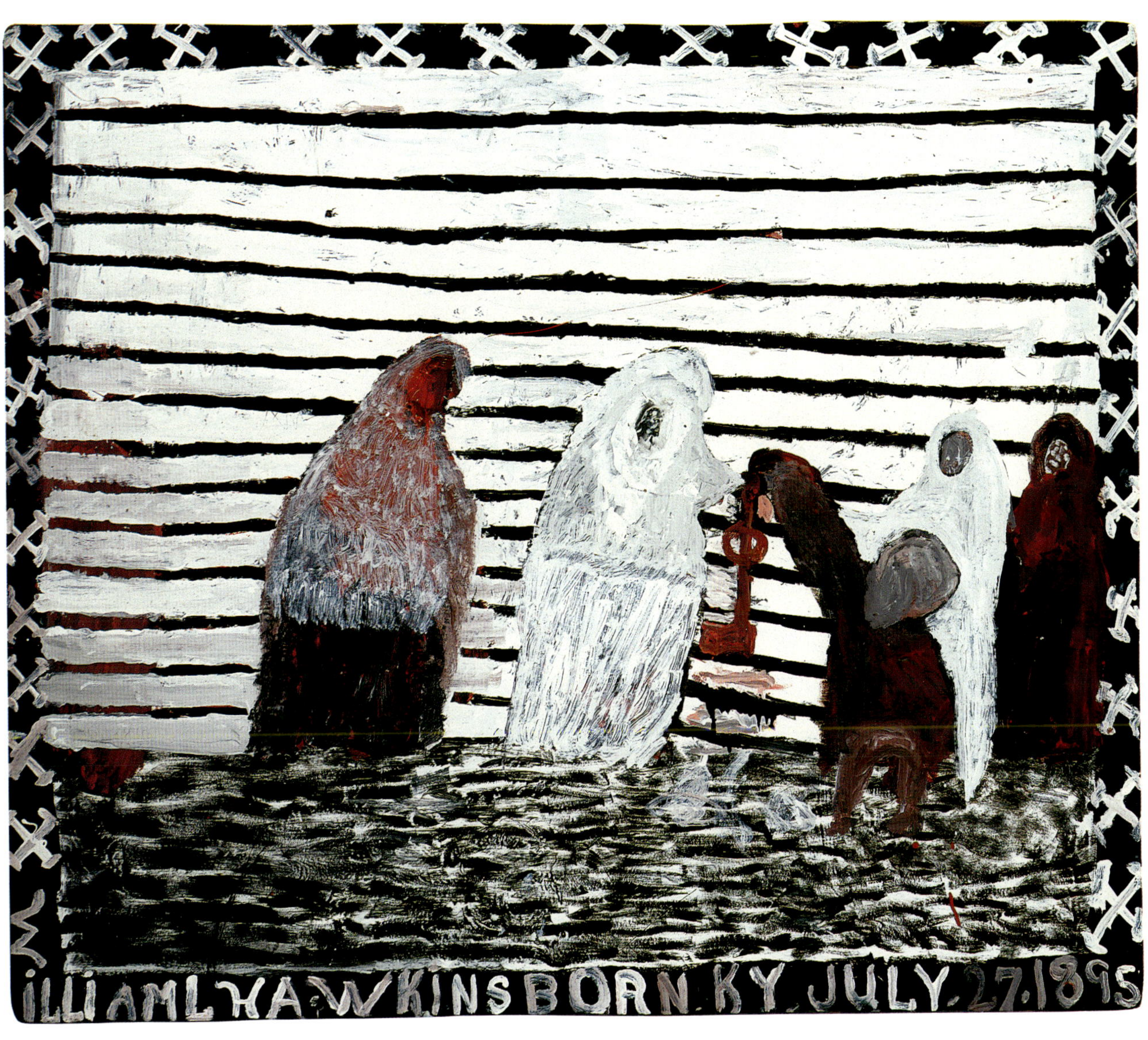

Christ Giving the Key to St. Peter, 1989

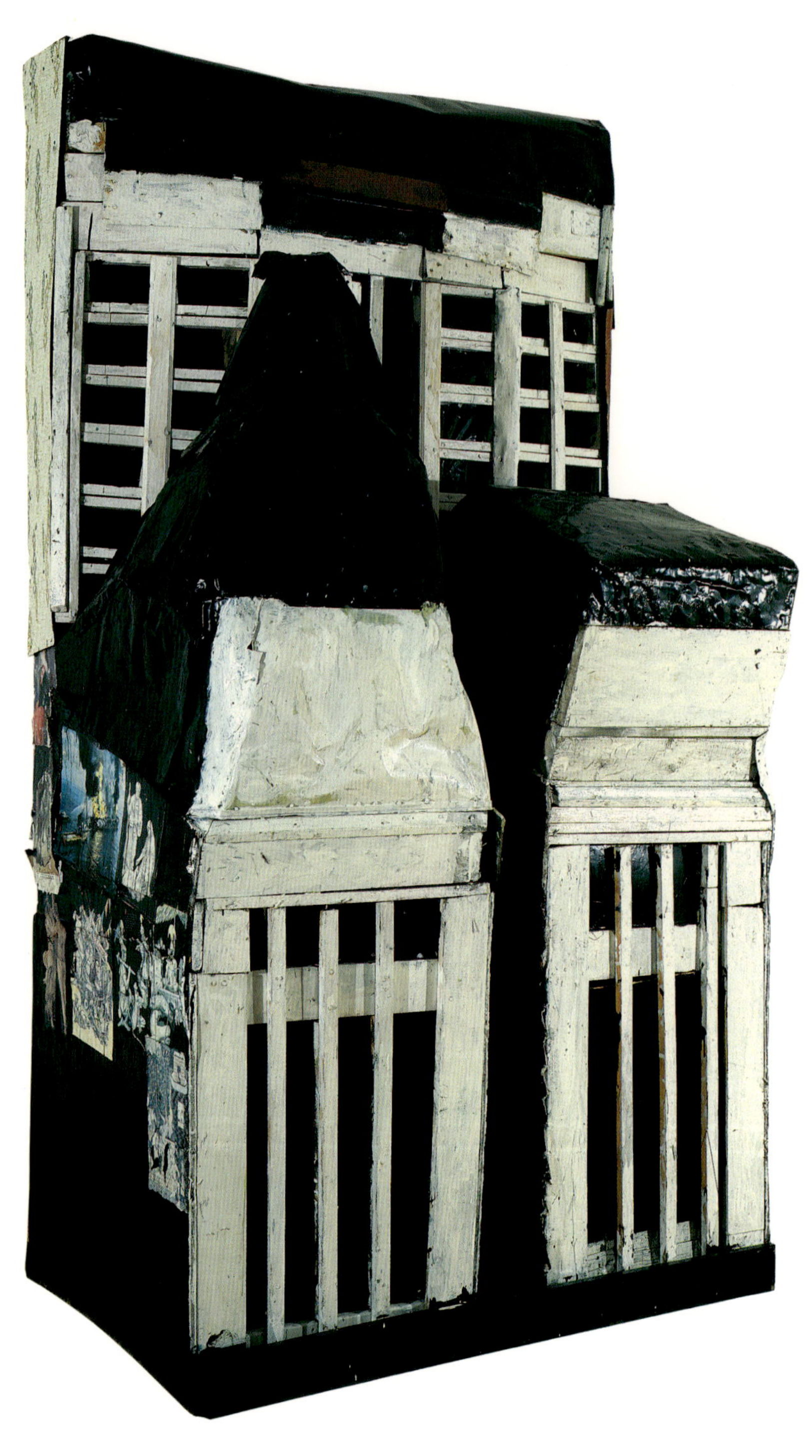

Columbus Skyline, 1989

Enamel, collage, wood, and tin construction, 92″ x 51″ x 33″

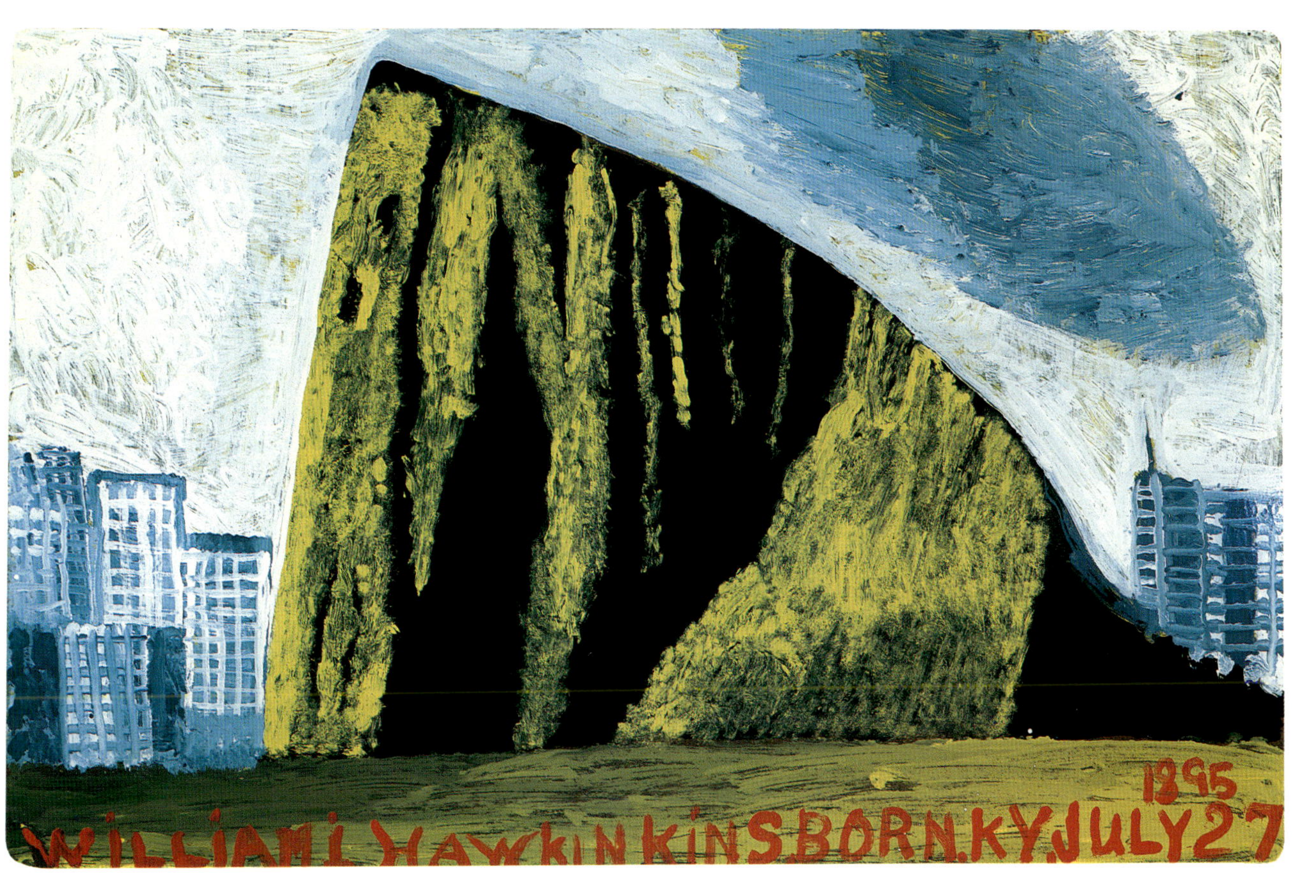

Prudential N.Y.C. 1985

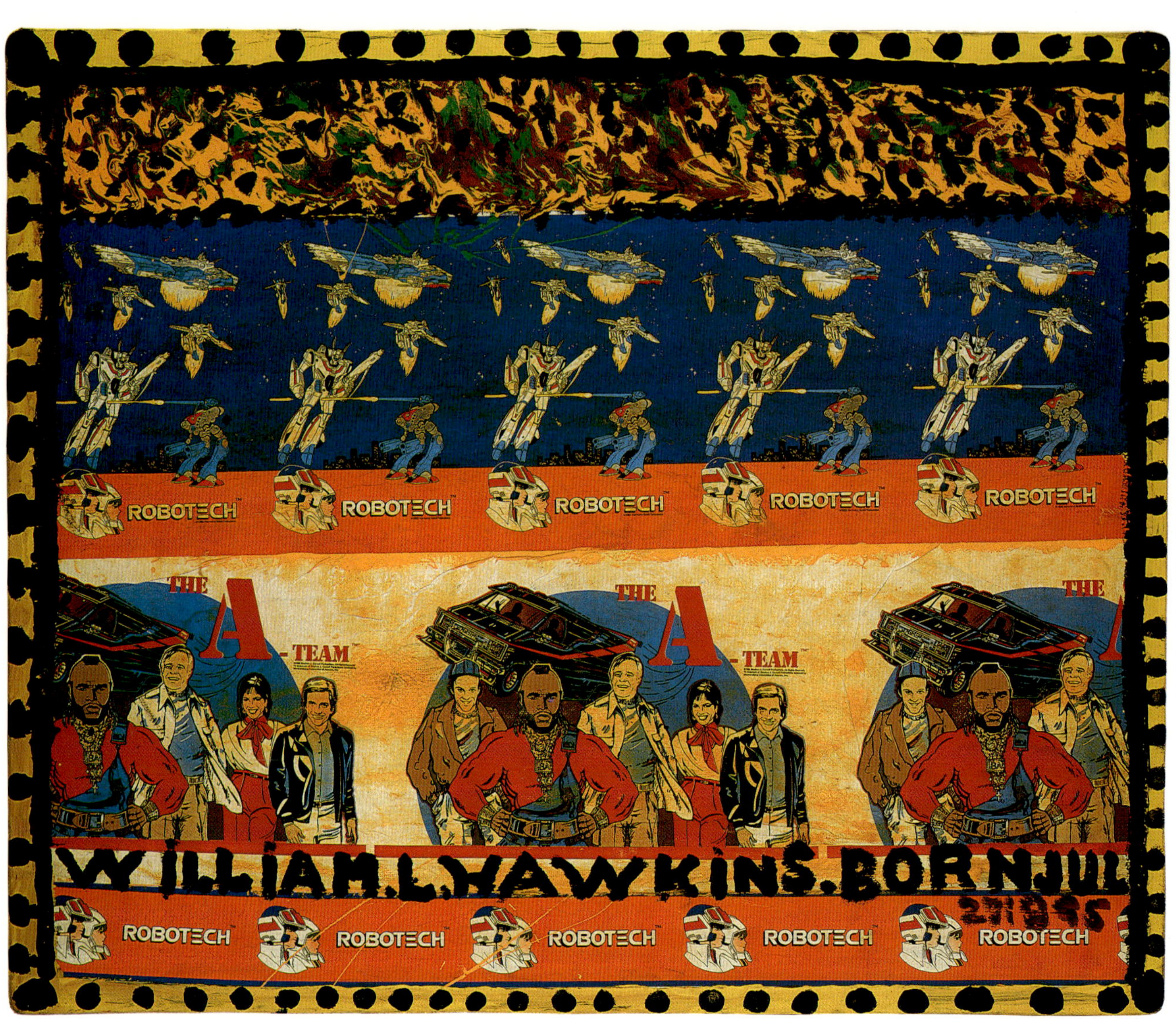

Robotech Collage, 1988

Enamel and collage on Masonite, 39½″ x 48″

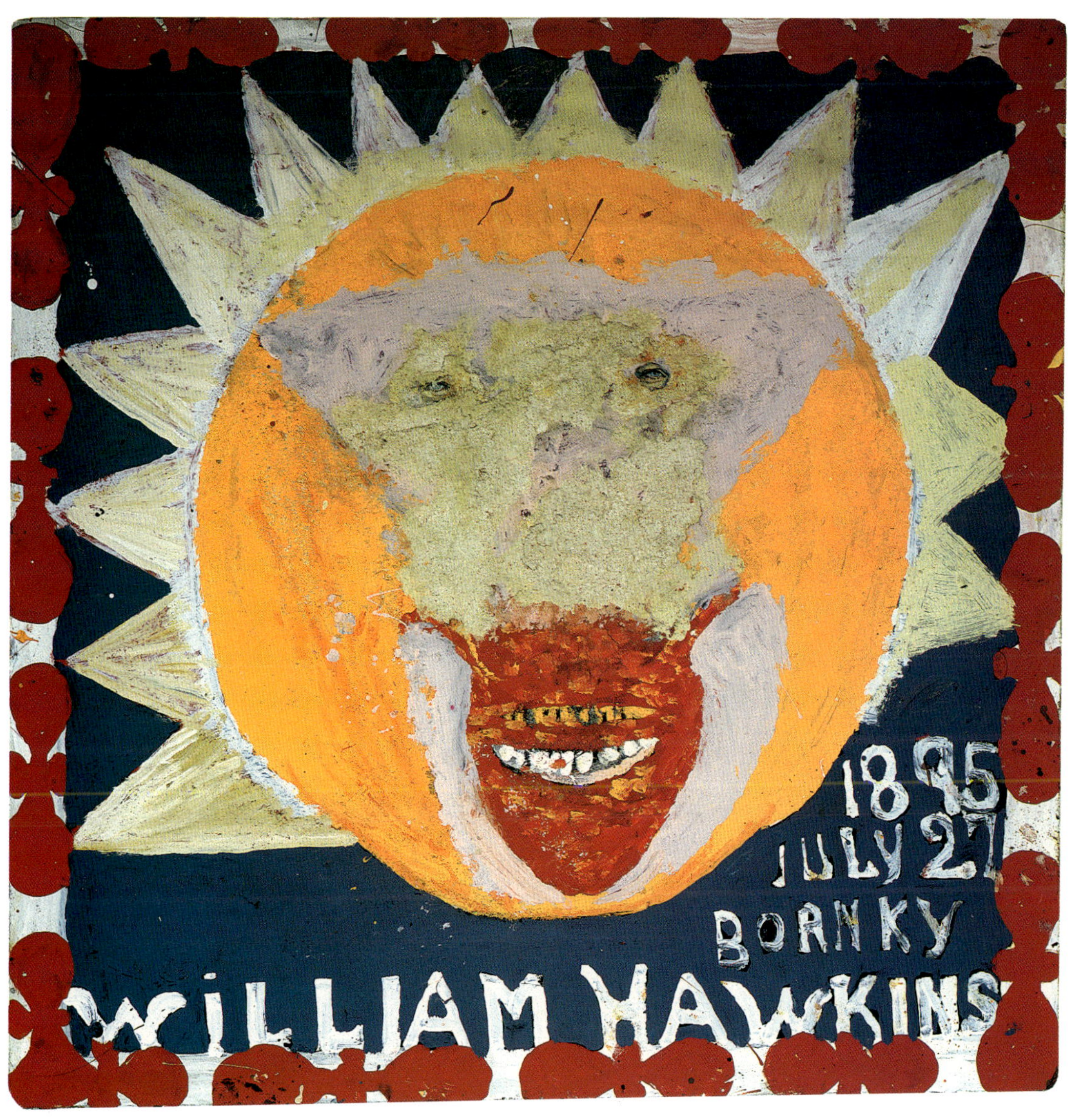

Sun 1988

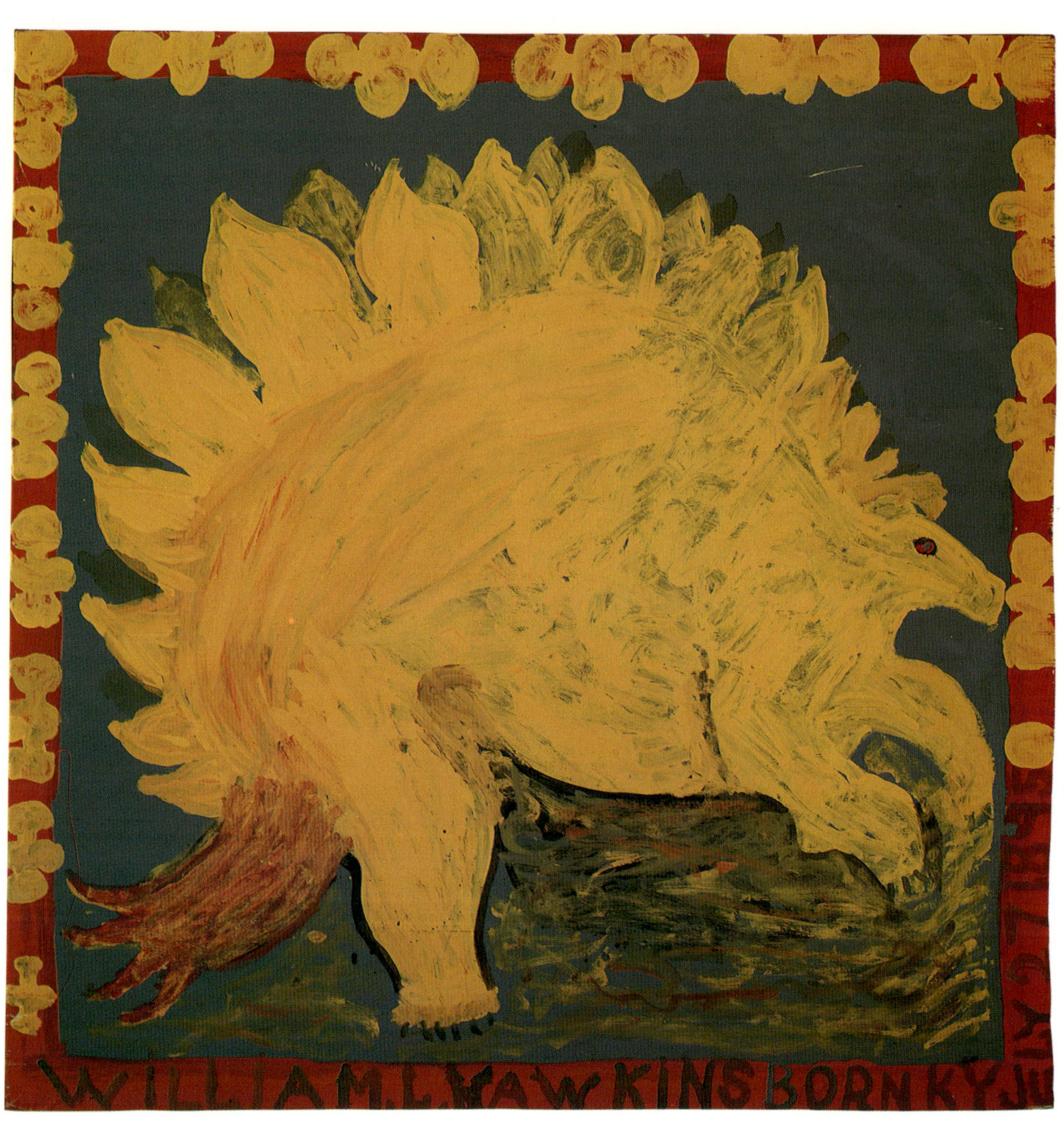

Yellow Dinosaur, 1989

Enamel on plywood, 48″ x 48″

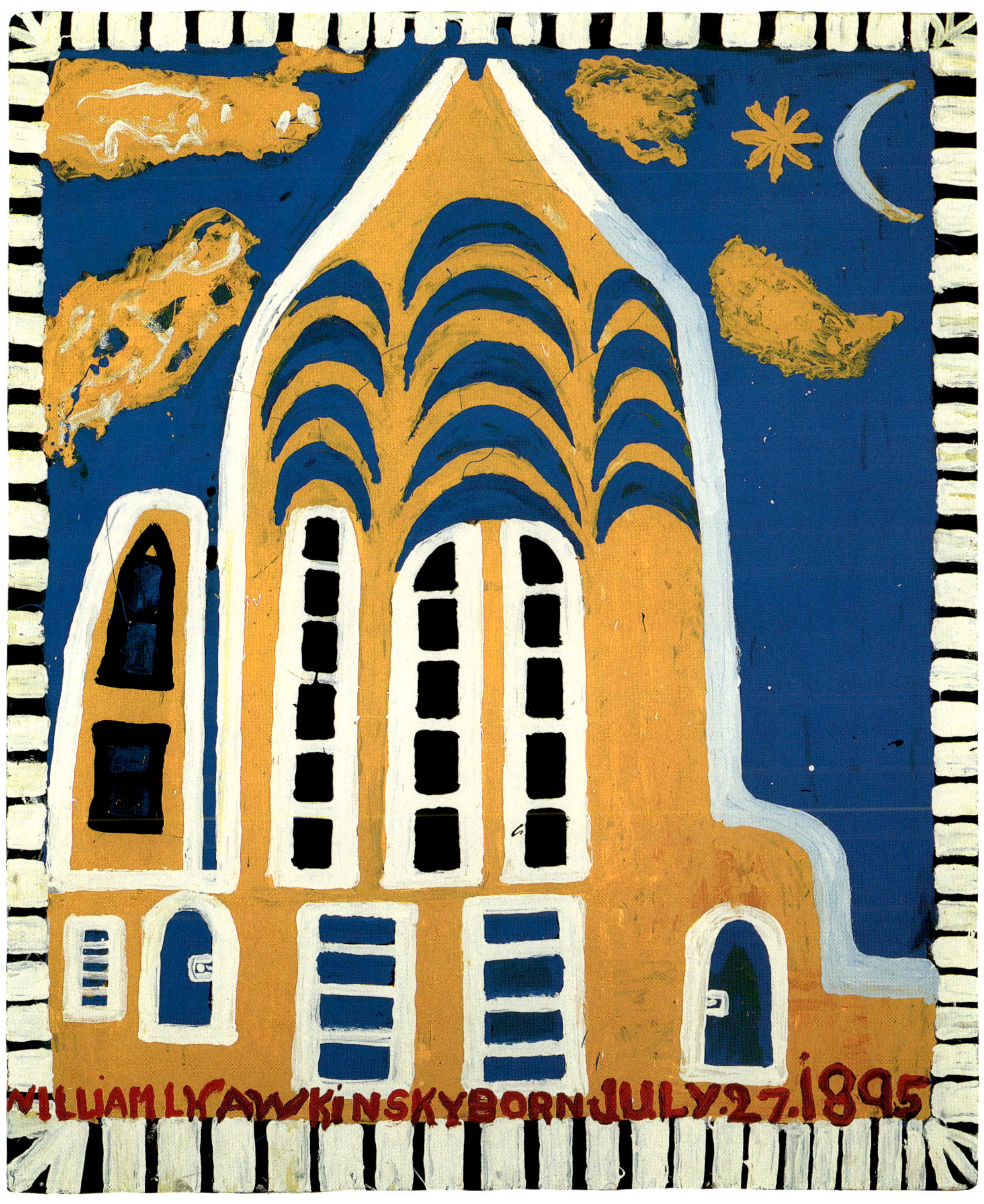

Chrysler Building, 1988

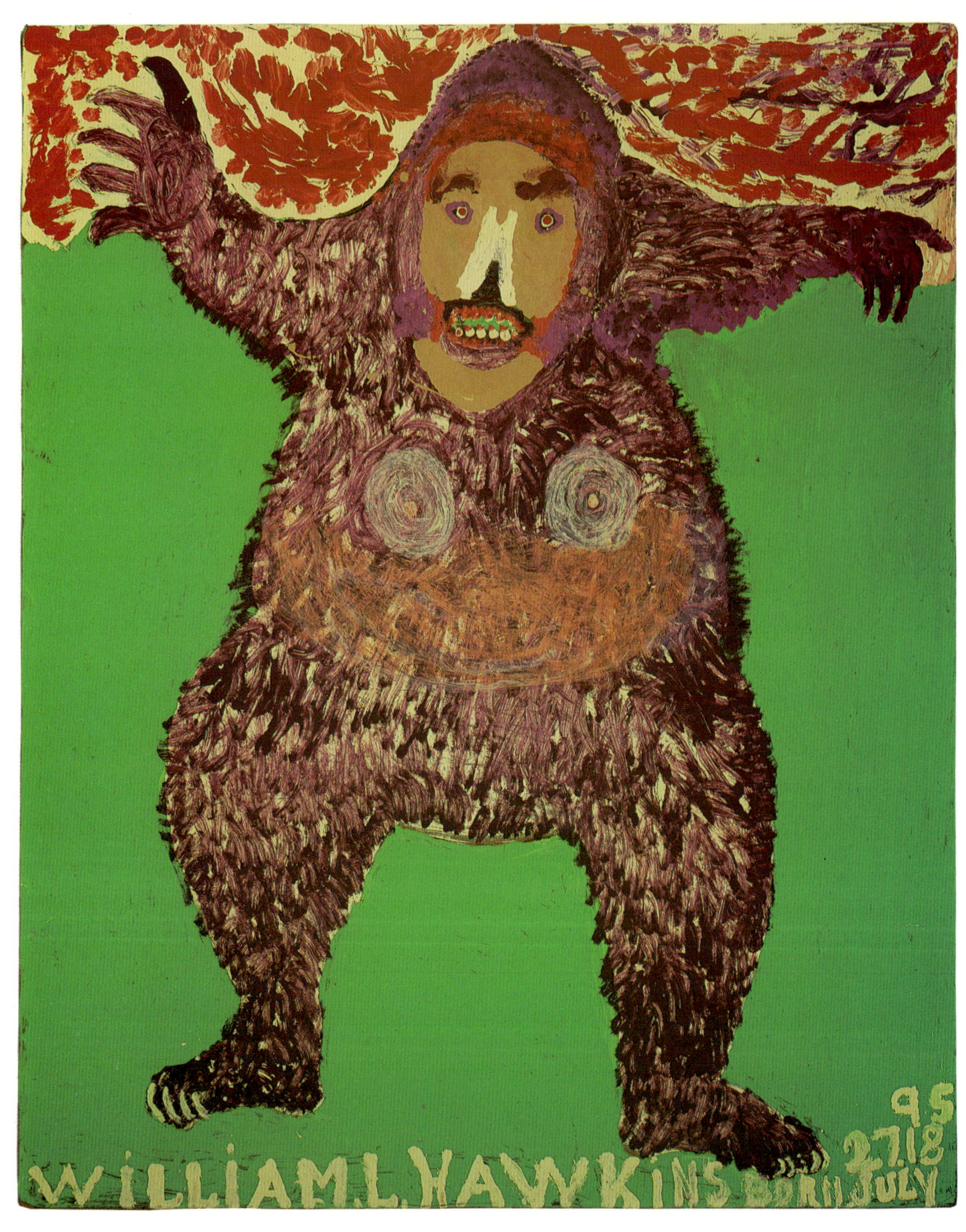

King Kong, 1985

Enamel on Masonite, 56″ x 46″

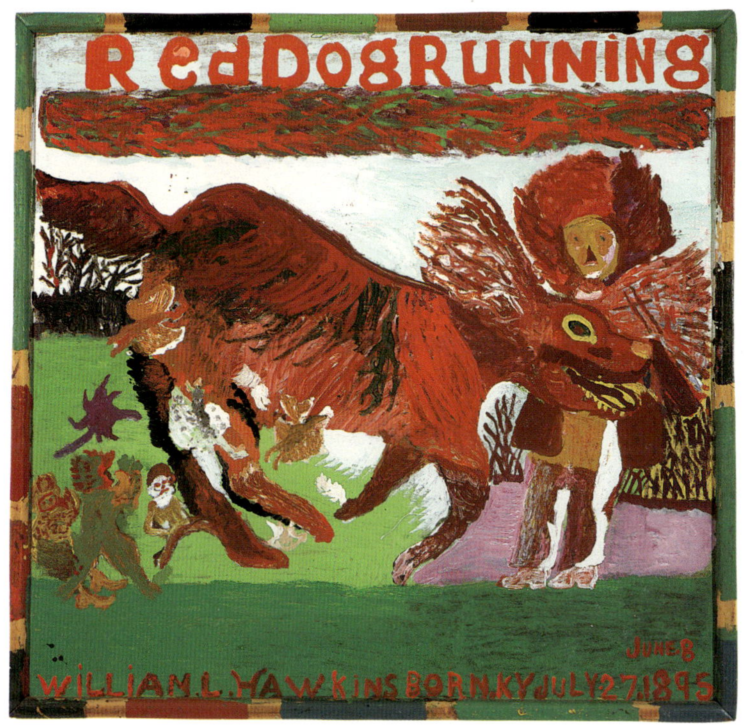

Red Dog Running # 2, 1984
Enamel on found board, 46″ x 43½″

Red Dog Running #1, 1984
Enamel on found board, 40″ x 49″

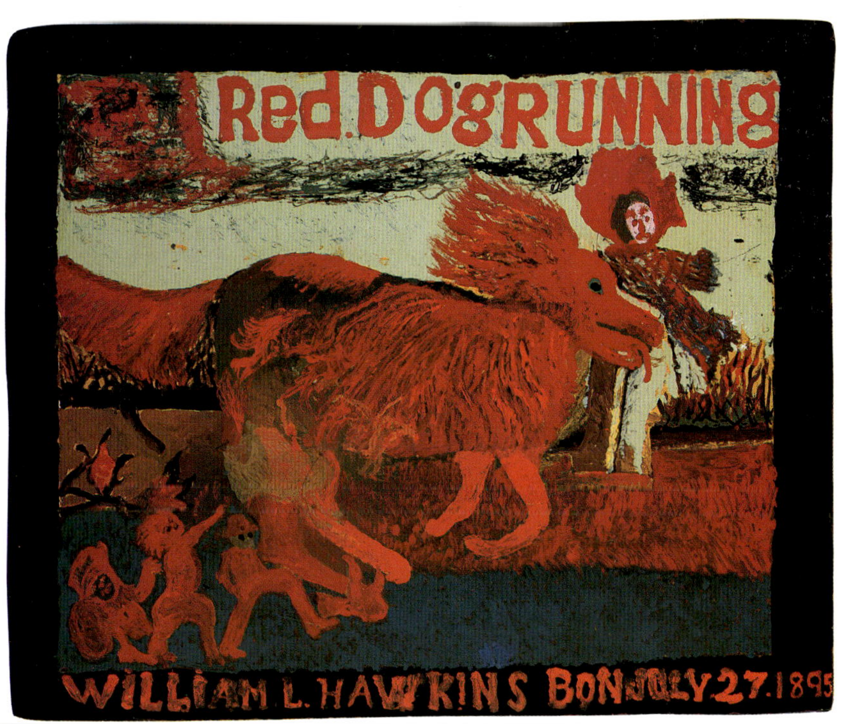

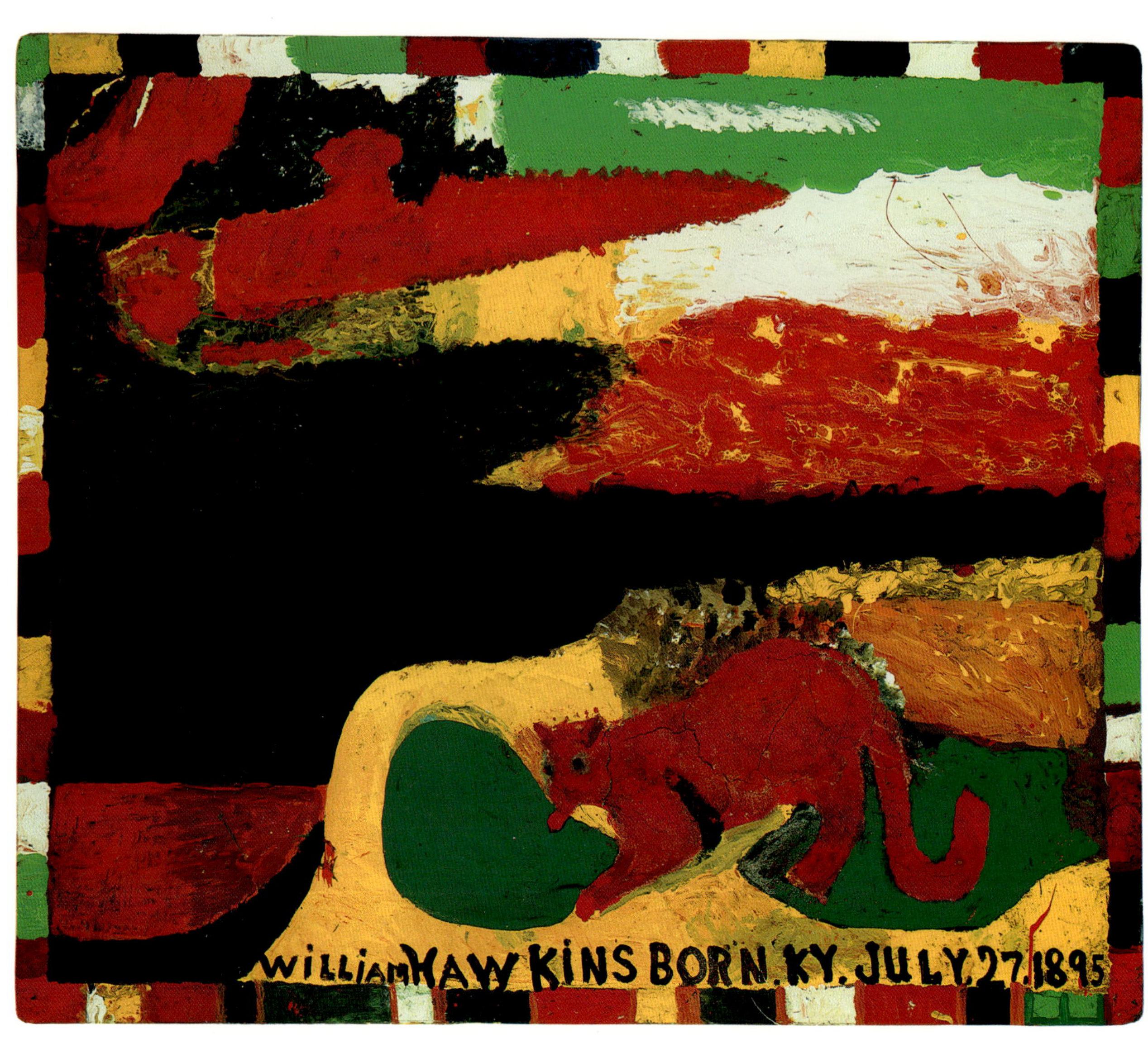

Mountain Lion Drinking Water, 1985

Enamel and mixed media on Masonite, 48″ x 56½″

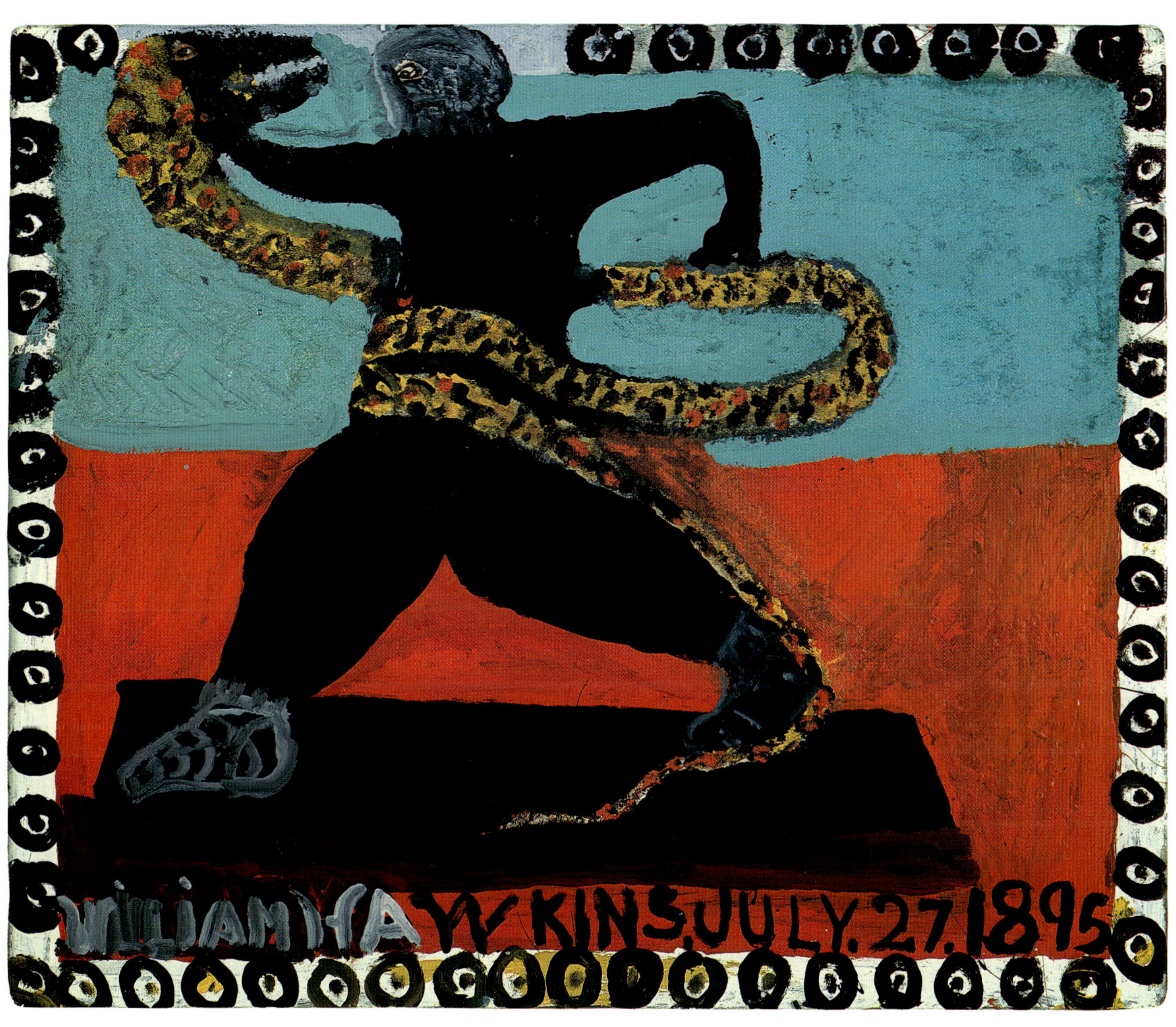
WILLIAM HAWKINS.JULY.27.1895

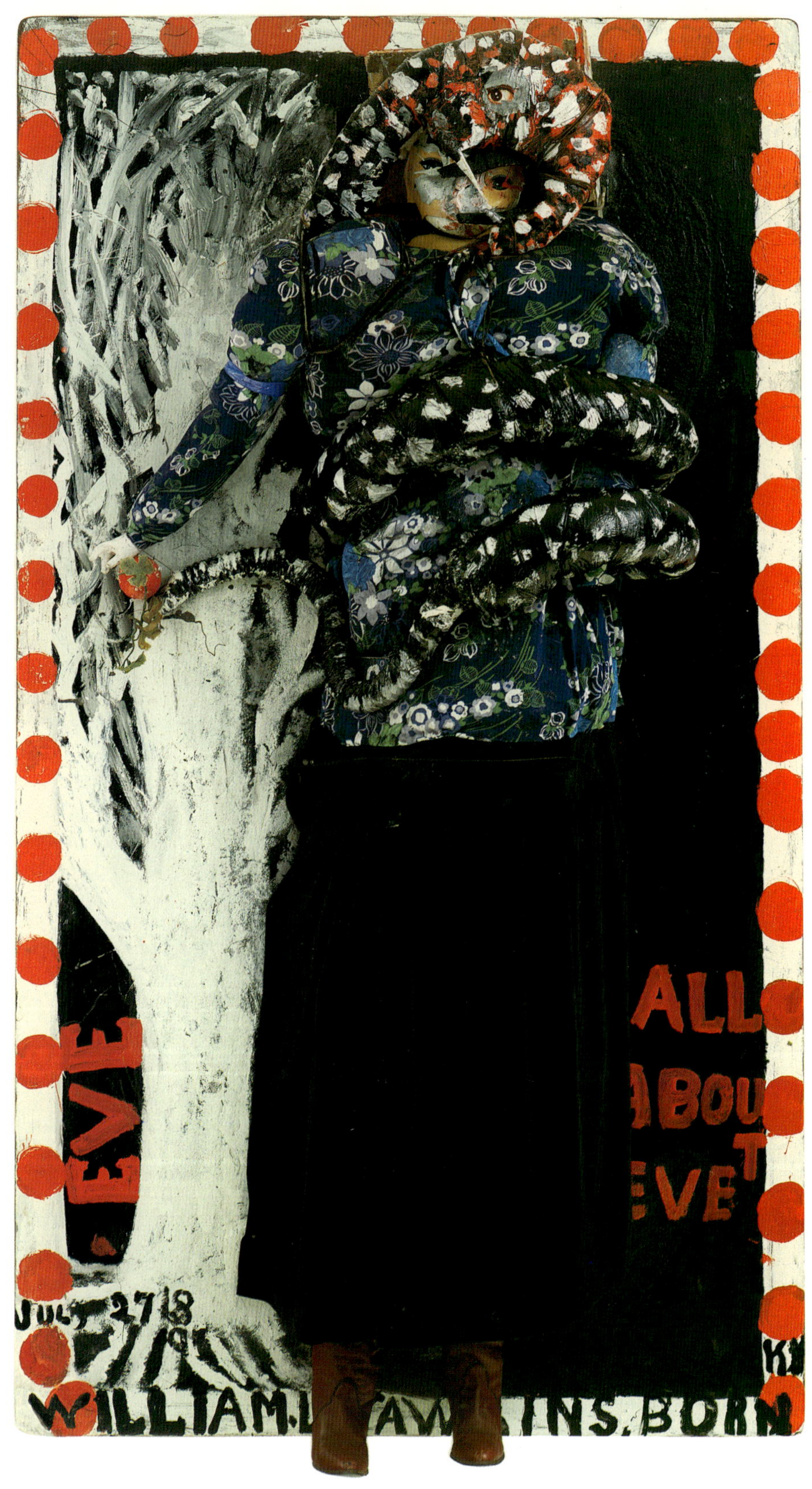

All About Eve, 1989

Enamel and mixed-media construction on Masonite, 84″ x 48″ x 12″

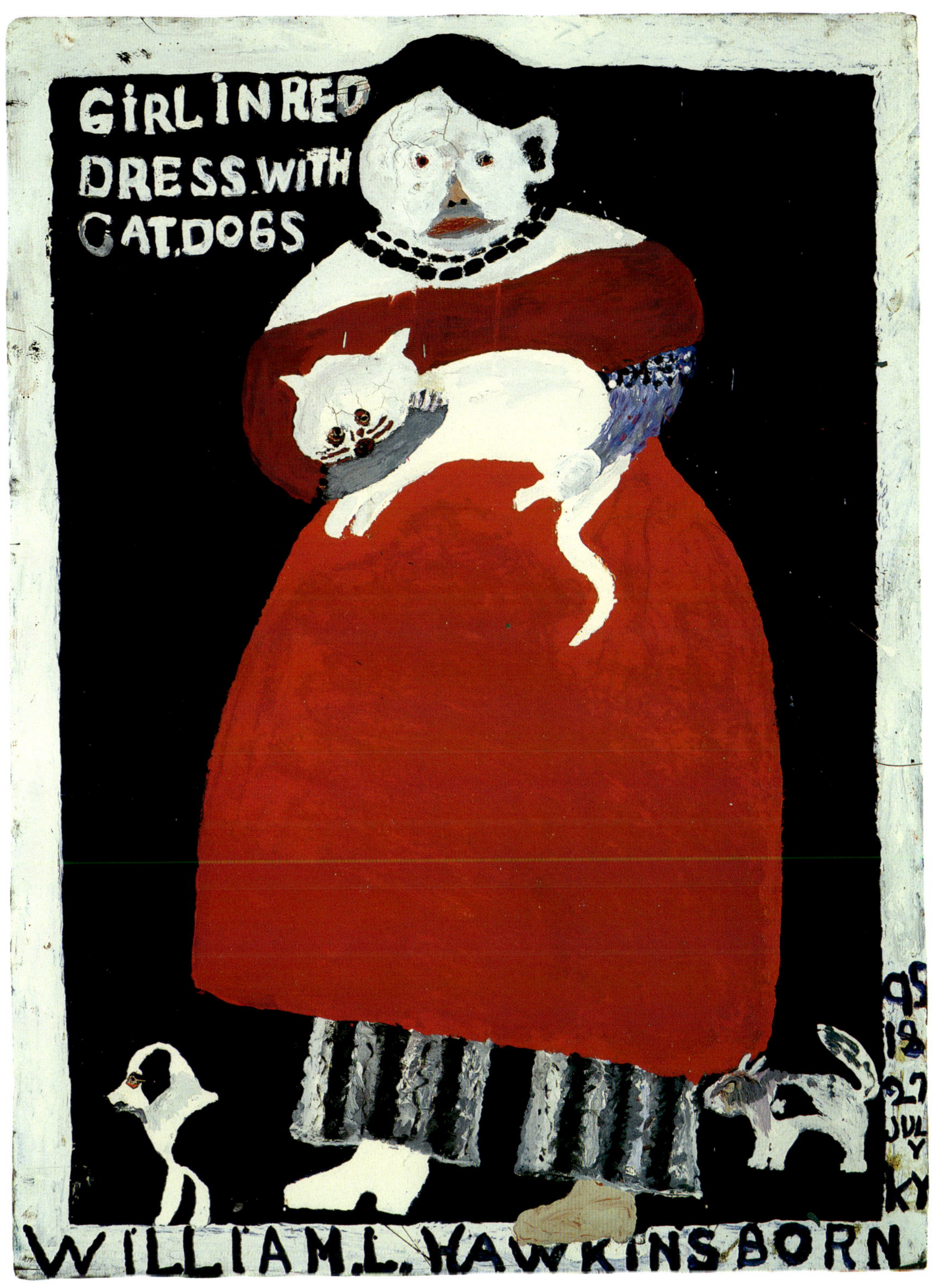

Girl in Red Dress with Cat and Dogs, 1985

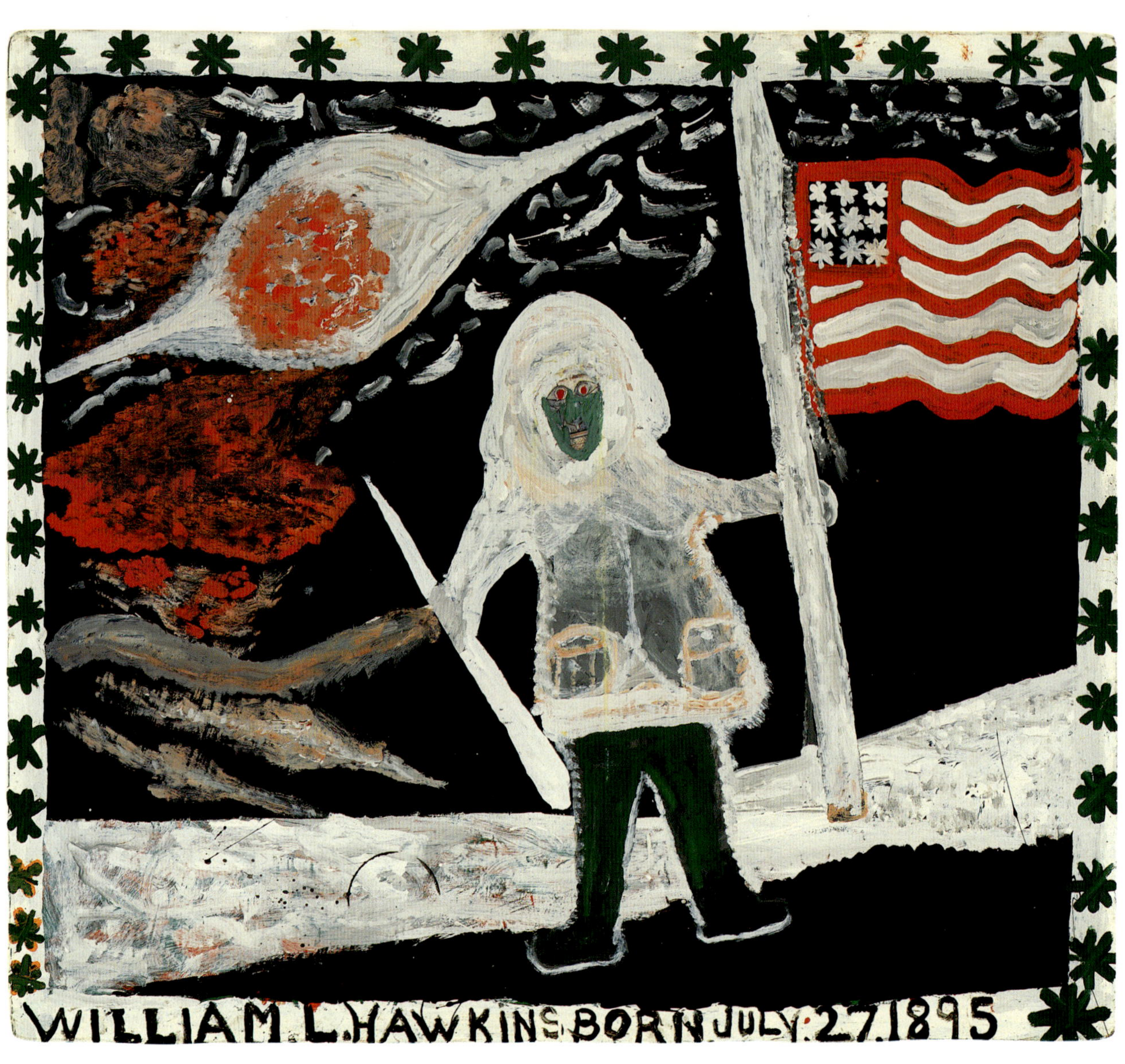

Conquest of the Moon #2, 1986

Enamel on Masonite, 44½″ x 50½″

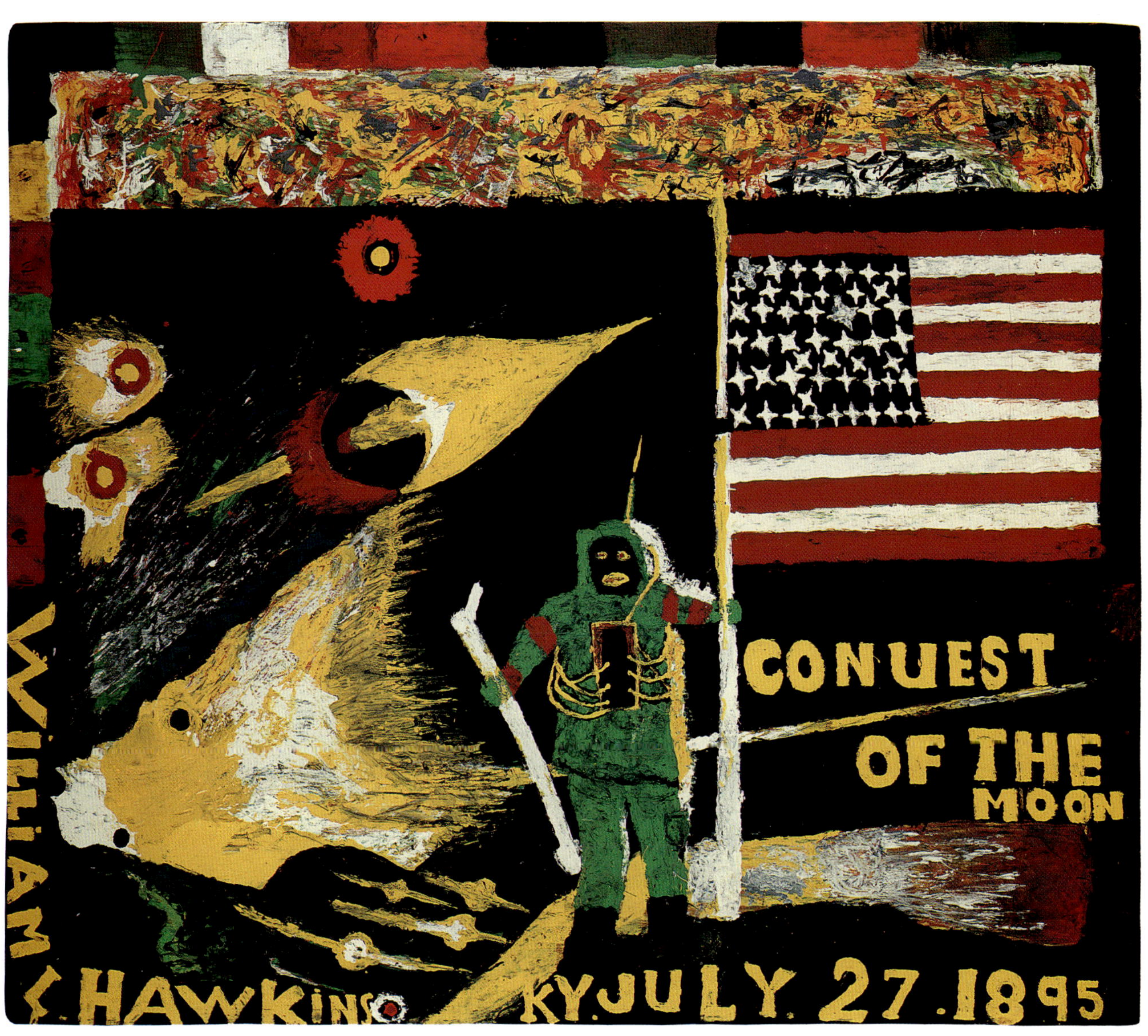

Conquest of the Moon #1, 1984

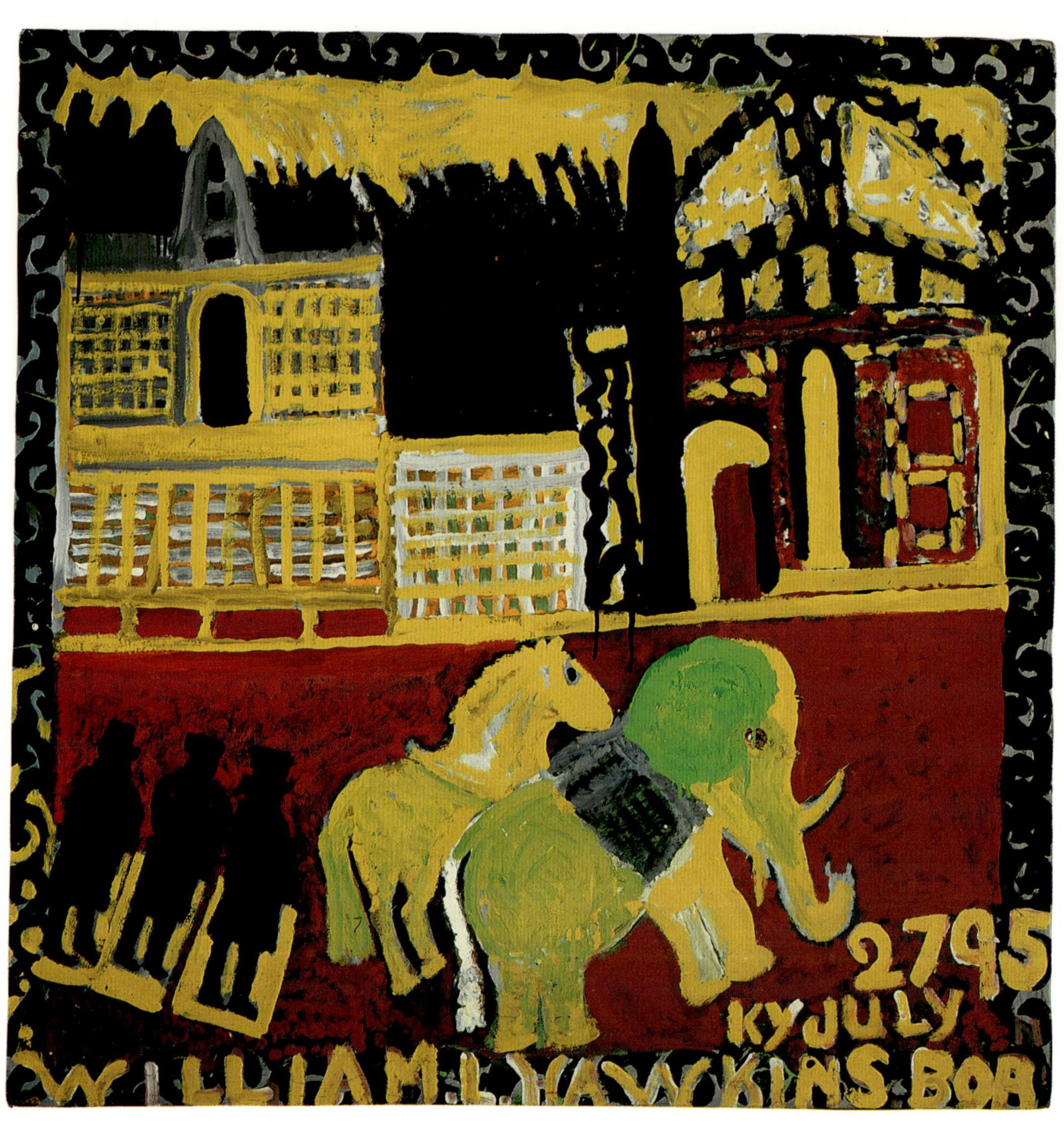

Indian Courtyard, 1988

Enamel and collage on Masonite, 48″ x 48″

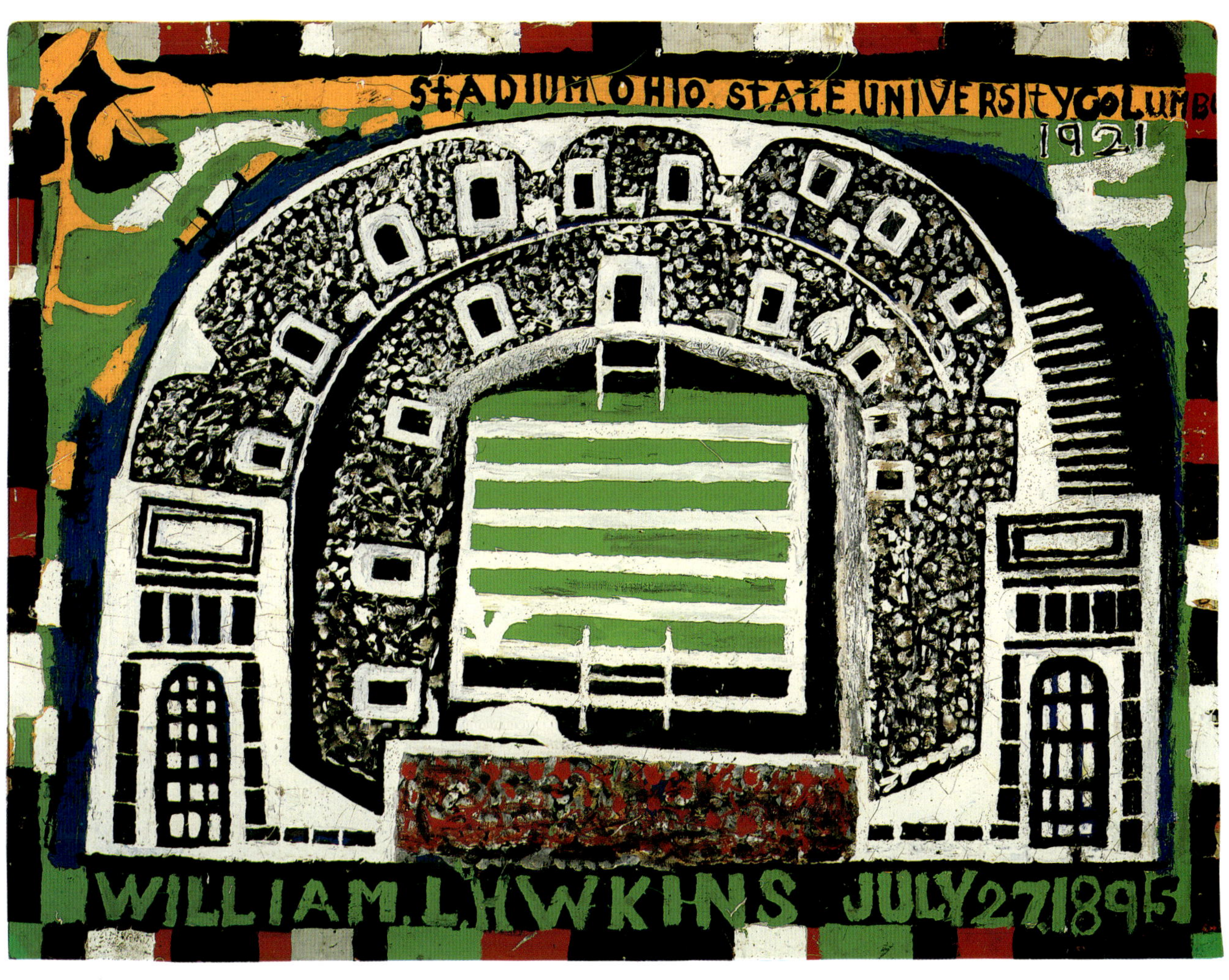

Ohio Stadium #1, 1983

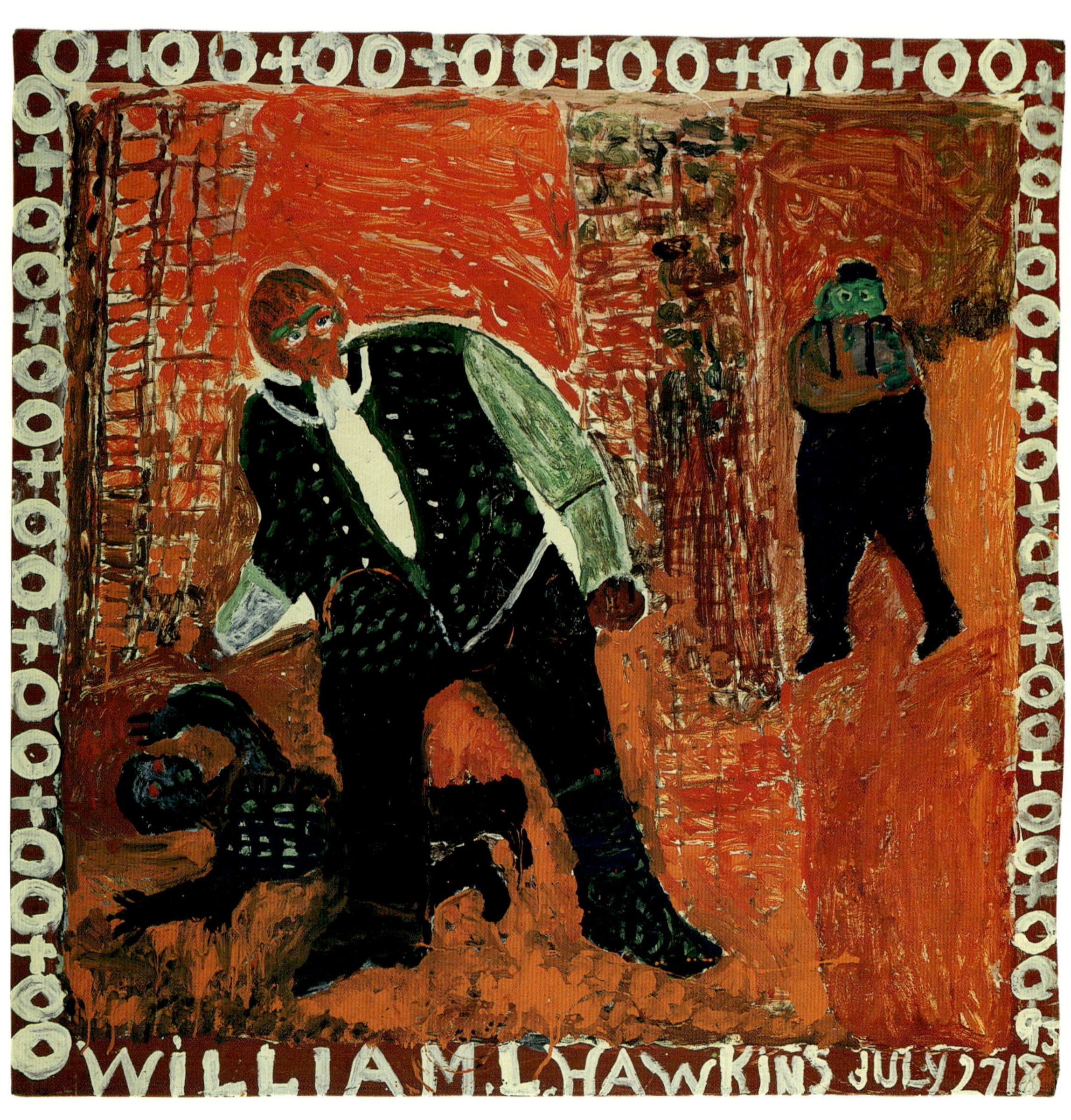

The Fight, 1987

Enamel and collage on Masonite, 48″ x 49″

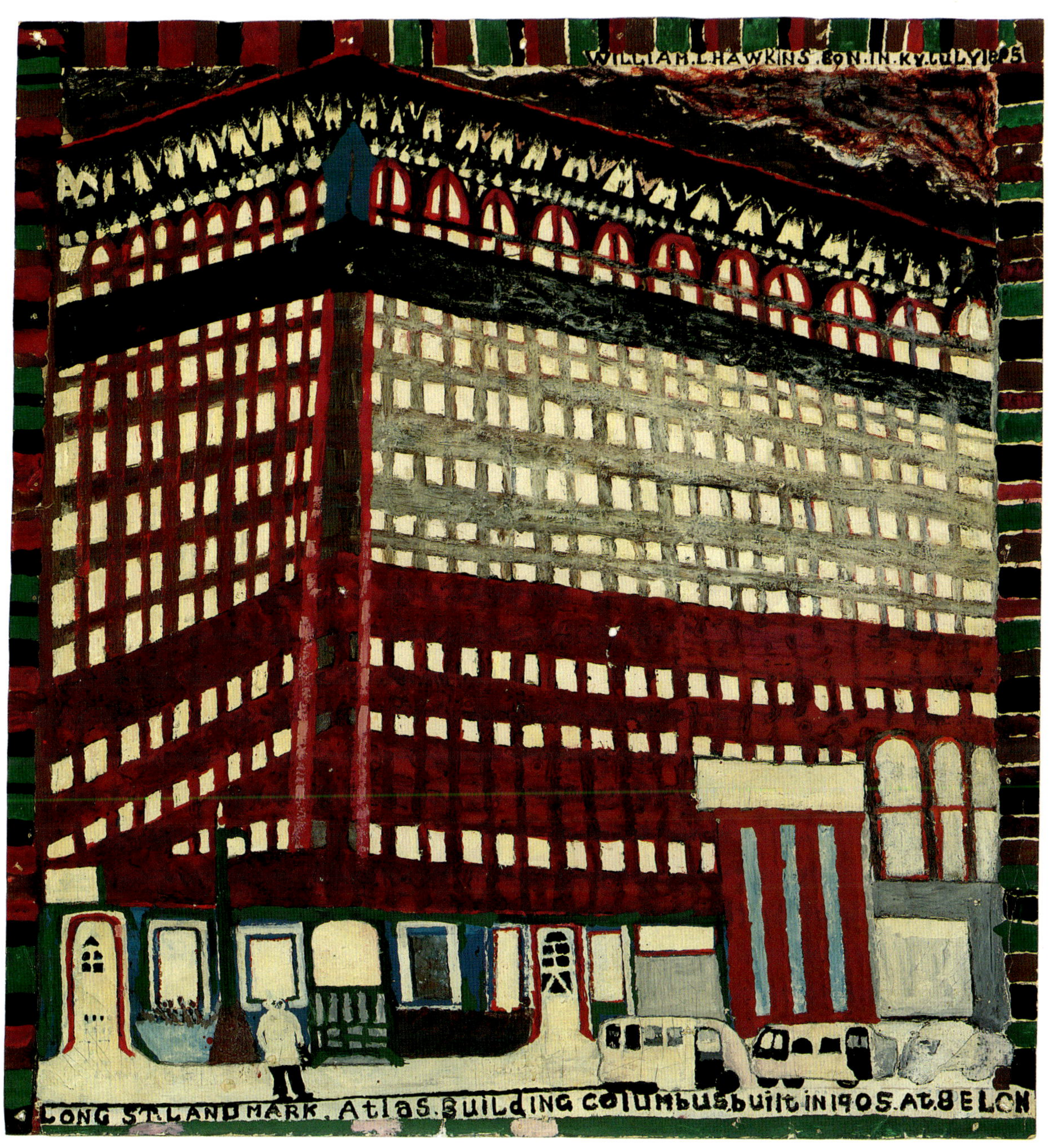

Atlas Building, 1979

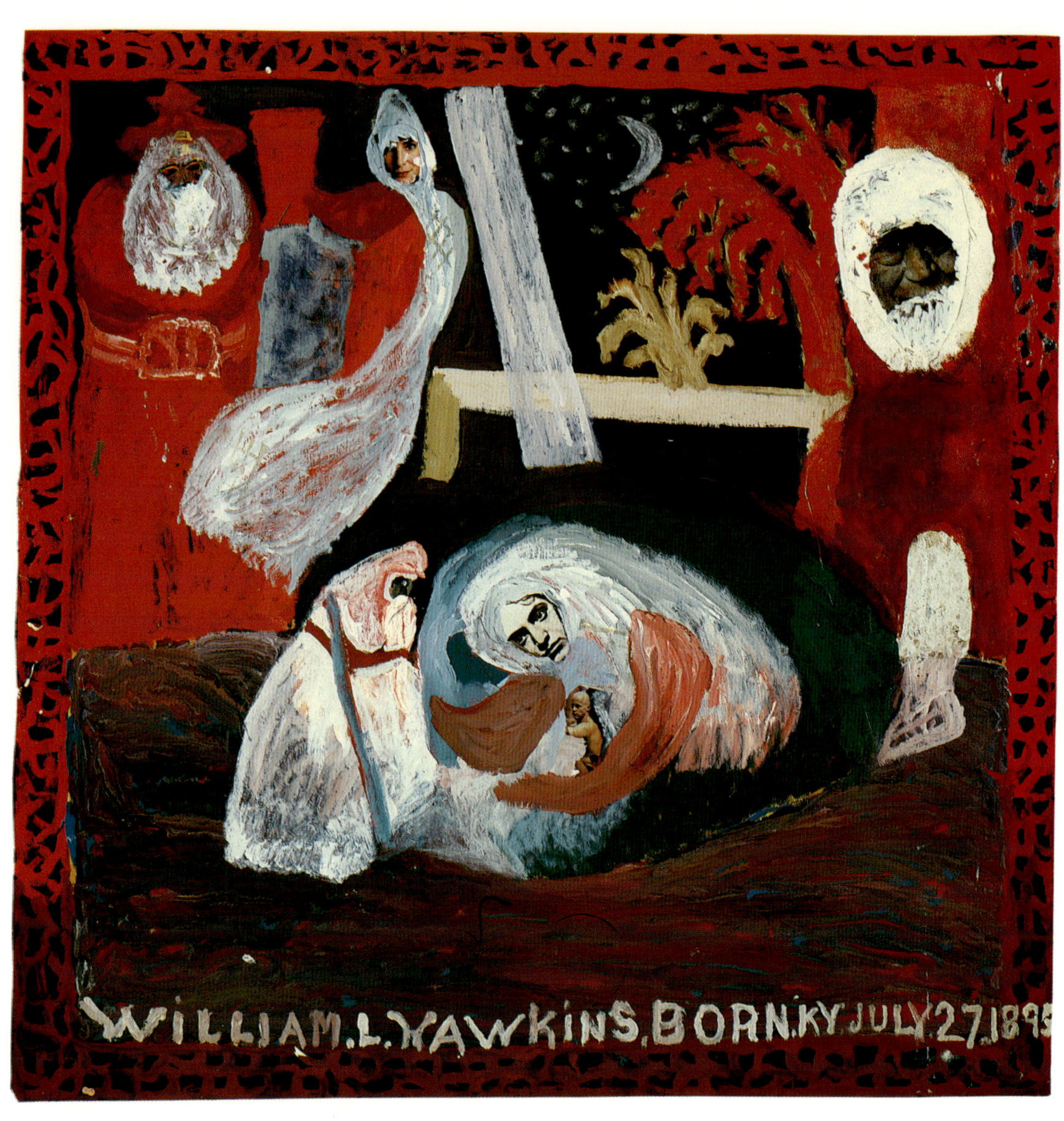

Nativity with Collage #3, 1989

Enamel and collage on plywood, 48″ x 48″

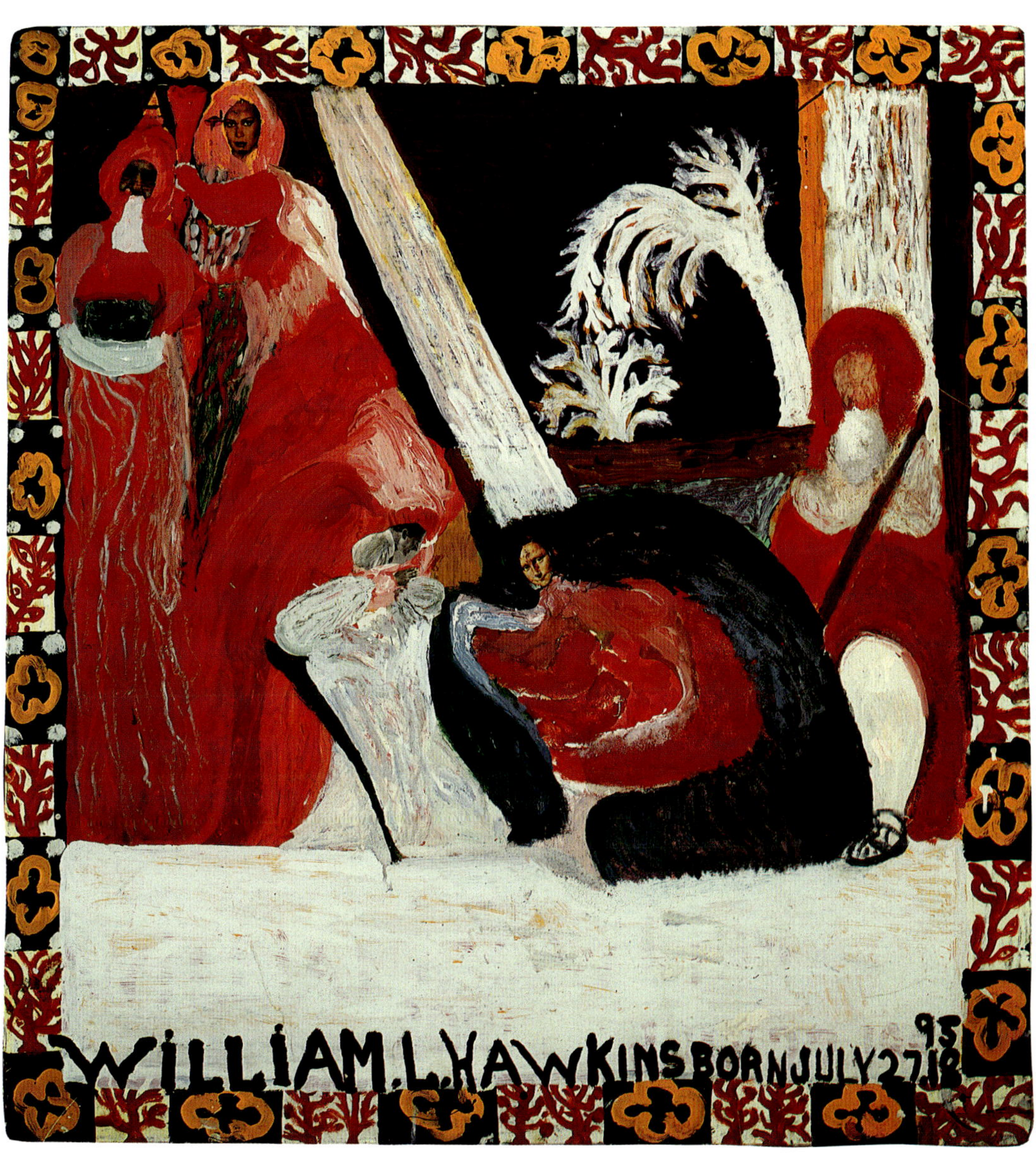

Adoration of the Wise Men #2, 1984

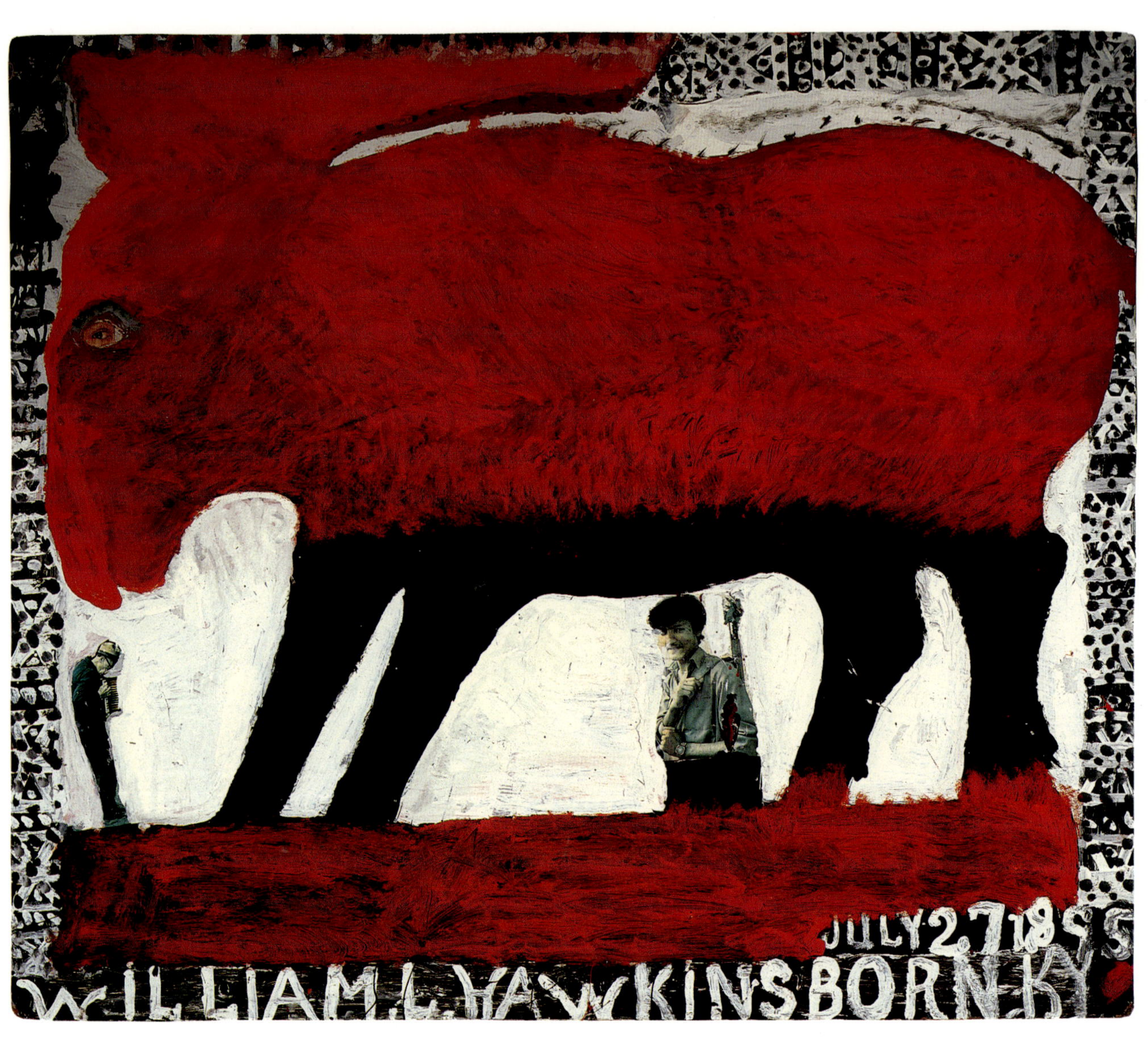

Orange Moose, 1989

Enamel and collage on Masonite, 48″ x $56\frac{1}{2}$″

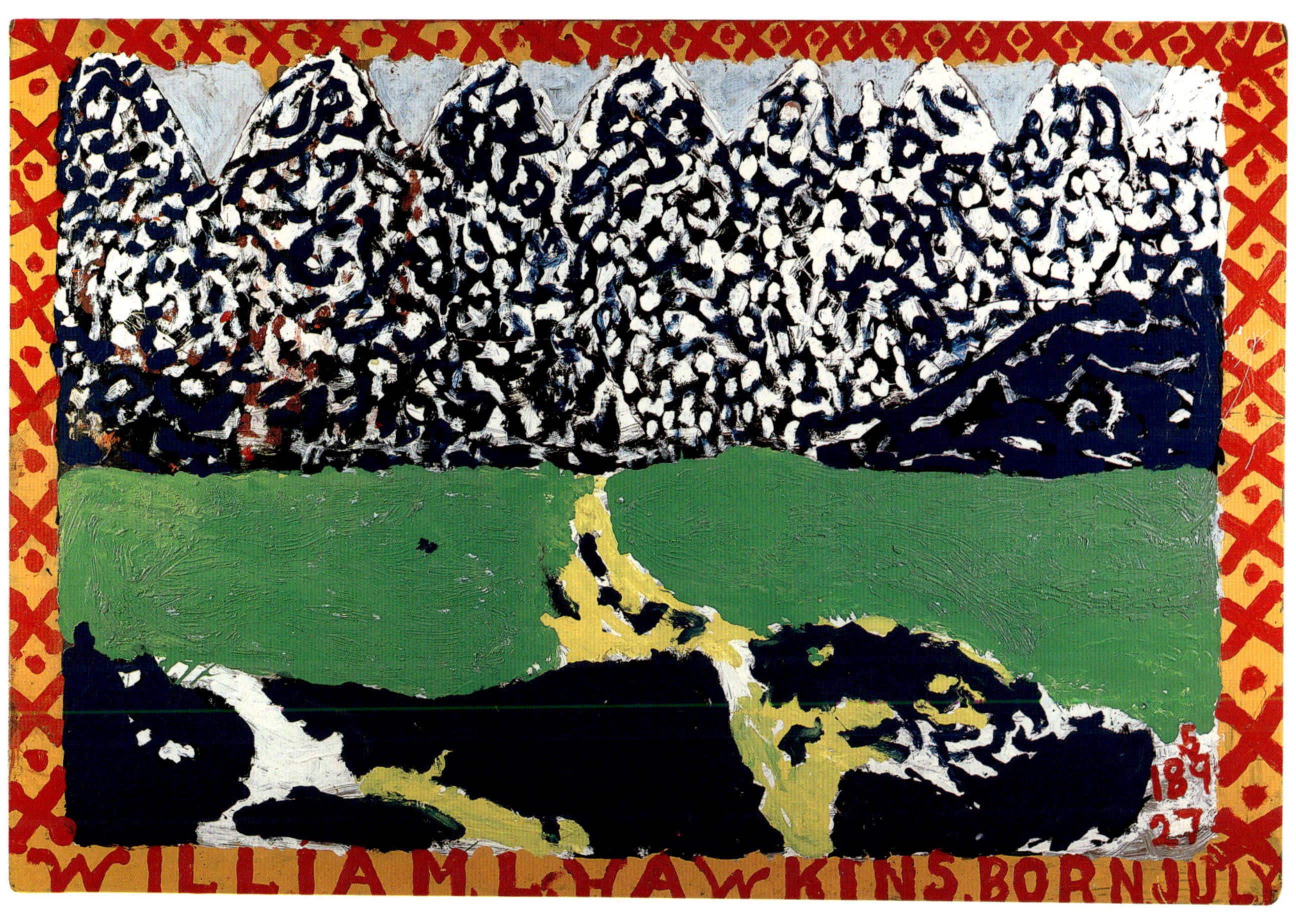

The Alps, 1987

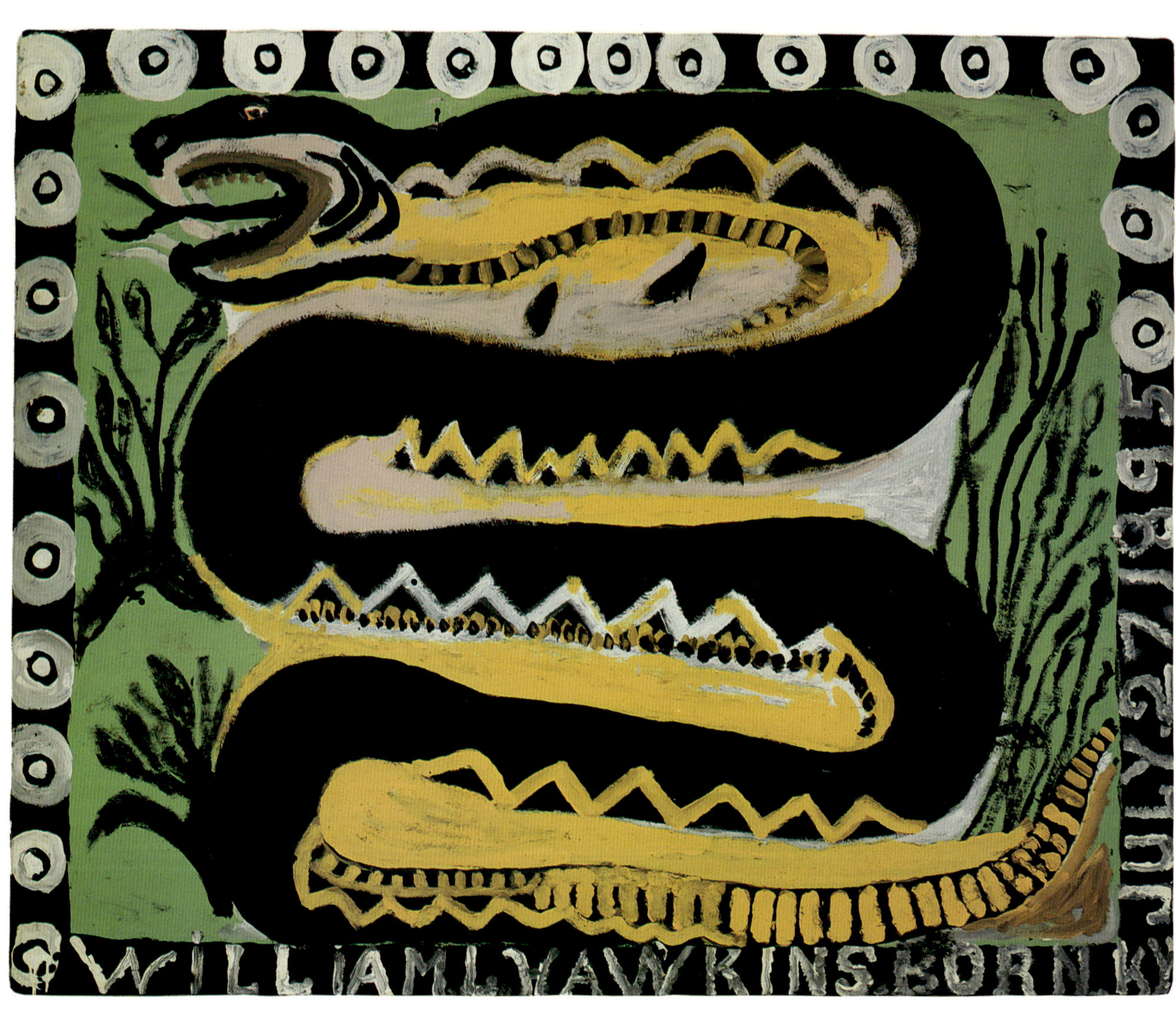

Rattlesnake #3, 1988

Enamel and collage on Masonite, 48″ x 60″

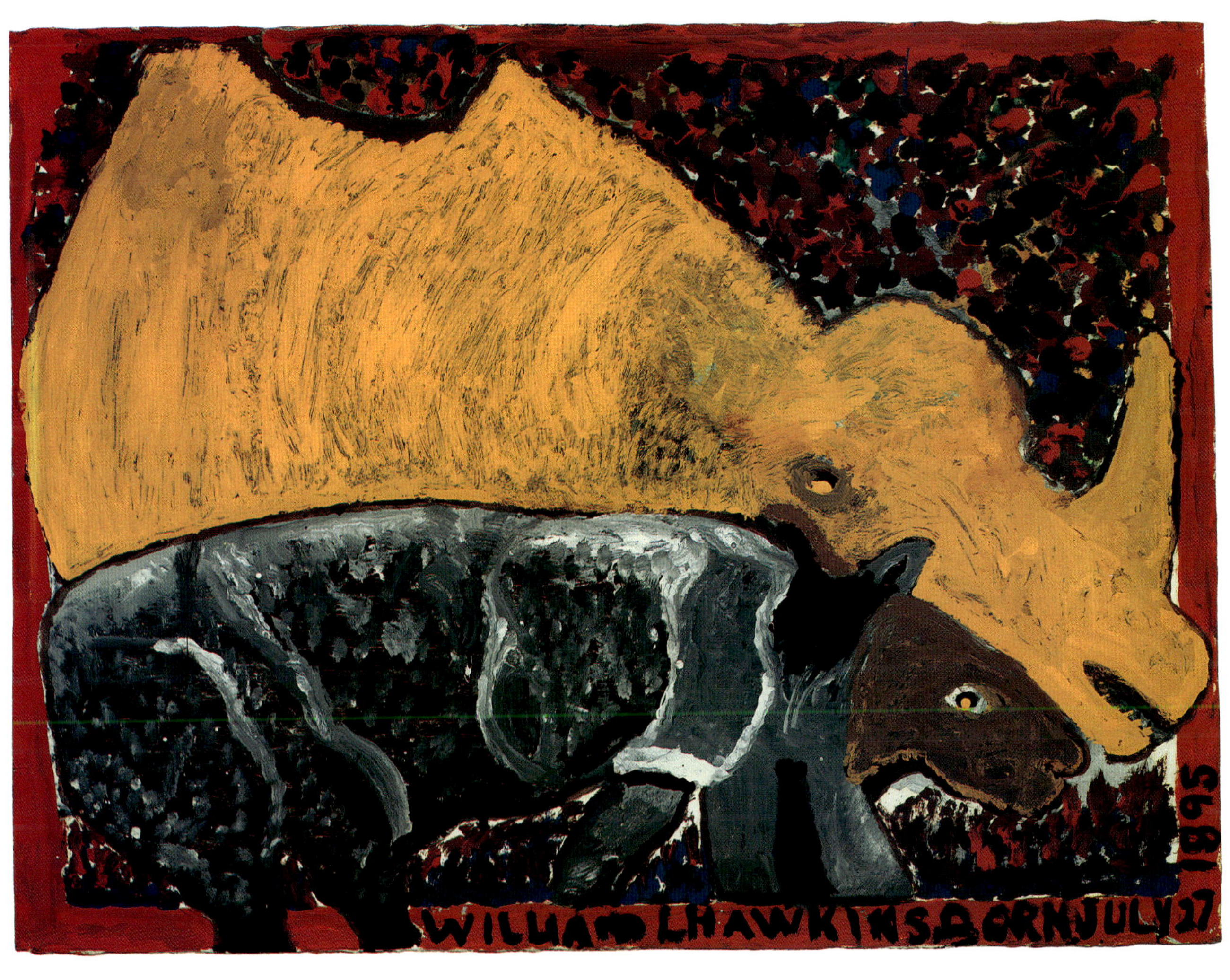

Two Rhinos, 1985

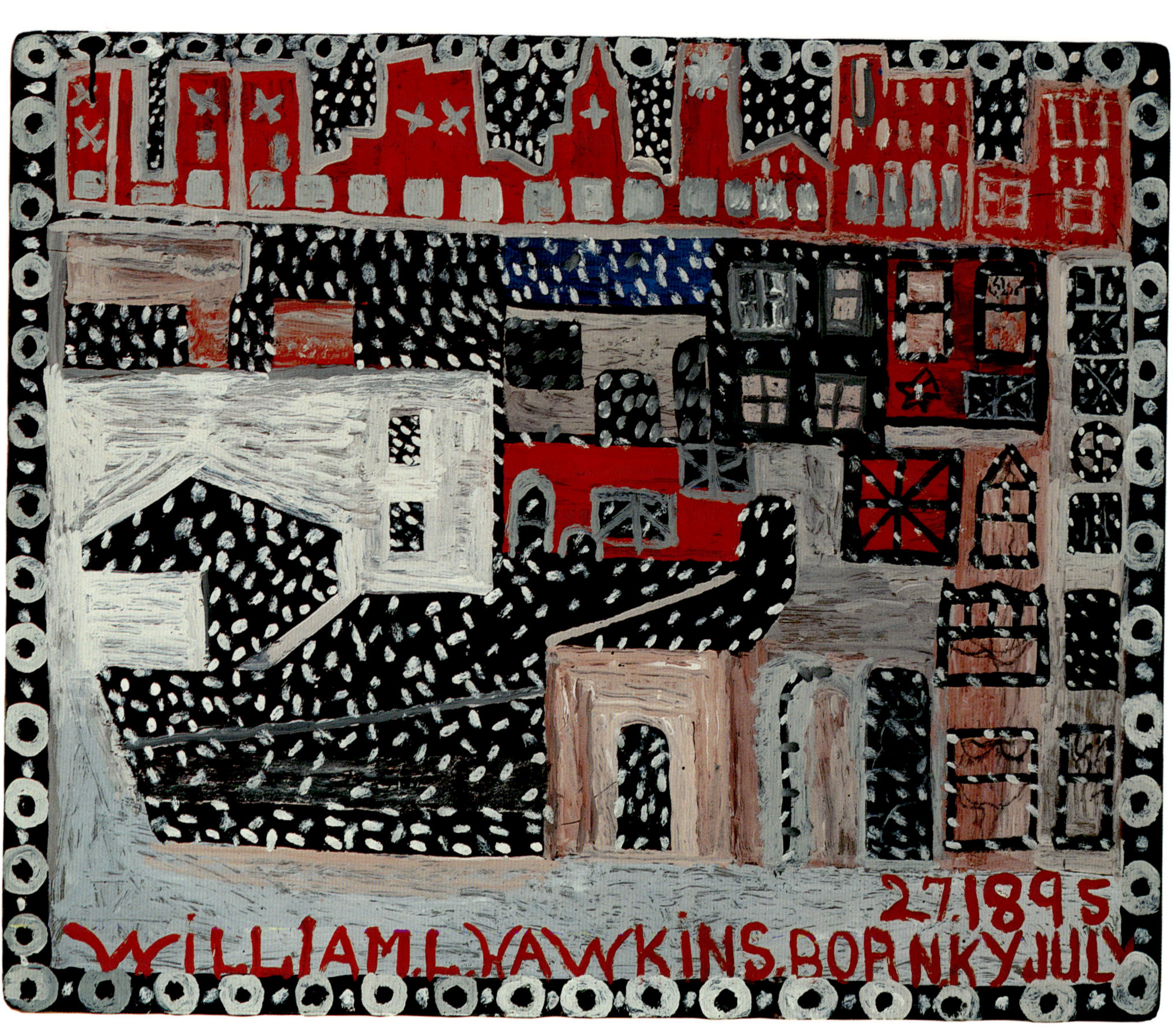

Speckled Buildings, 1989

Enamel on Masonite, $39\frac{1}{2}''$ x 48″

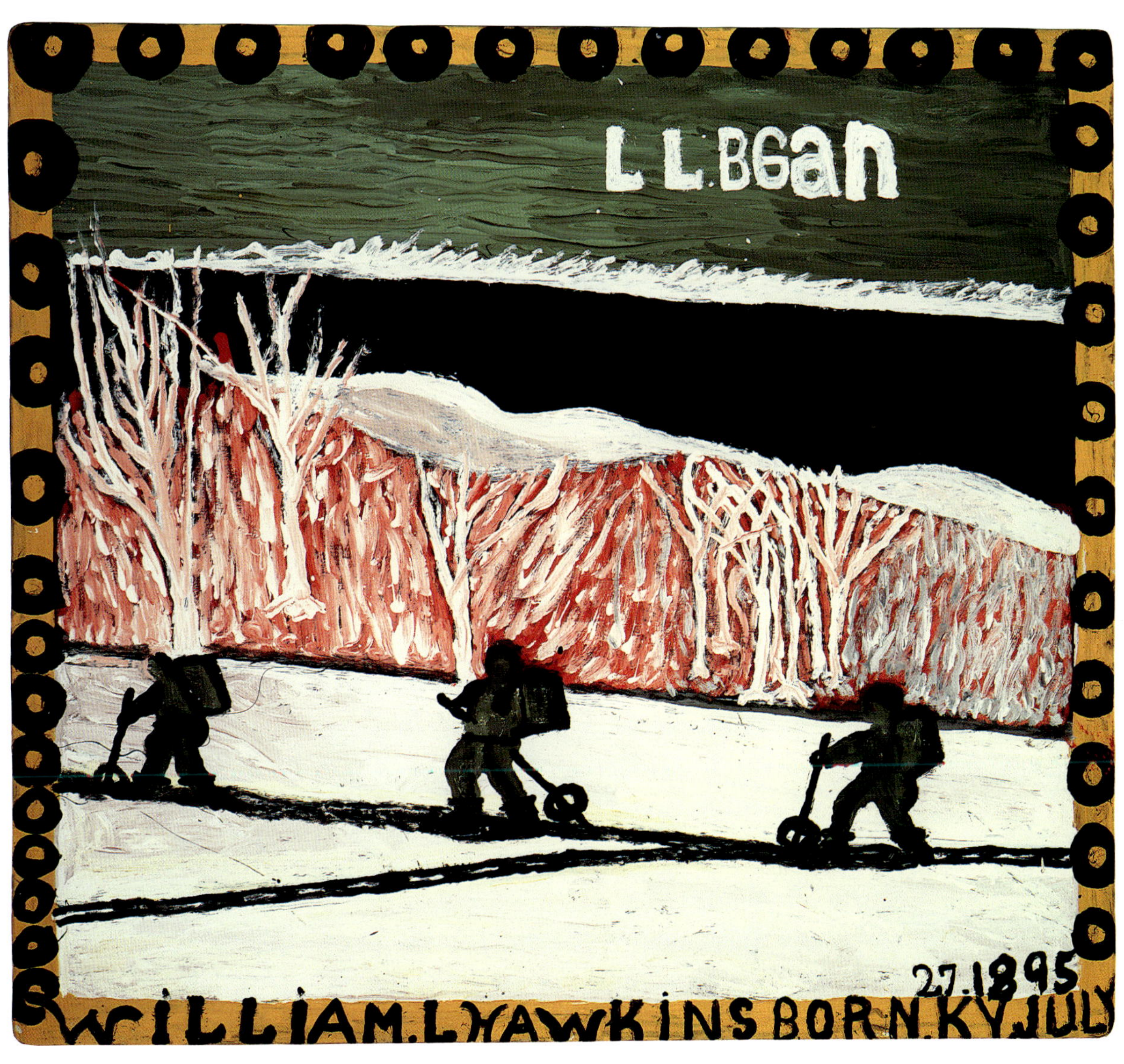

L.L. Bean, 1989

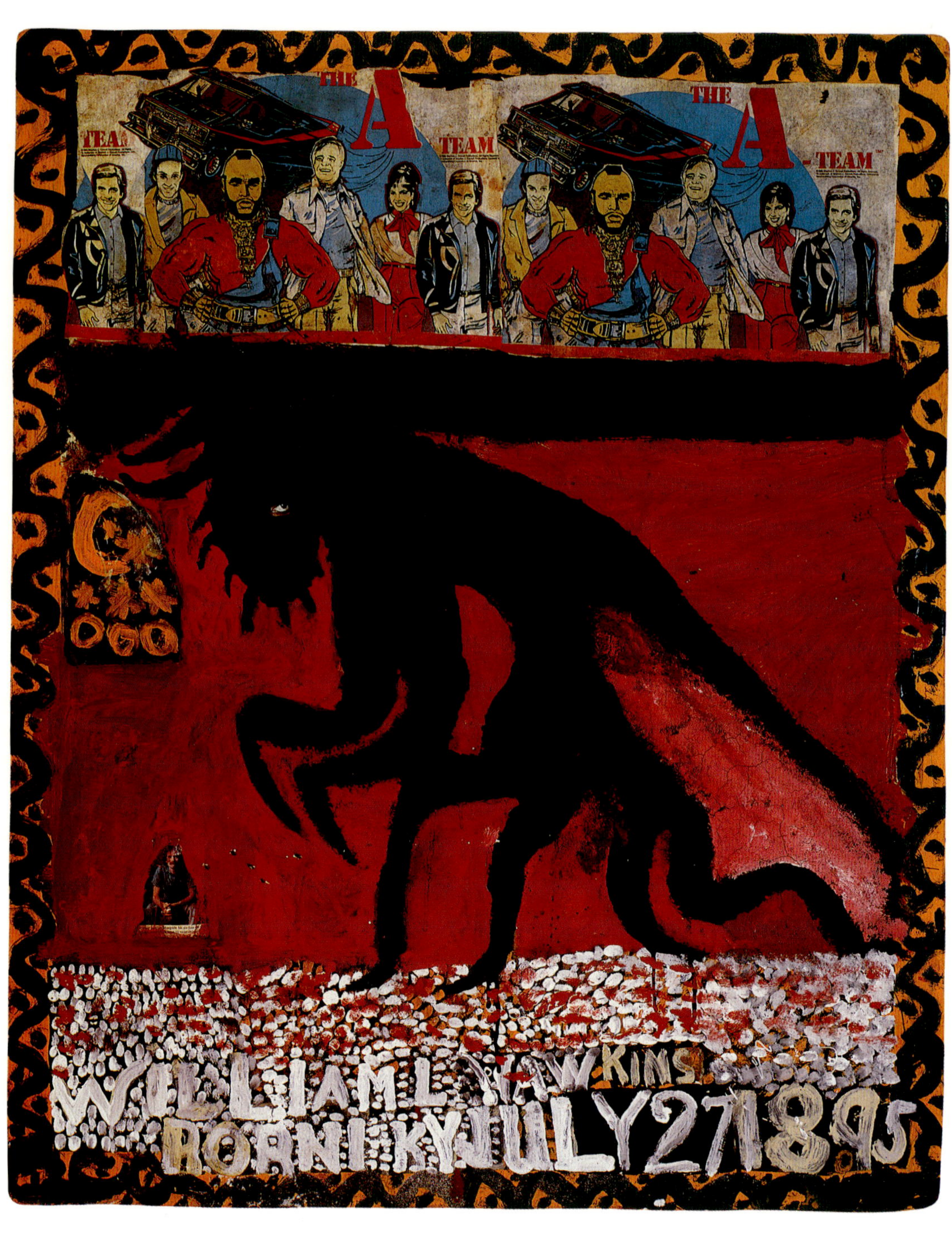

Praying Mantis, 1989

Enamel and collage on Masonite, 48″ x 39½″

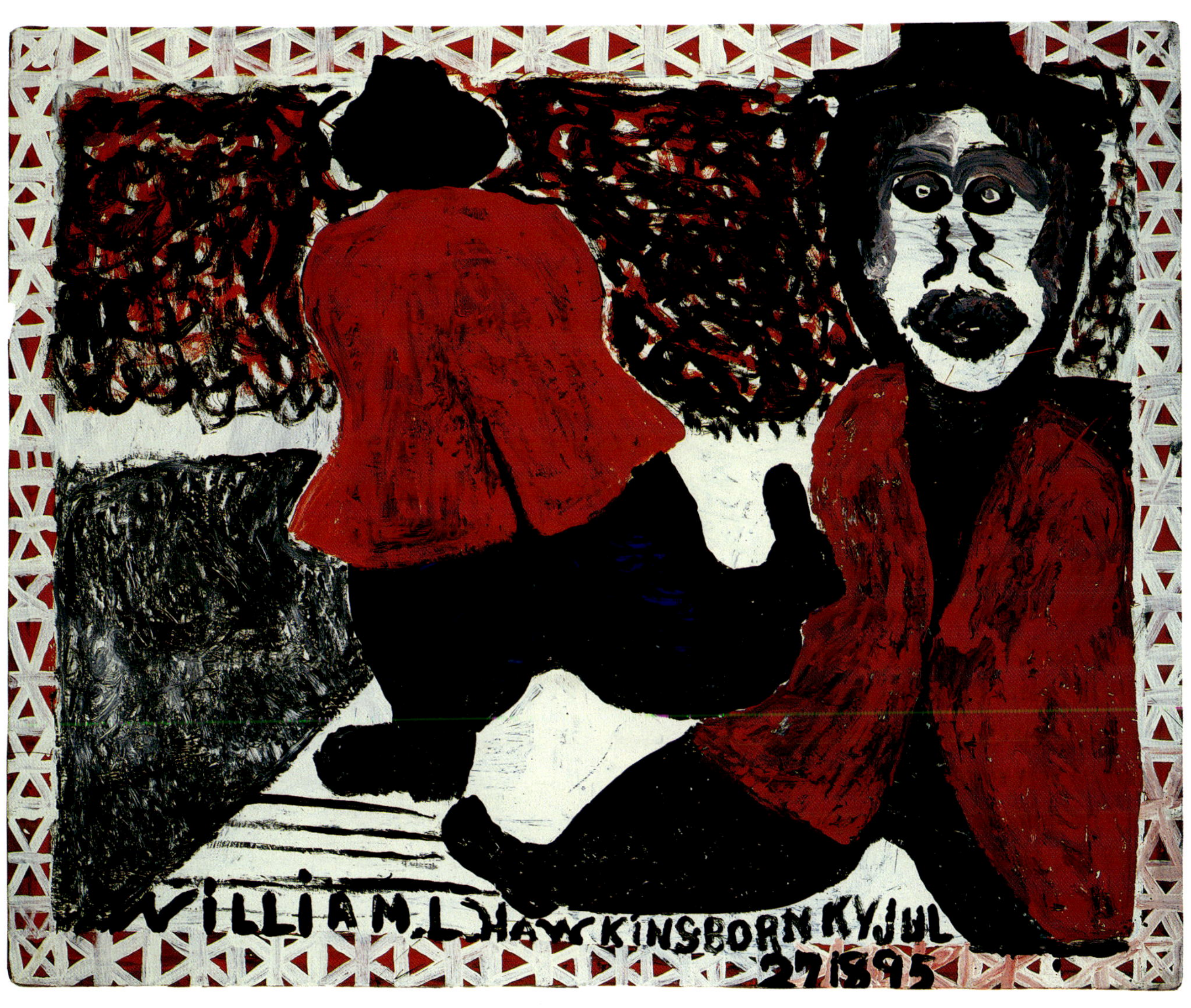

Charlie Chaplin, 1988

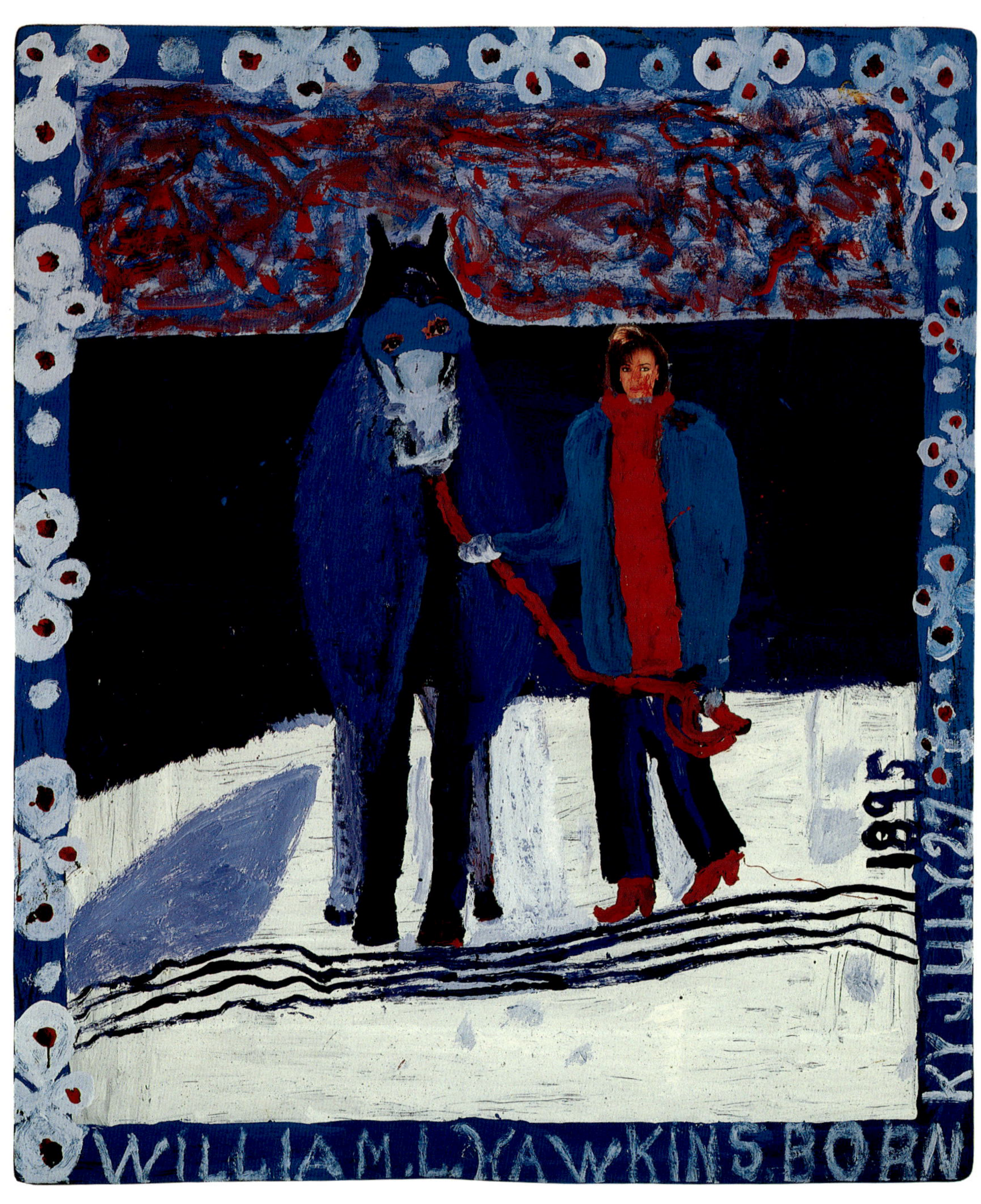

Woman Walking Horse, 1989

Enamel and collage on Masonite, 46″ x 39½″

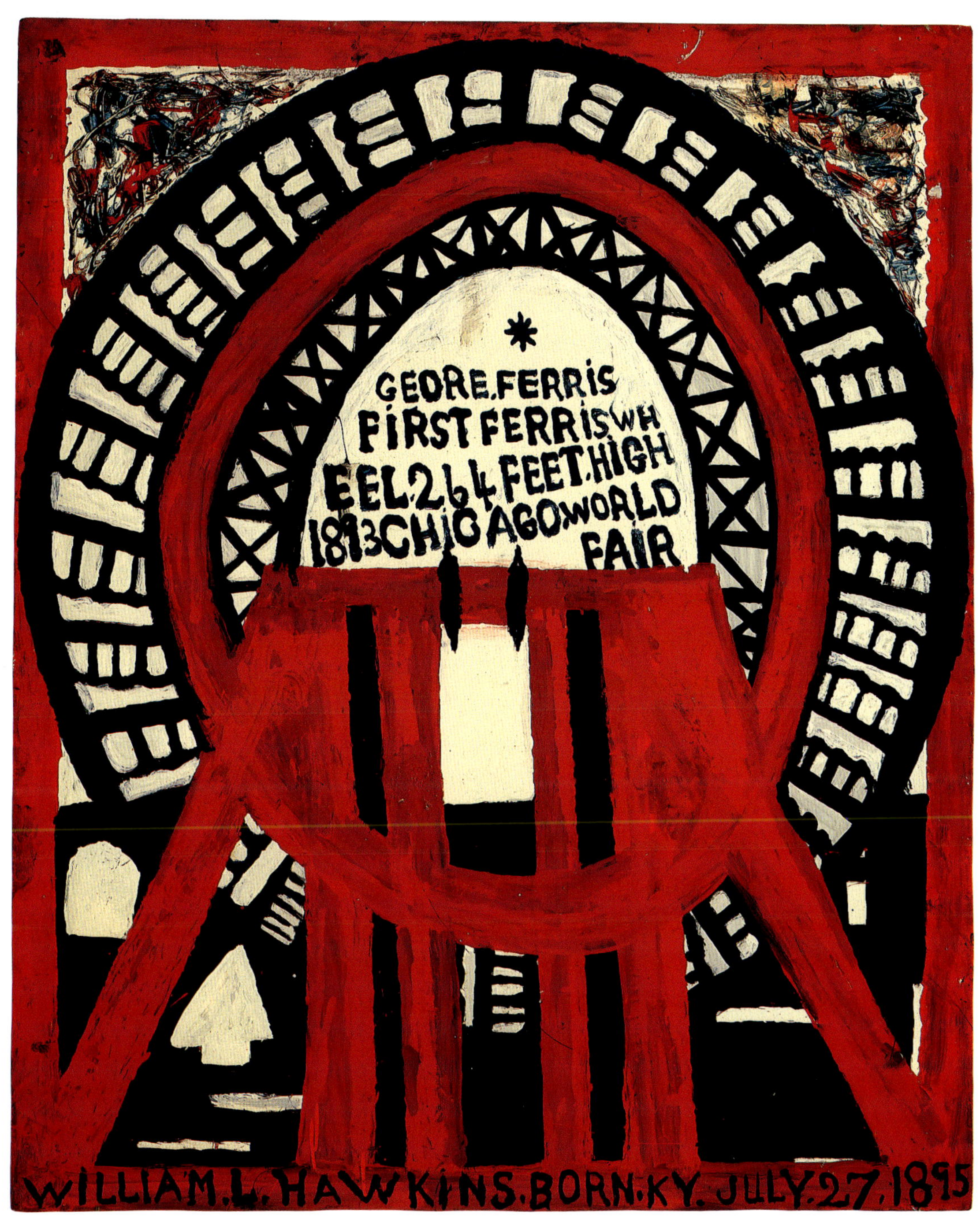

Ferris Wheel #2, 1985

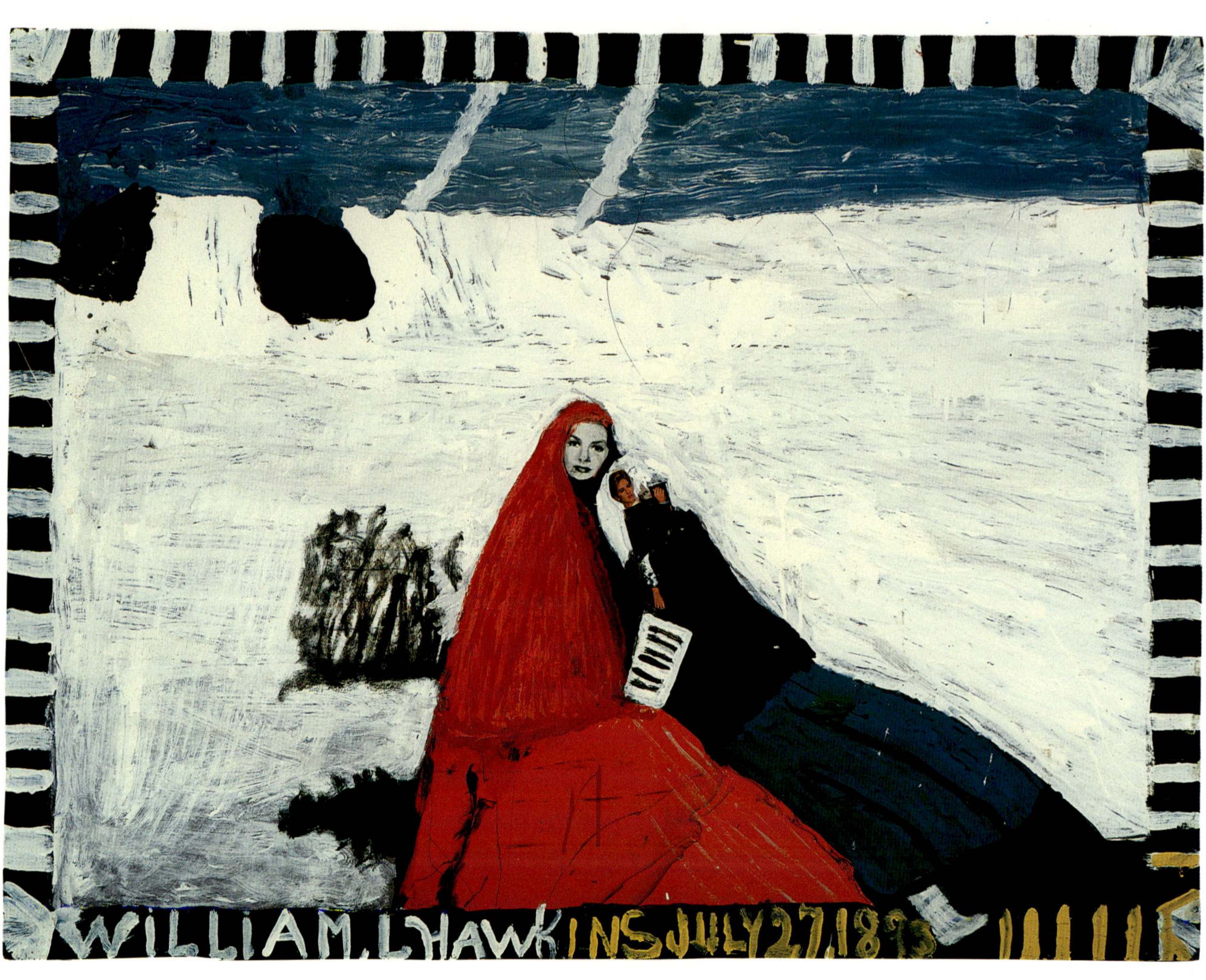

Two Figures with Collage Faces, 1987

Enamel and collage on Masonite, 36″ x 48″

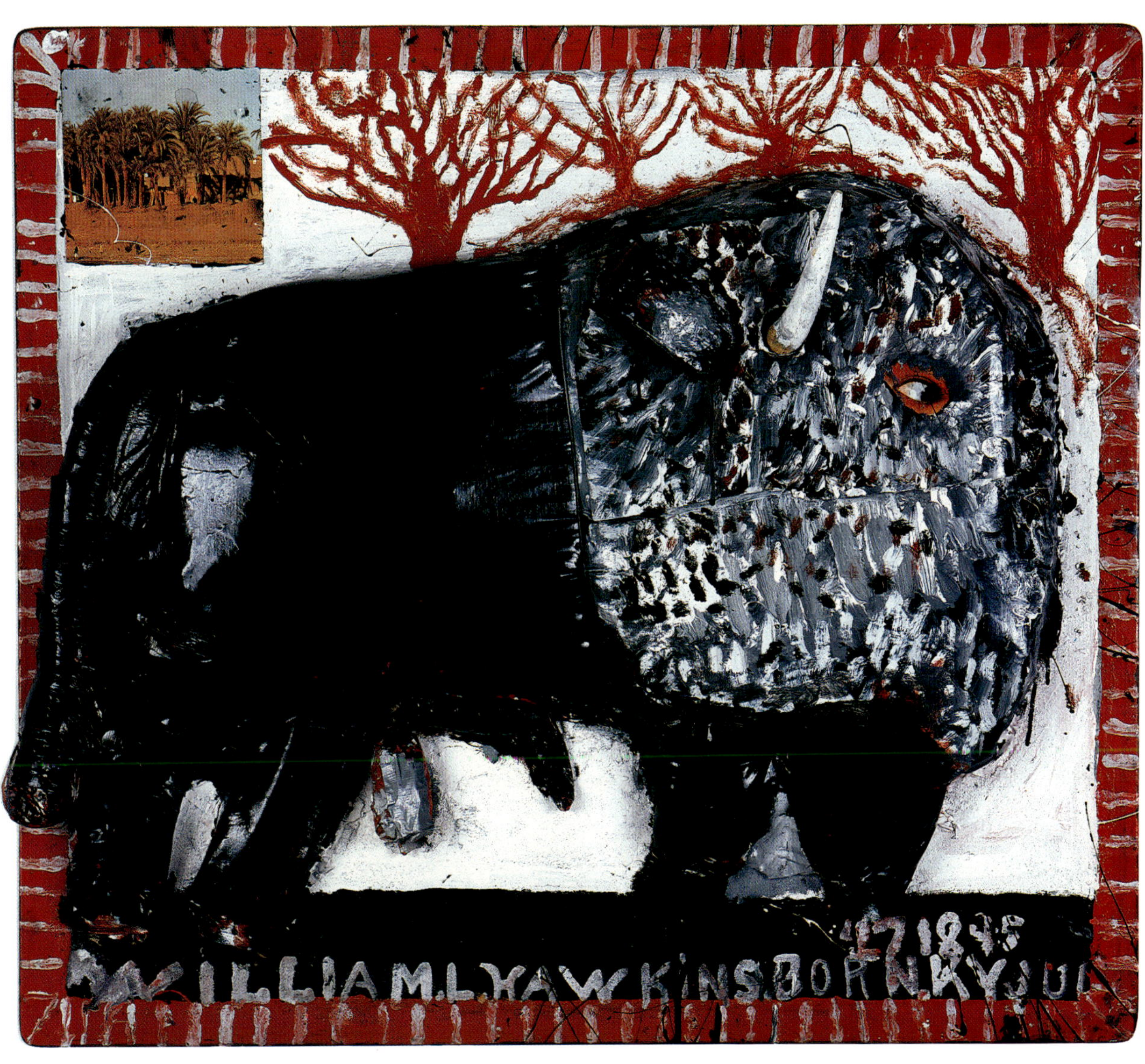

Buffalo #6, 1989

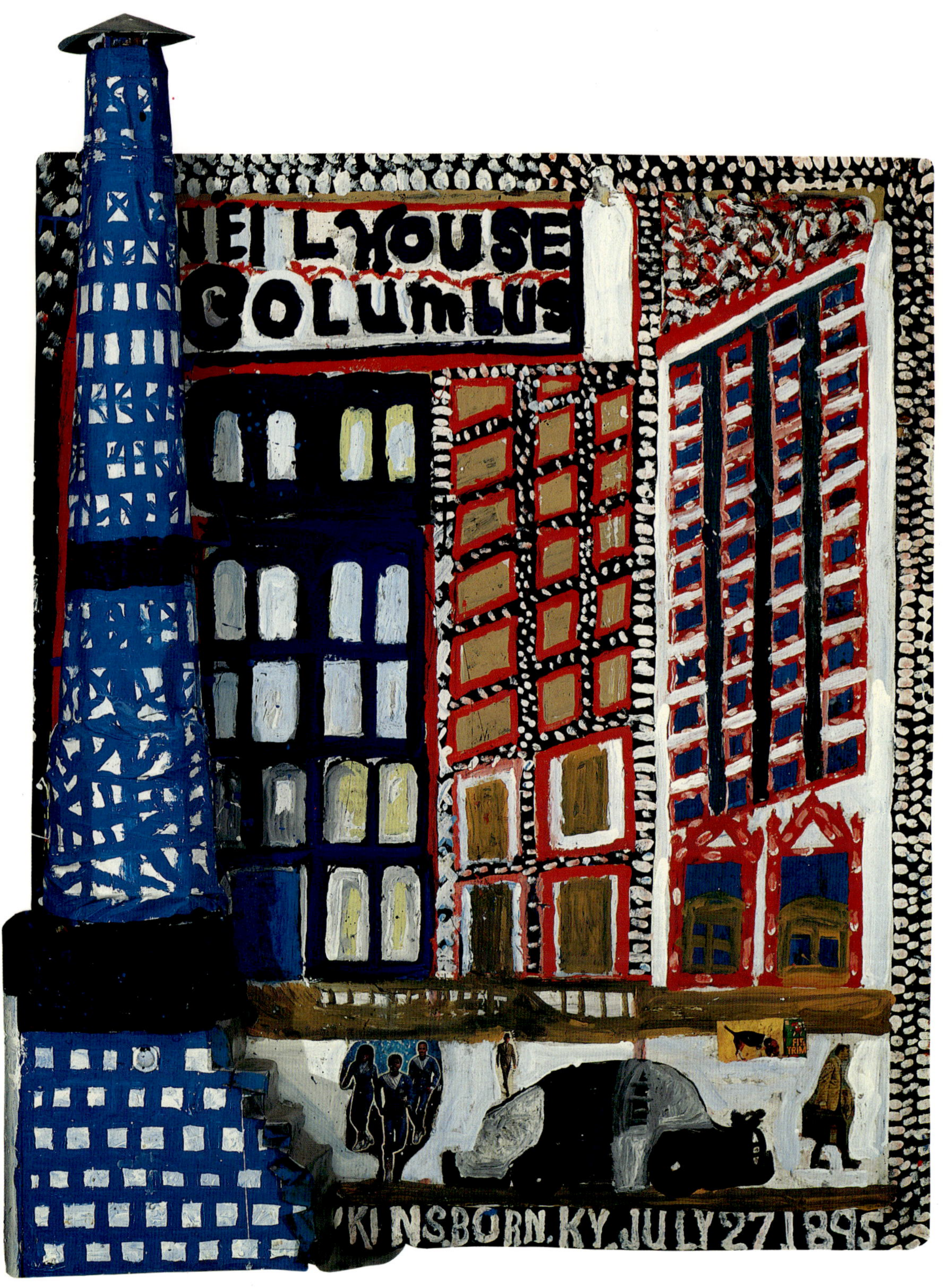

Neil House with Chimney #2, 1989

Enamel, collage, and mixed-media construction on Masonite, 64″ x 48″ x 5″

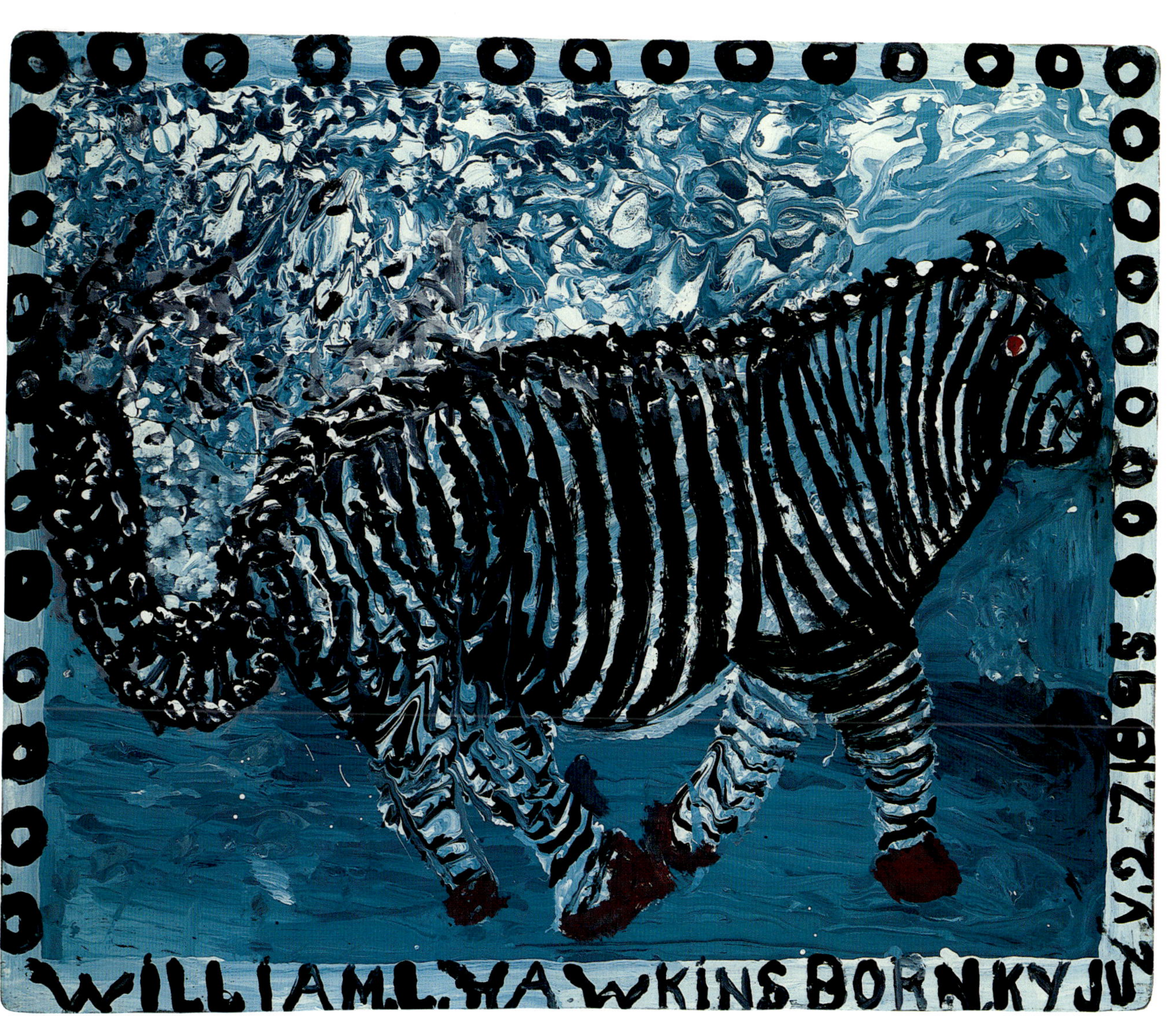
WILLIAM.L.HAWKINS BORN.KY JU

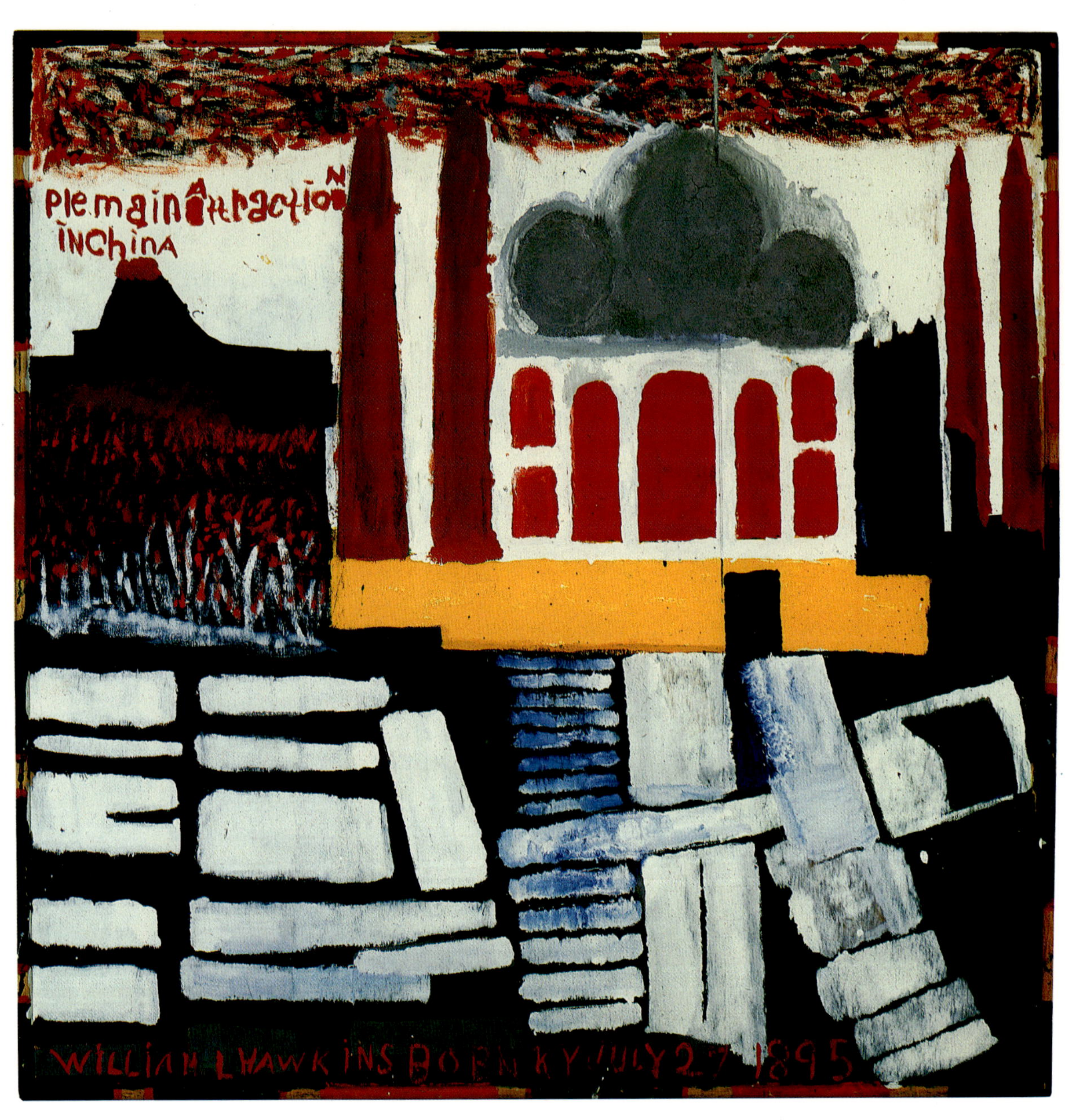

Taj Mahal, 1984

Enamel and mixed media on plywood, 48″ x 48″

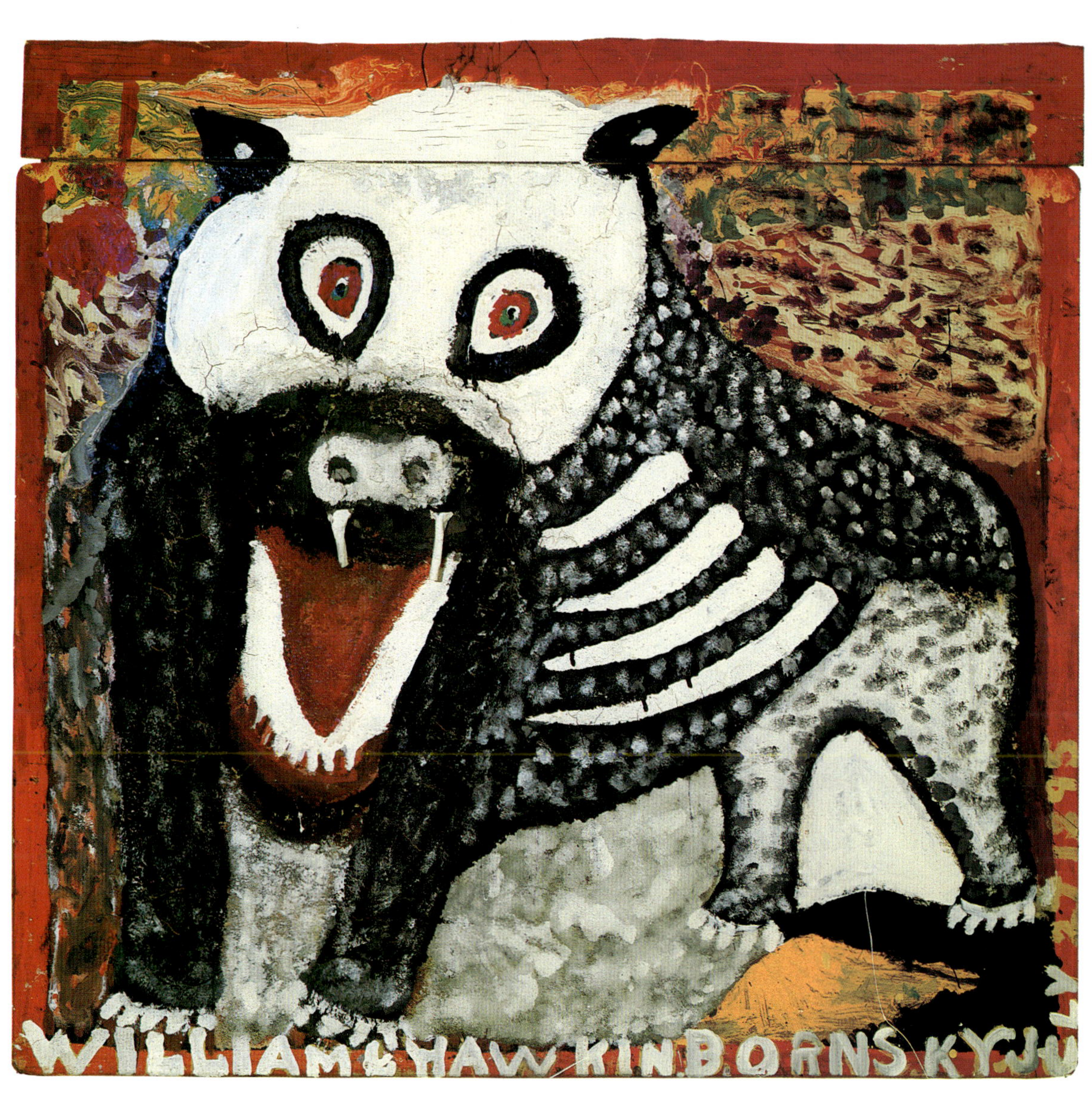
WILLIAM L HAWKIN BORNS KY JU
LY

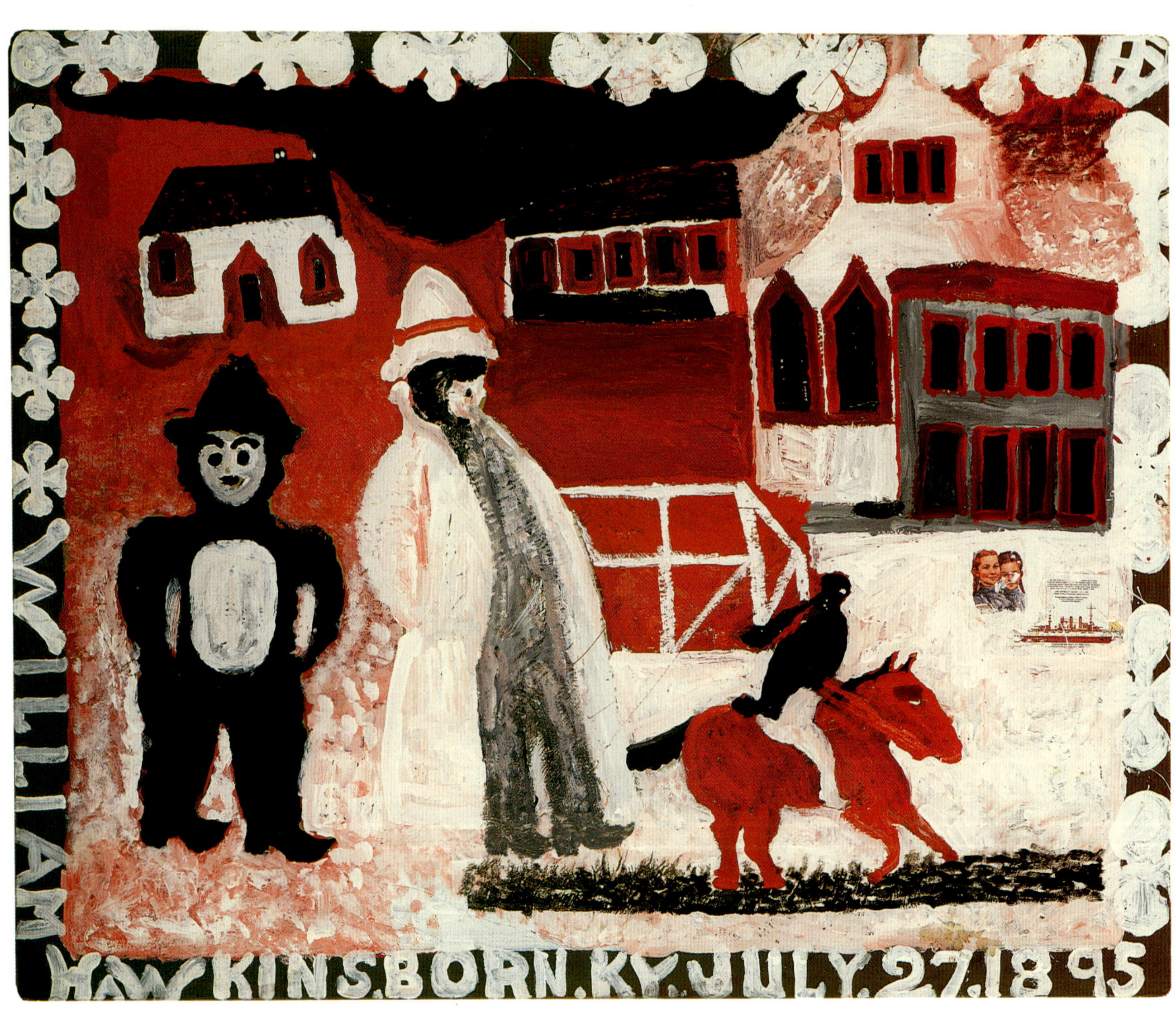

New England Landscape, 1988

Enamel on Masonite, 48″ x 60″

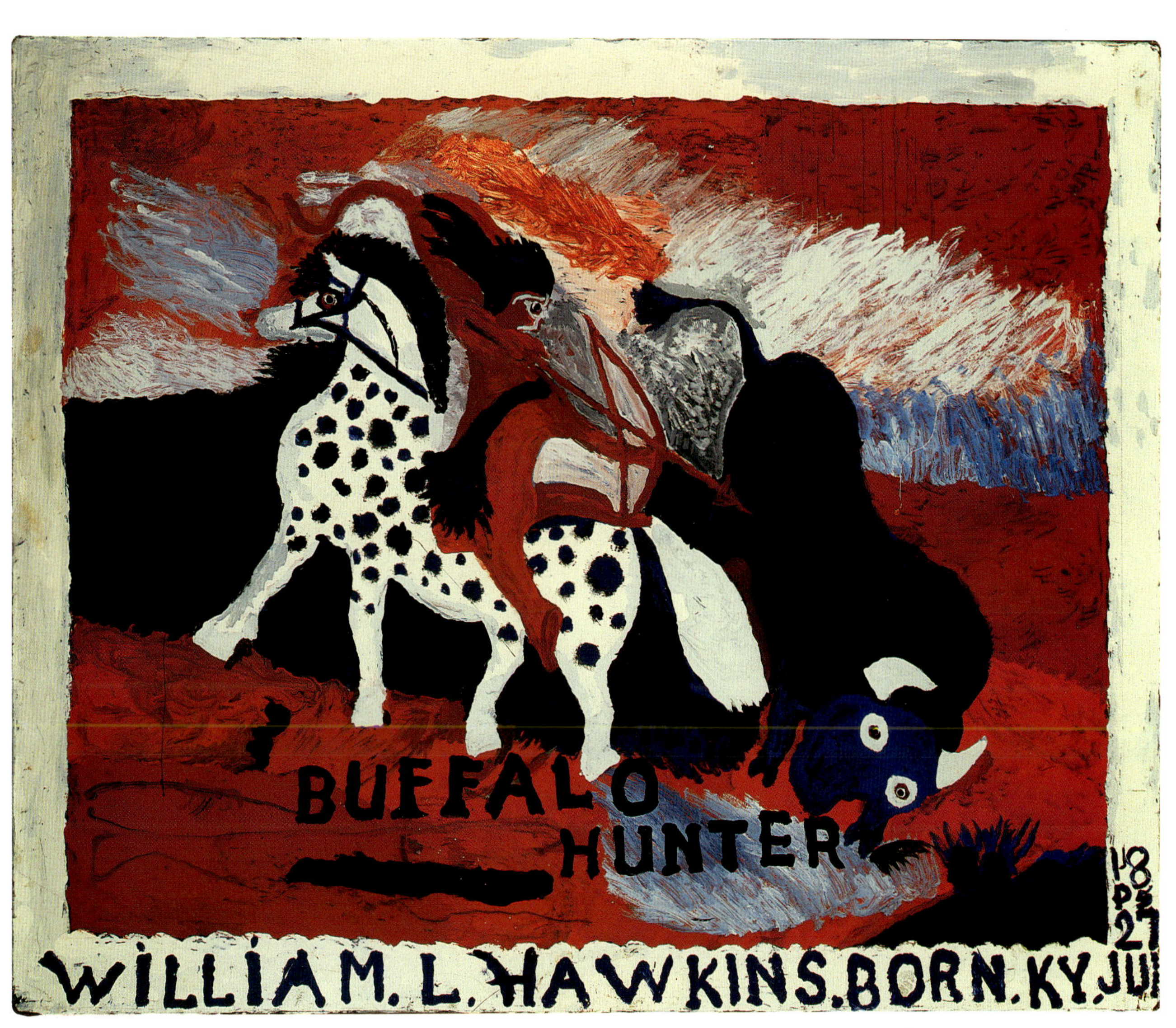
BUFFALO
HUNTER
WILLIAM. L. HAWKINS. BORN. KY. JU

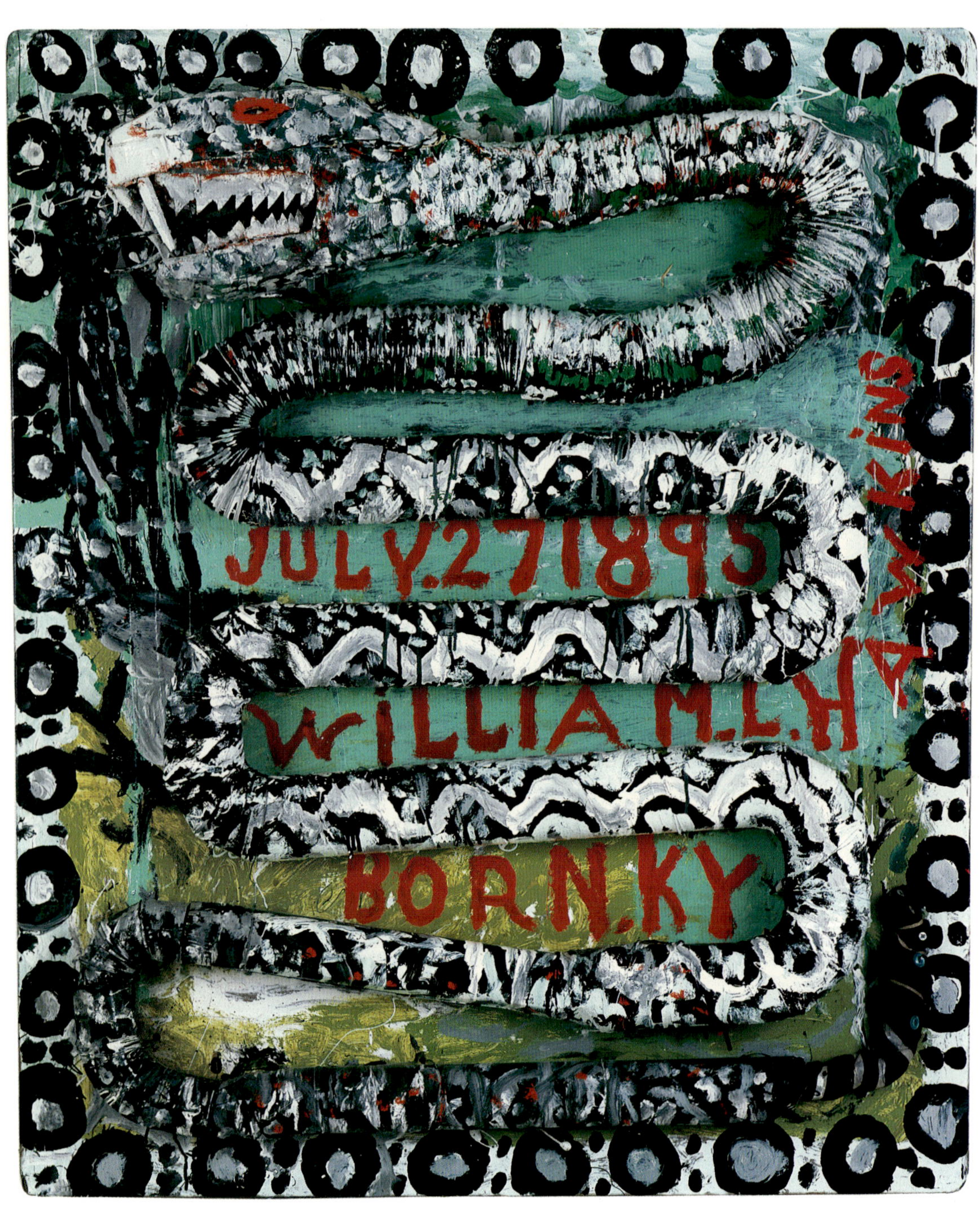

Dragon Snake, 1987

Enamel and mixed-media construction on Masonite, 56½″ x 48″ x 5″

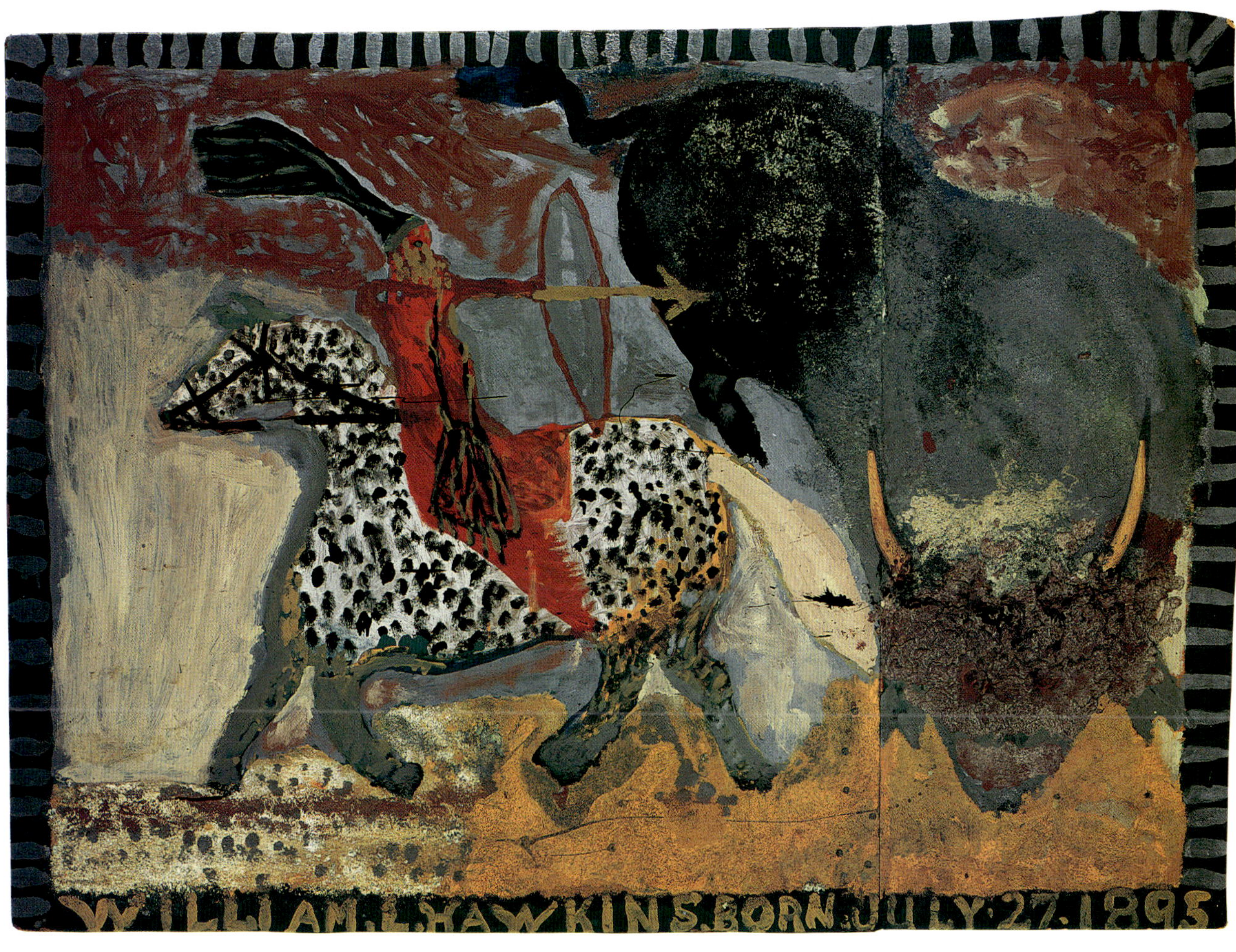

Indian Hunting Buffalo, 1983

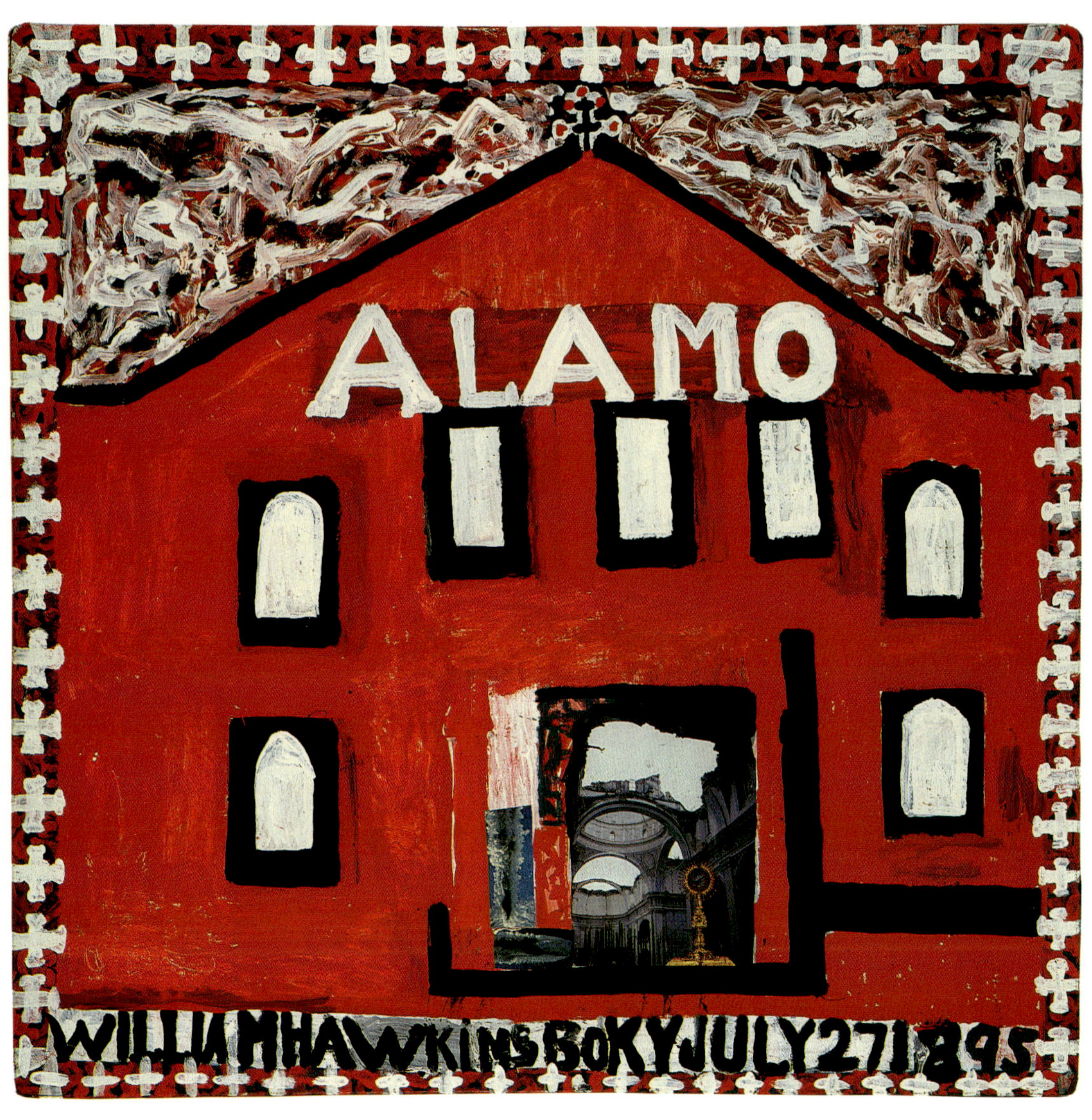

Alamo, 1986

Enamel and collage on Masonite, 48″ x 46½″

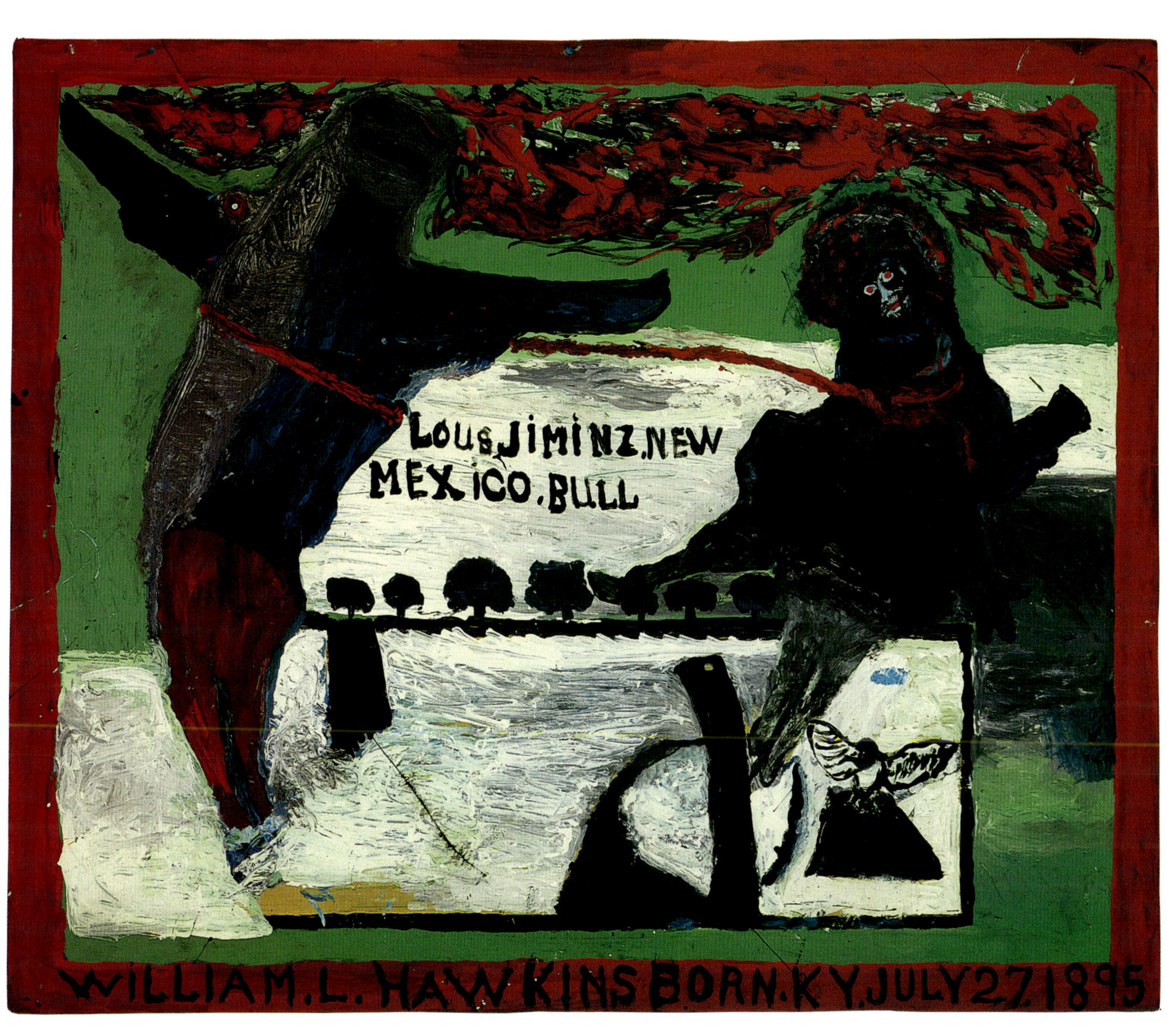
LOUS JIMINZ NEW
MEX ICO. BULL
WILLIAM. L. HAWKINS BORN. KY. JULY 27 1895

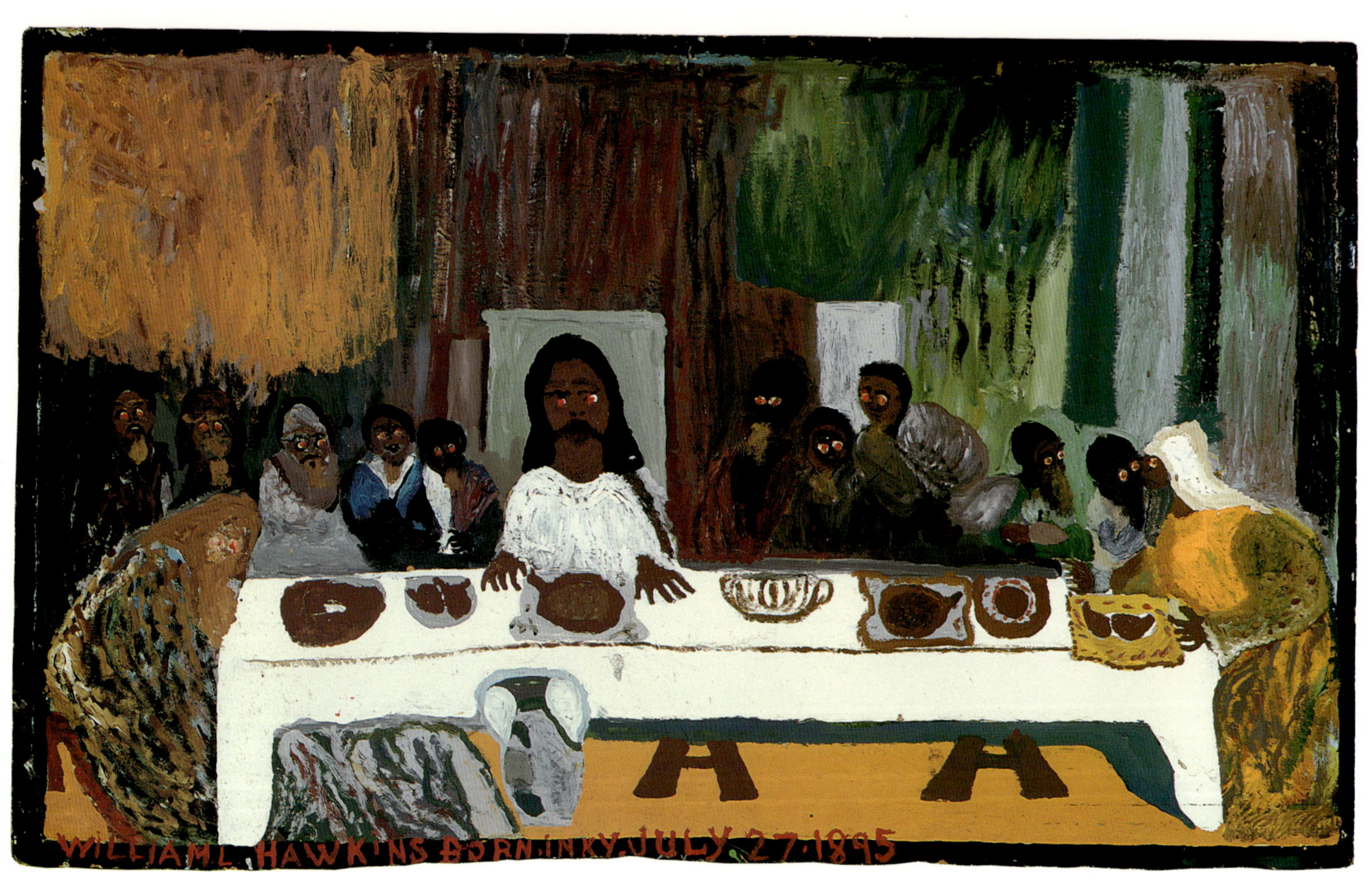

Last Supper #1, 1984

Enamel on particleboard, 38″ x 52″

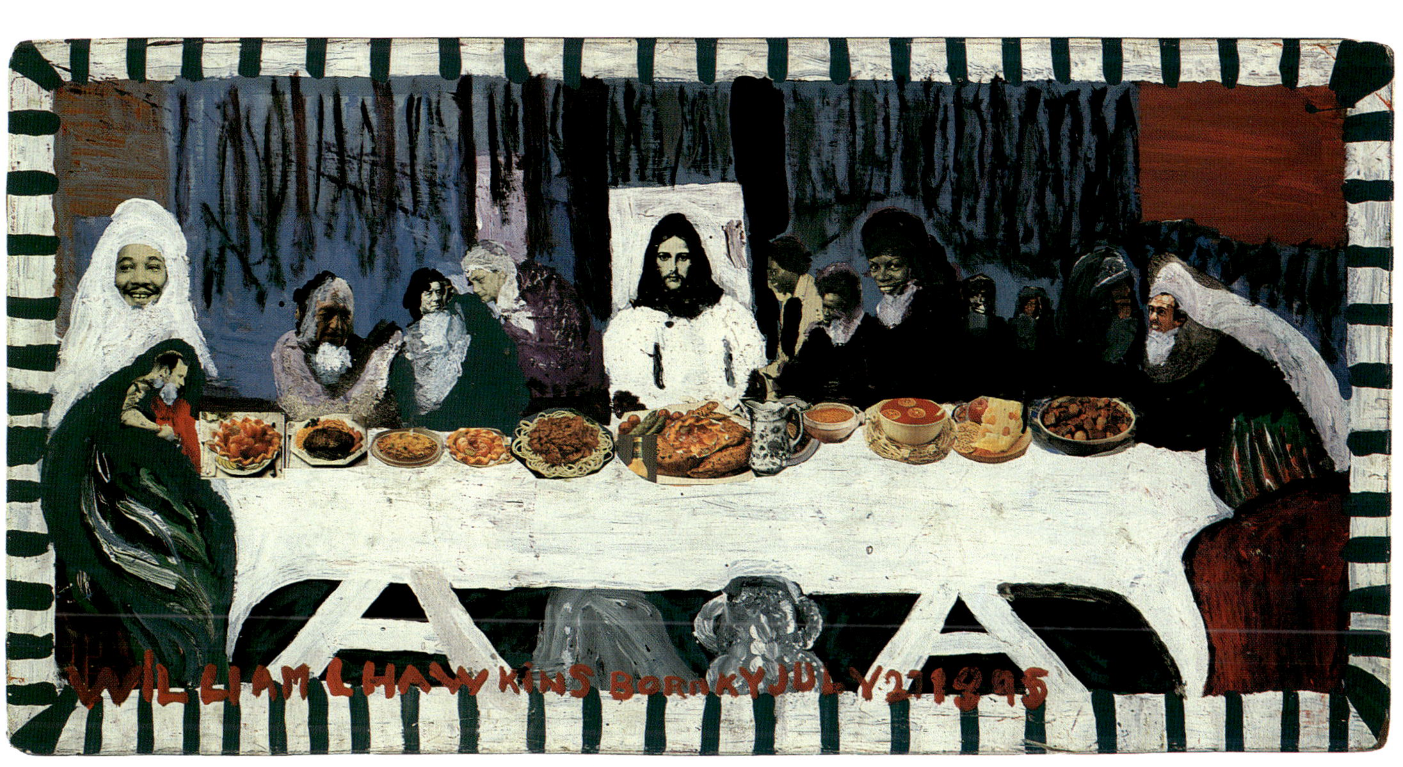

Last Supper #6, 1986

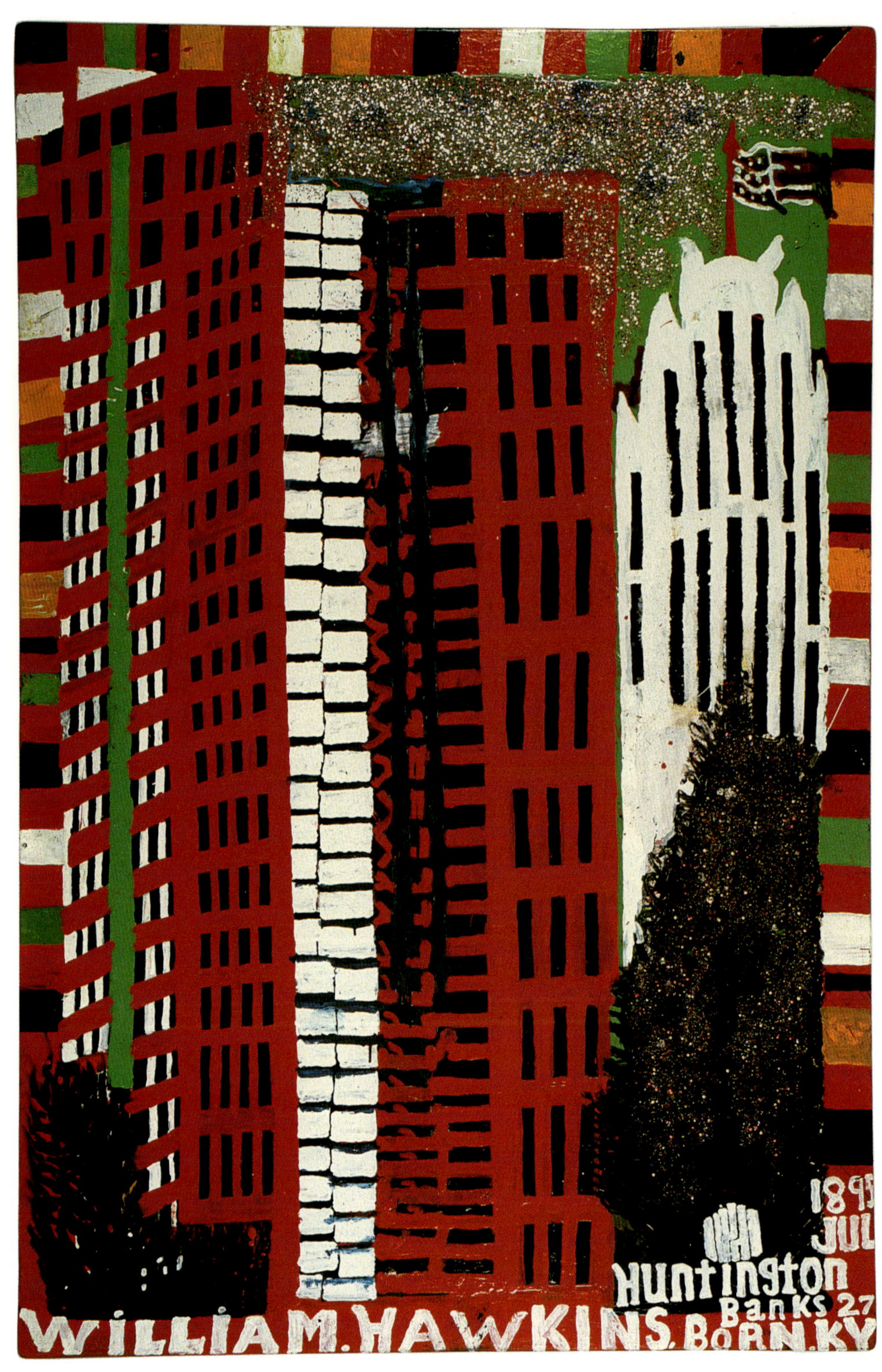

Huntington Bank #2, 1985

Enamel and mixed media on Masonite, 72″ x 48″

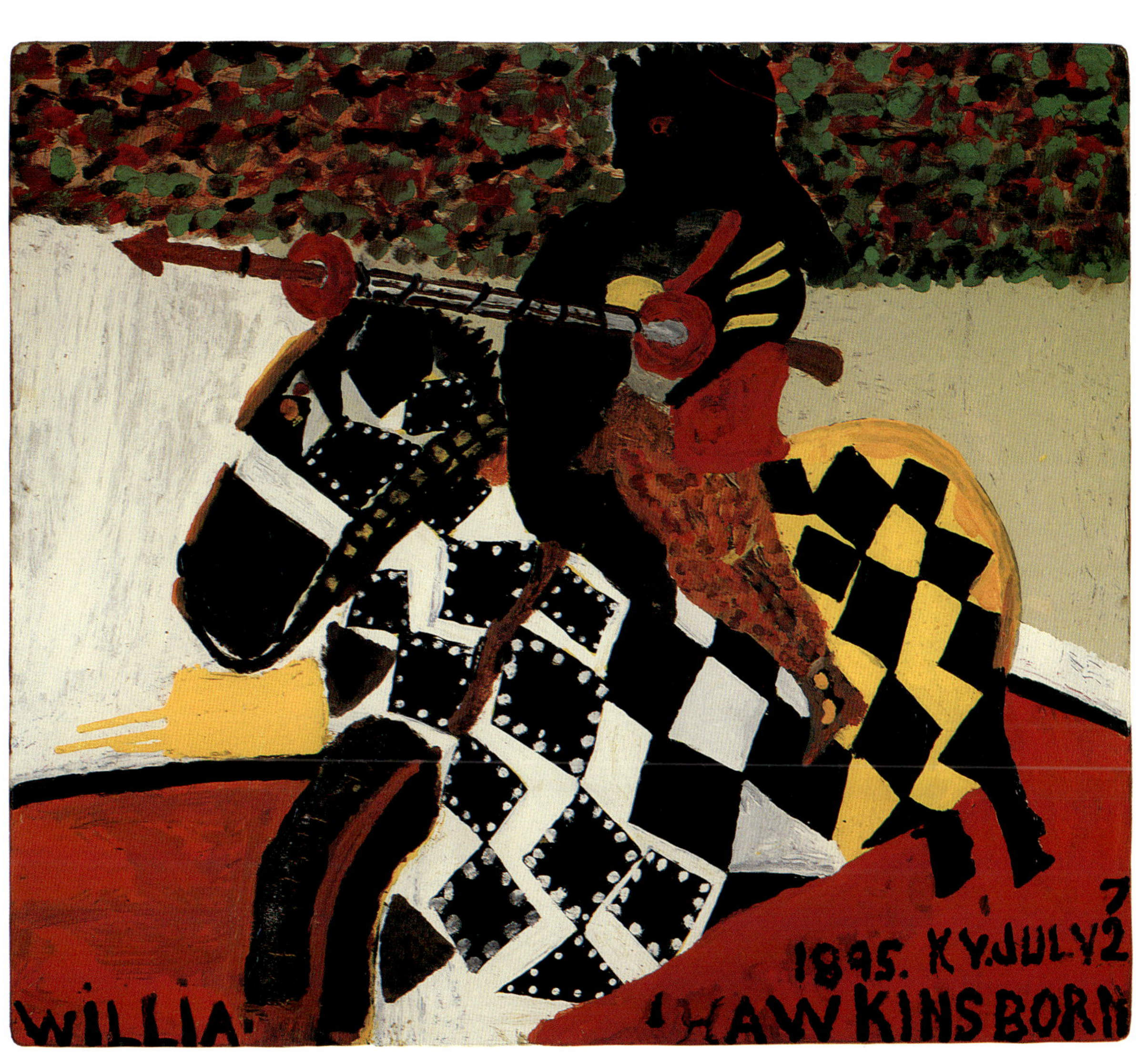

Jousting Knight #2, 1985

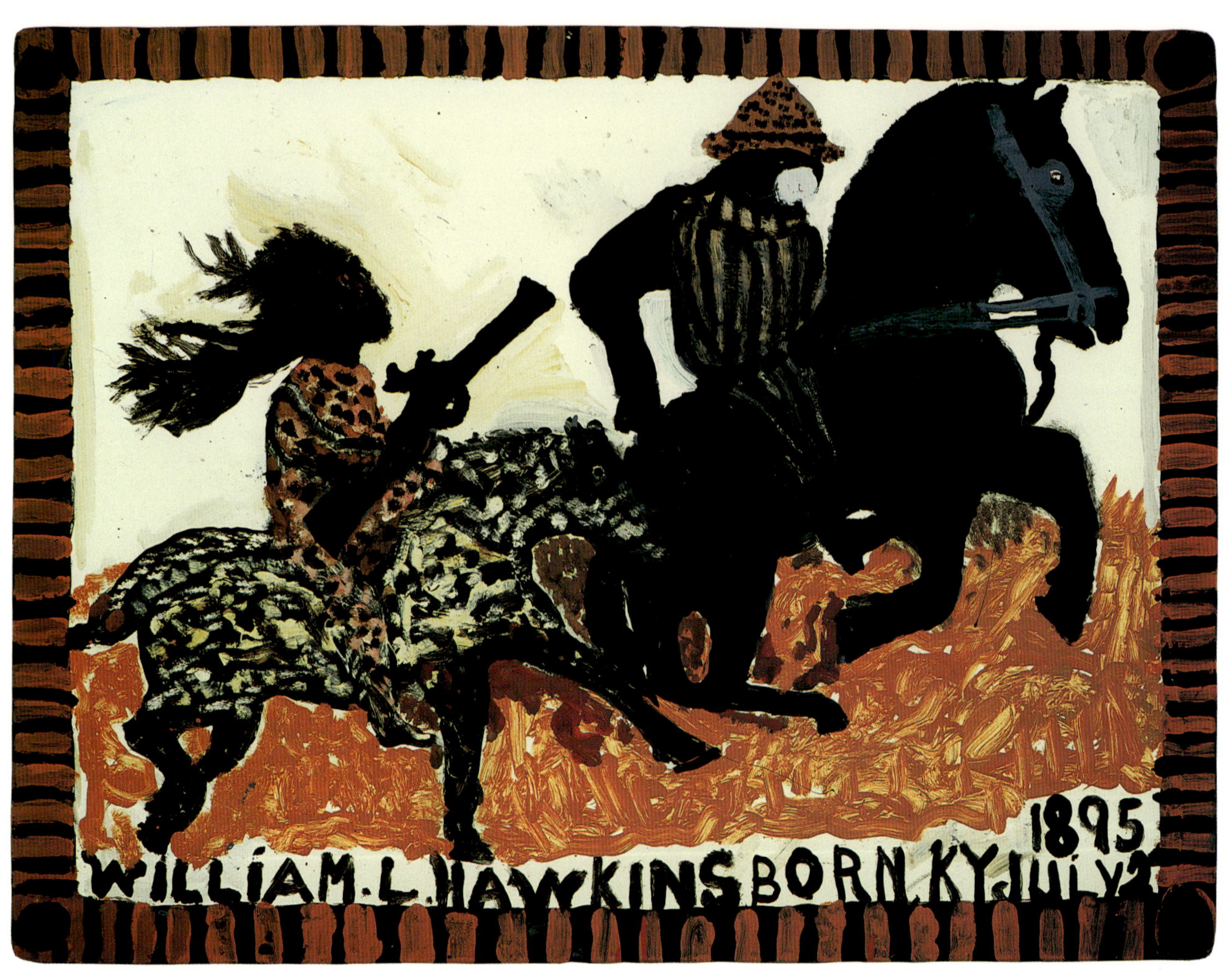

Indian Chasing White Man, 1988

Enamel on Masonite, 36″ x 48″

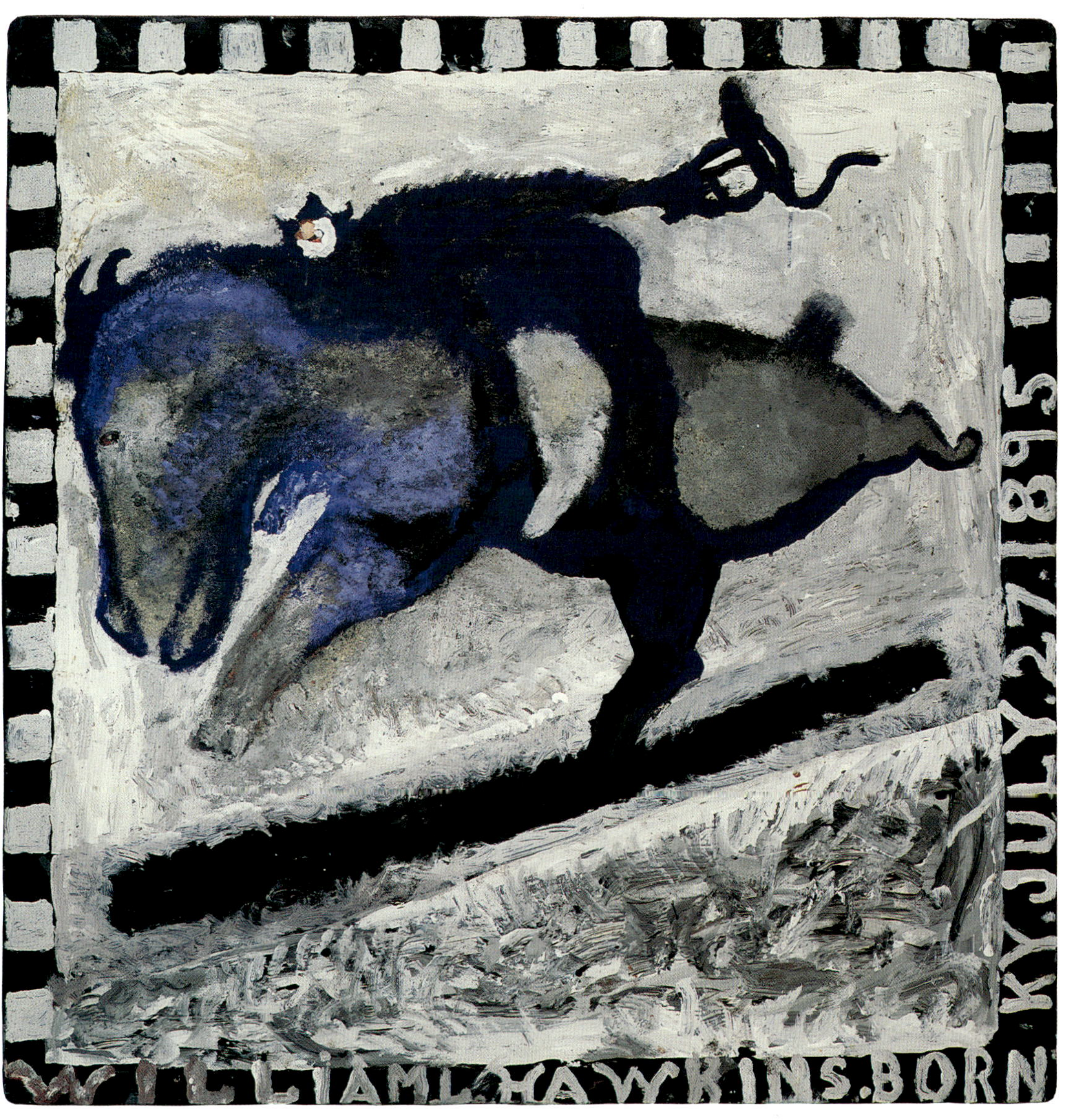

Bucking Bronco, 1989

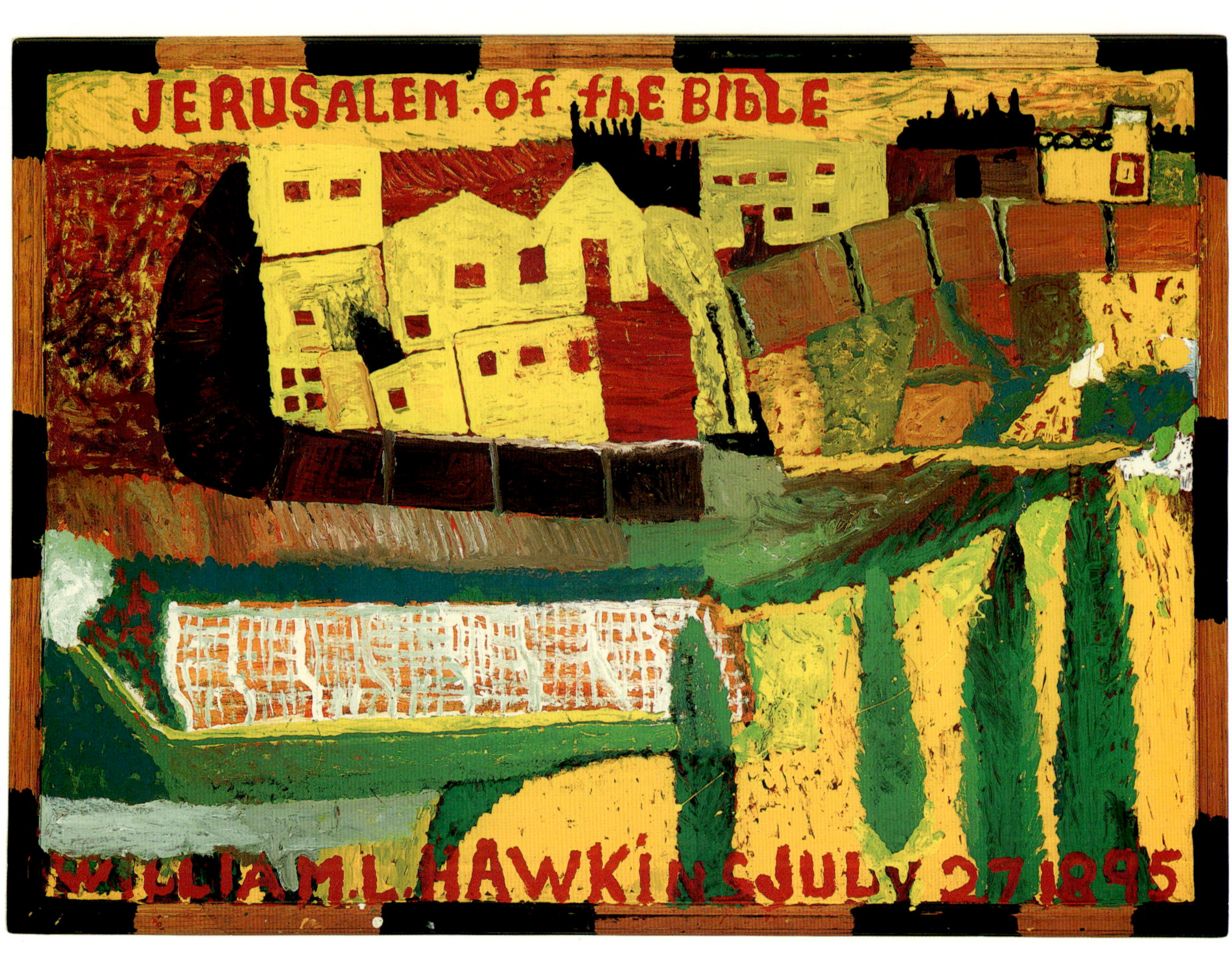

Jerusalem of the Bible #1, 1984

Enamel on Masonite, 33″ x $46\frac{1}{4}$″

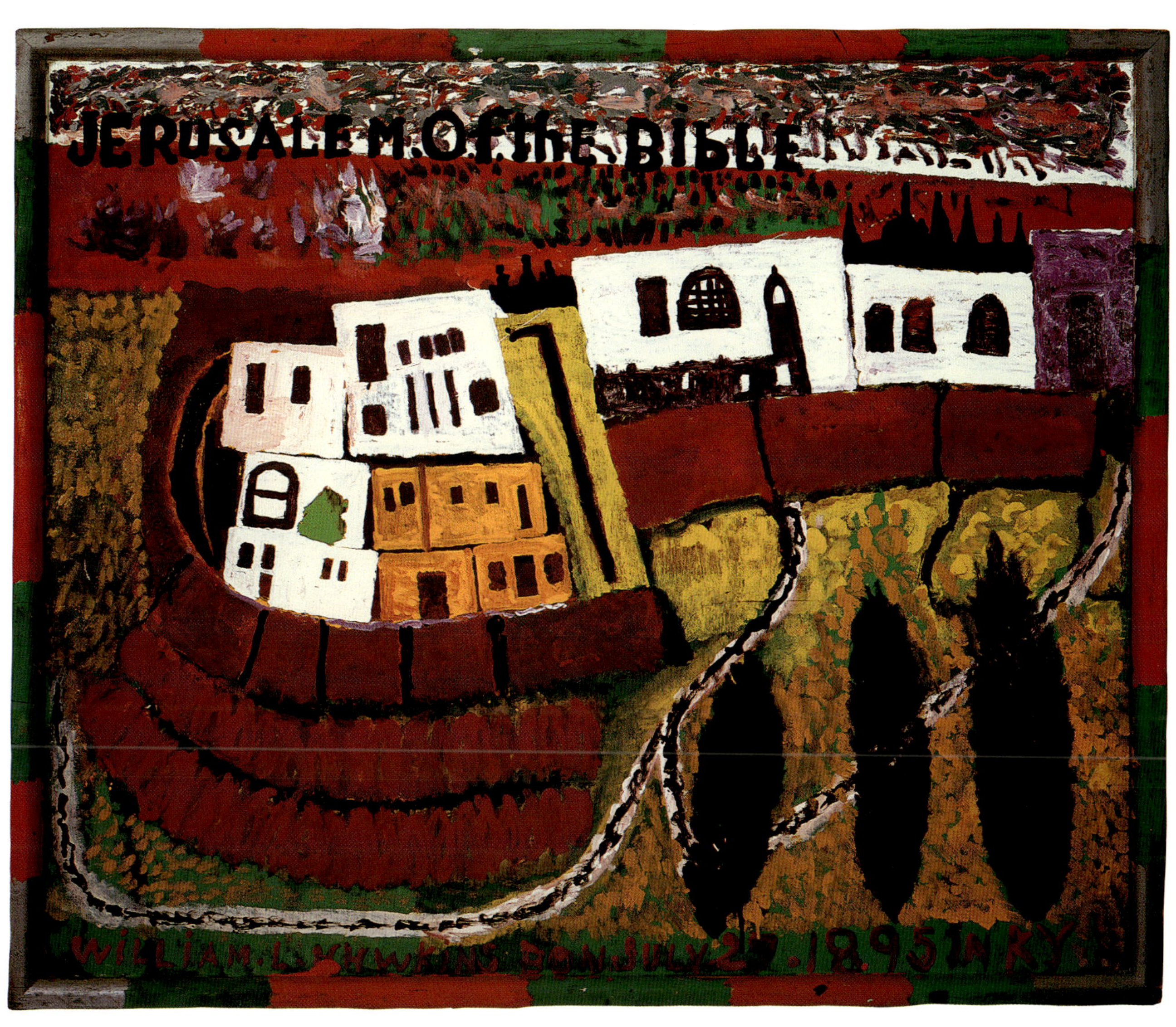

Jerusalem of the Bible #2, 1984

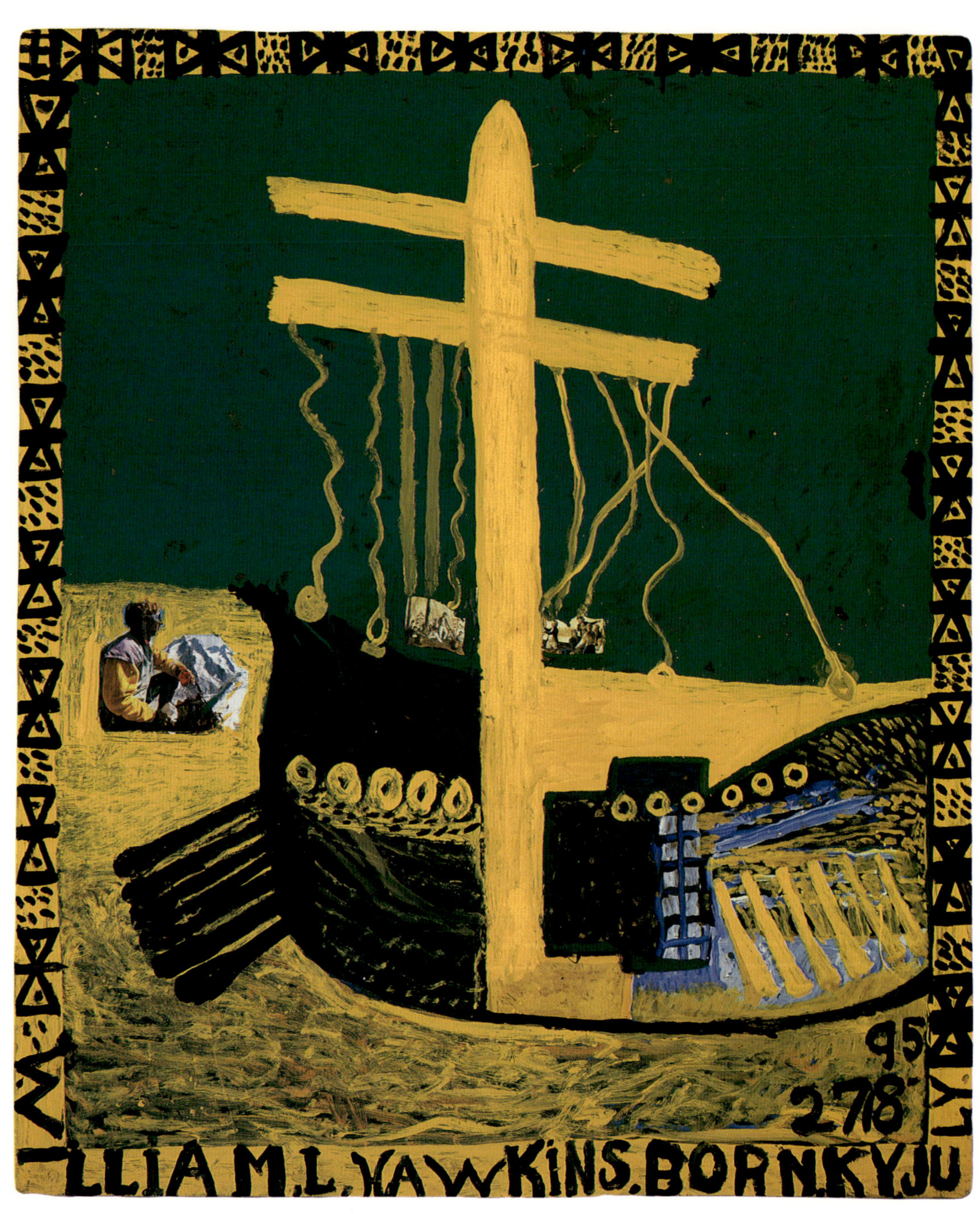

Ship with Yellow Mast, 1989

Enamel and collage on Masonite, 56½″ x 48″

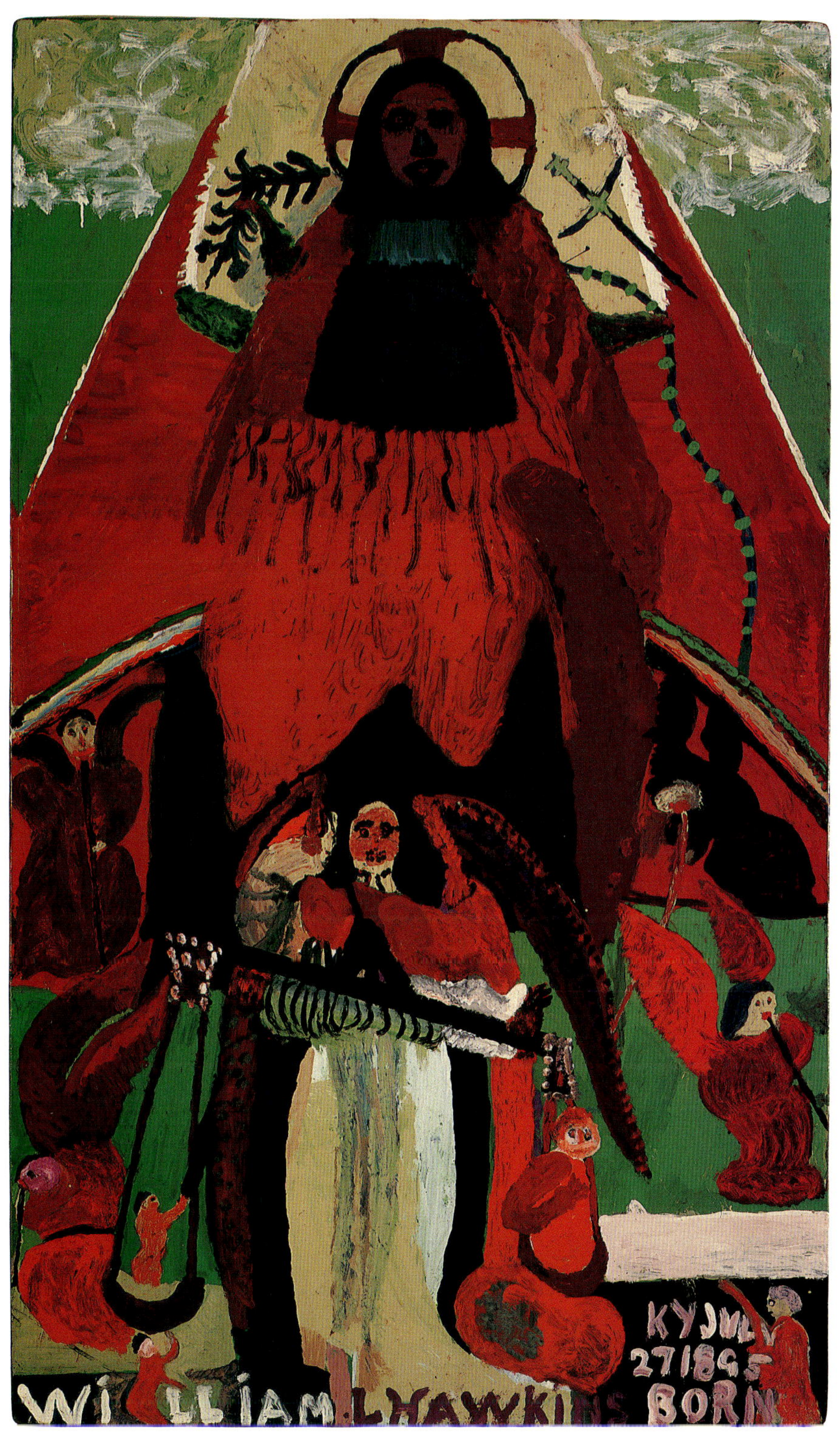

The Judgment, 1985

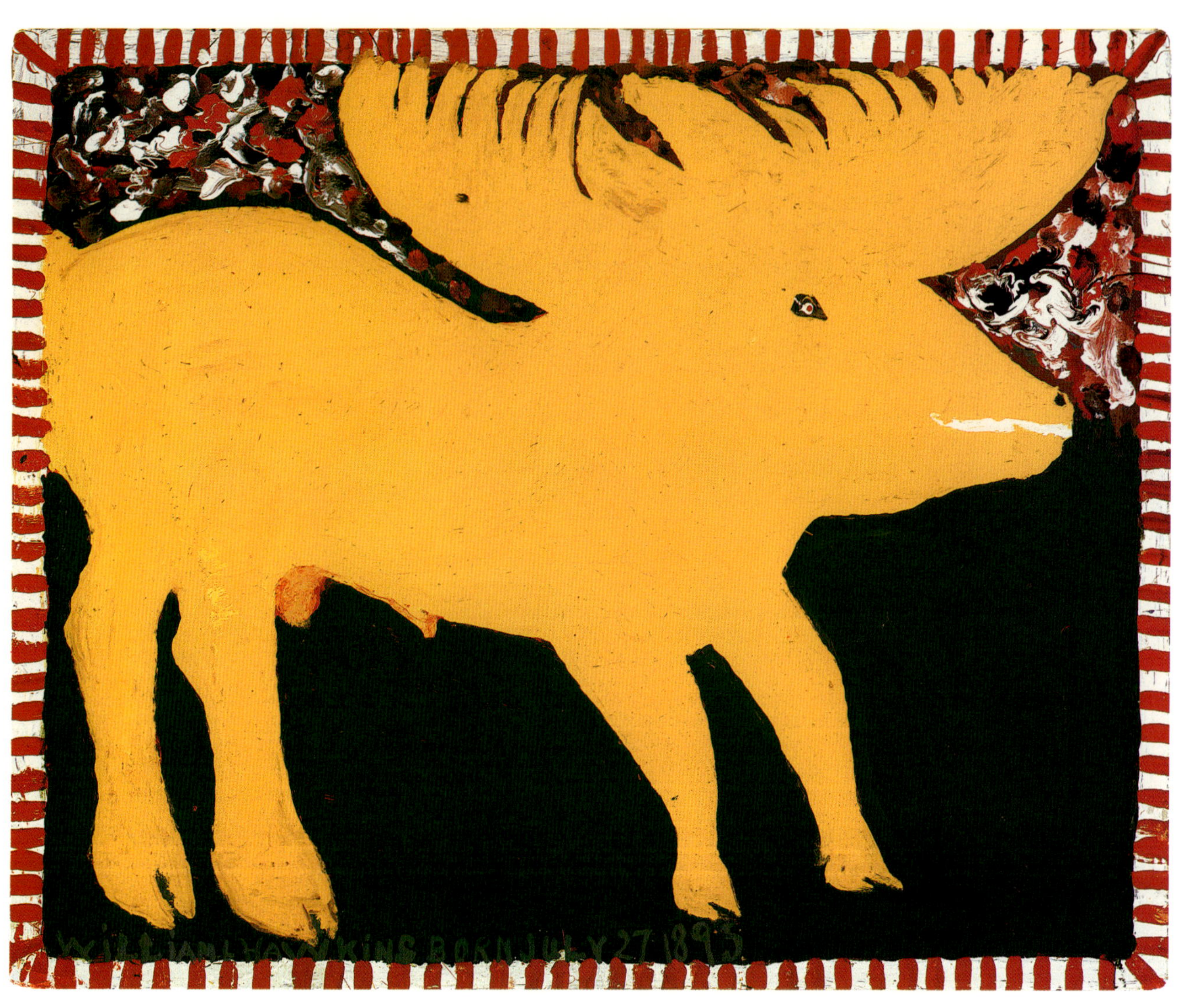

Yellow Buck, 1987

Enamel on Masonite, 48″ x 60″

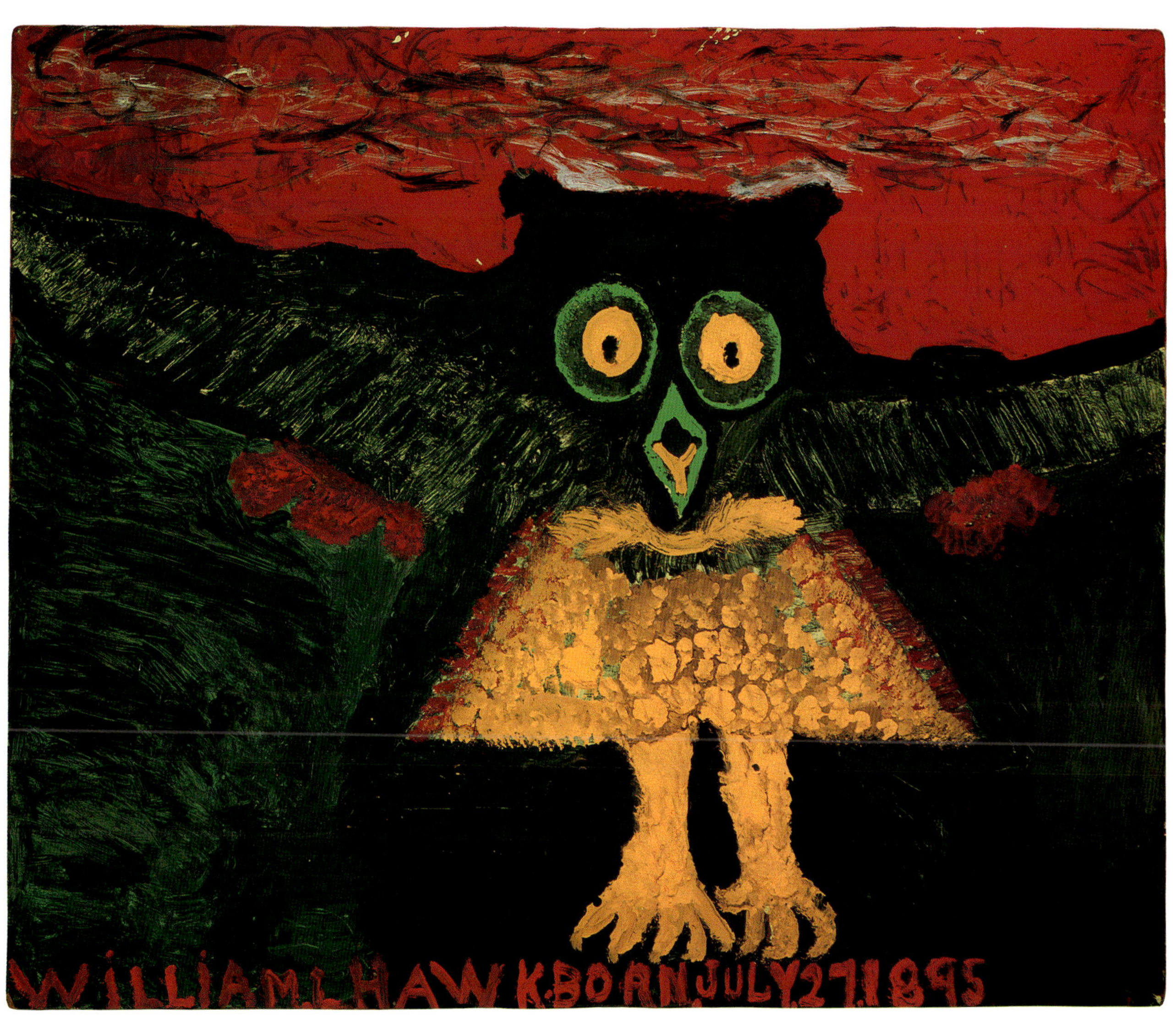

Great Horned Owl, 1985

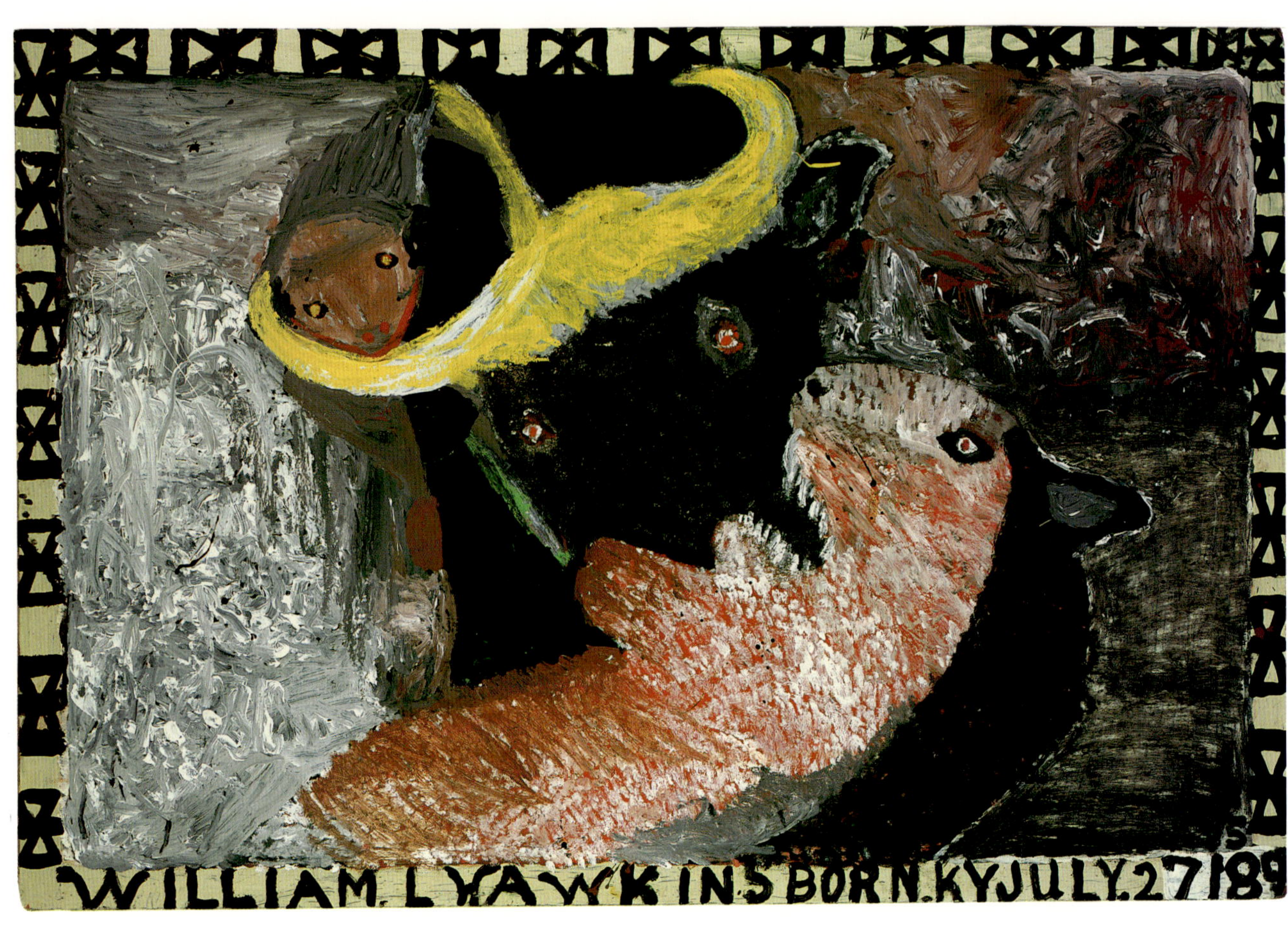

Lions Attacking Wildebeest, 1987

Enamel and mixed media on Masonite, 48″ x 72″

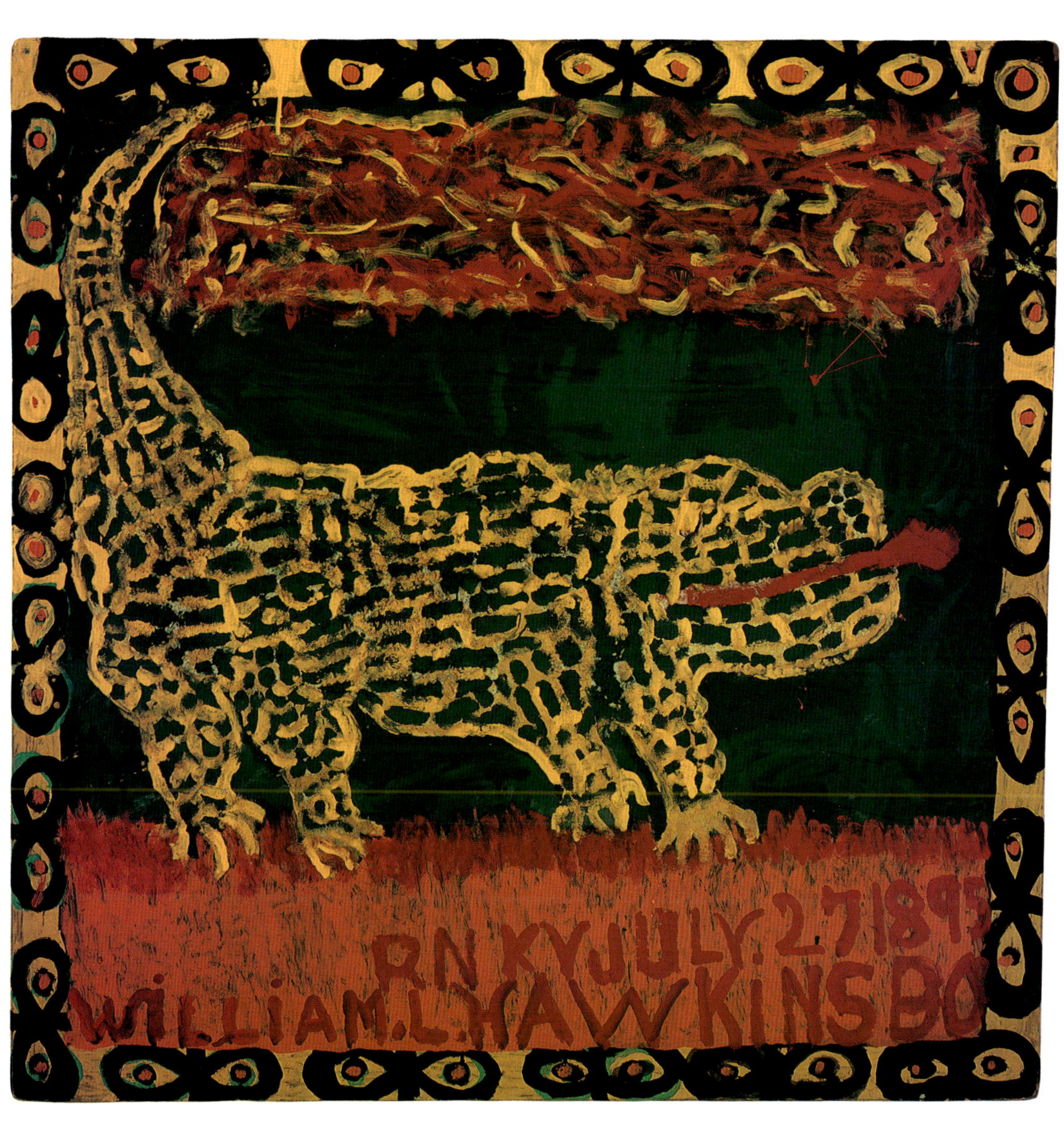

Alligator, [illegible]

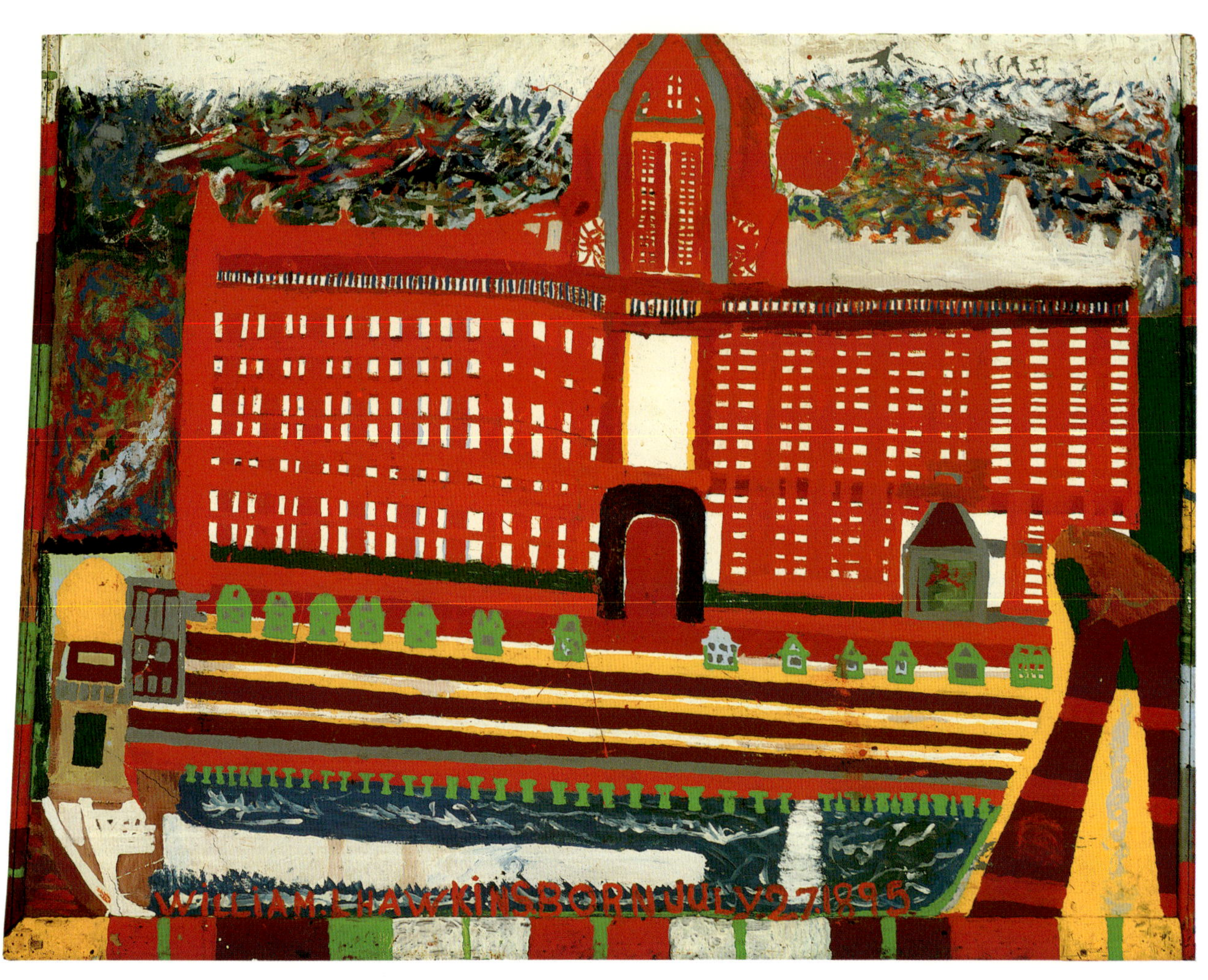

Wrigley Building, 1985

Enamel on particleboard, 49″ x 65″

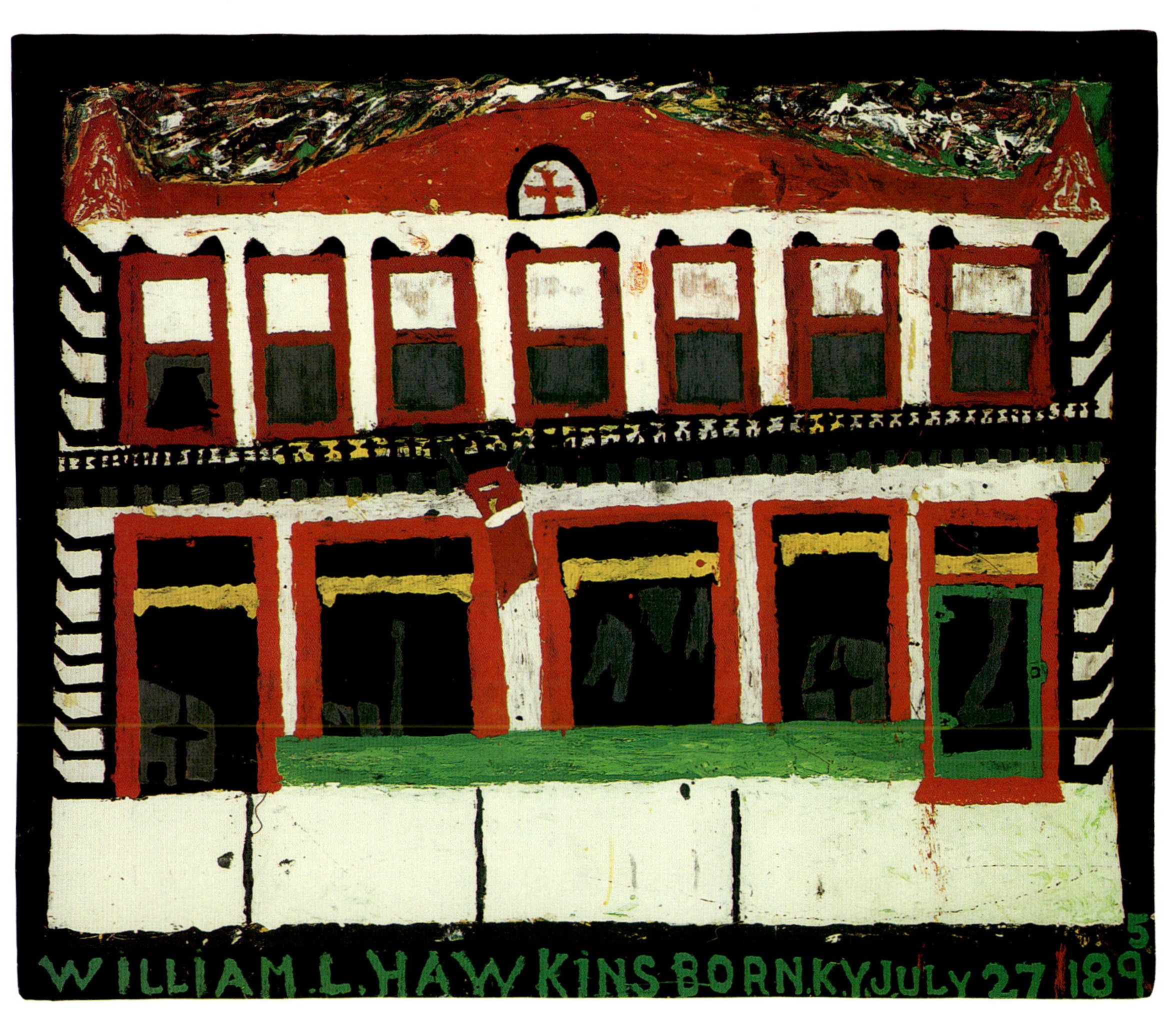
WILLIAM.L.HAWKINS BORN.KY.JULY 27 1895

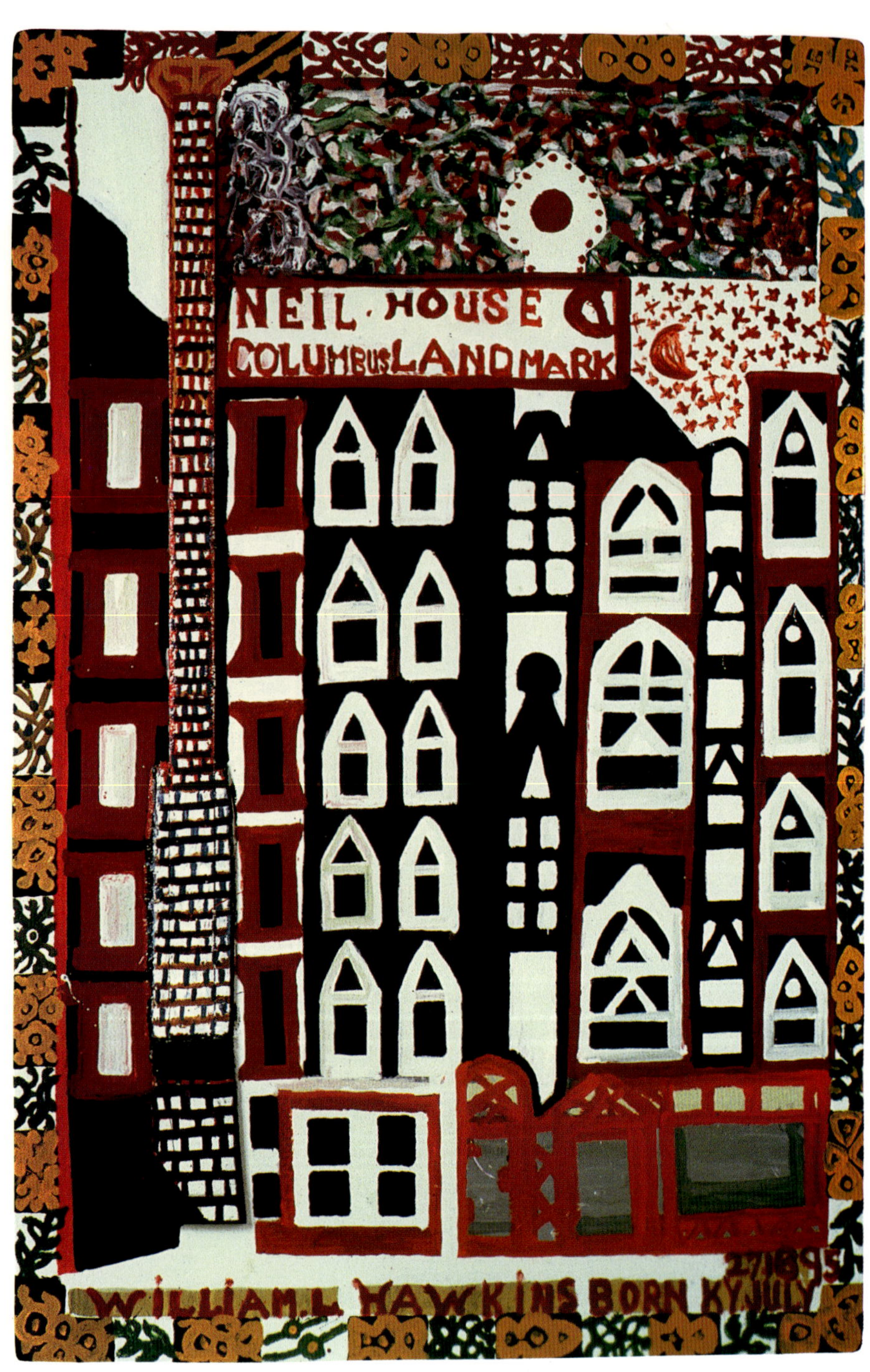

Neil House with Chimney, 1986

Enamel and composition material on Masonite, 72″ x 48″

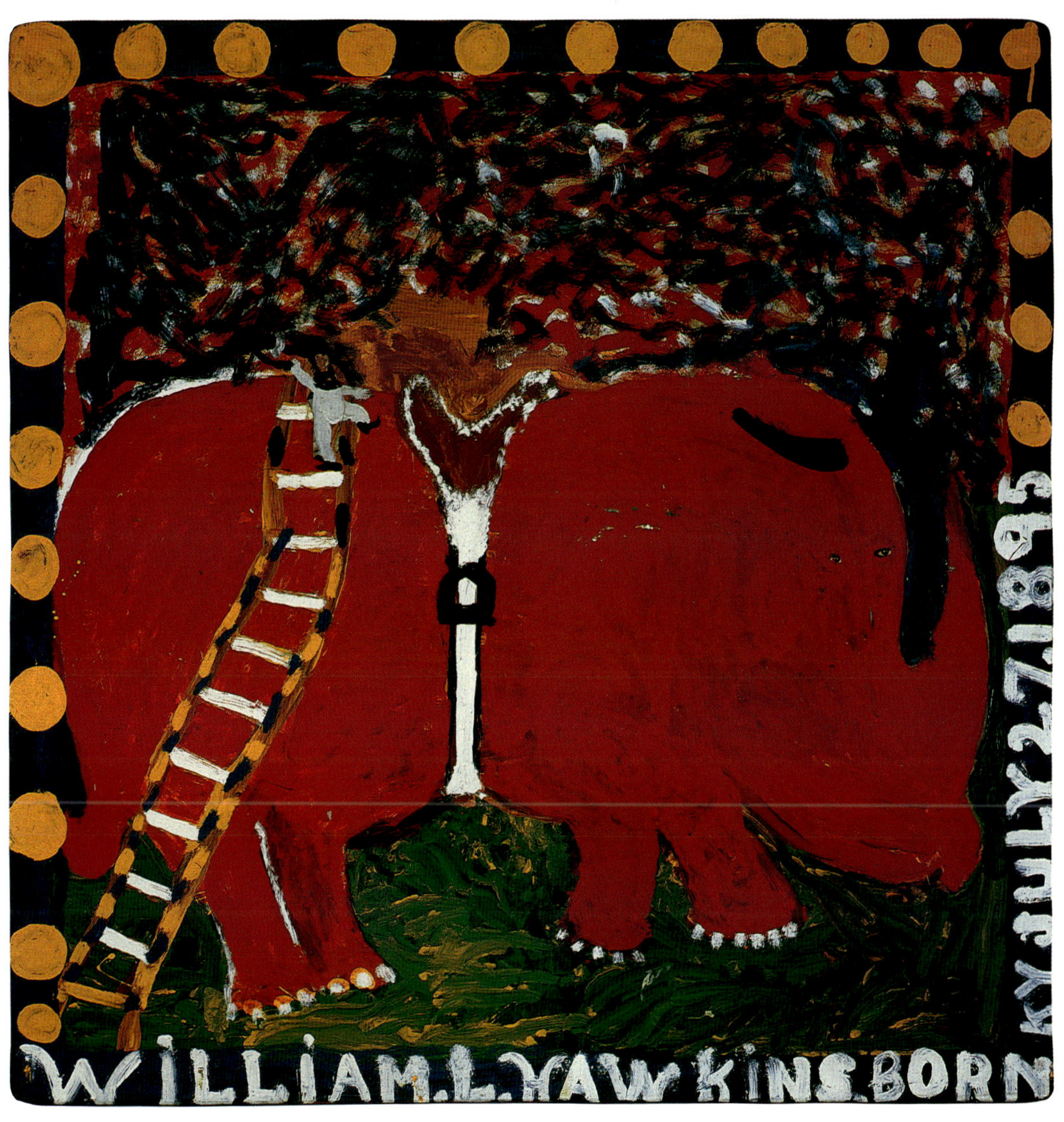

Rhino with Ladder #2, 1989

The Big Chair, 1988

Enamel and collage on Masonite, 50½″ x 50½″

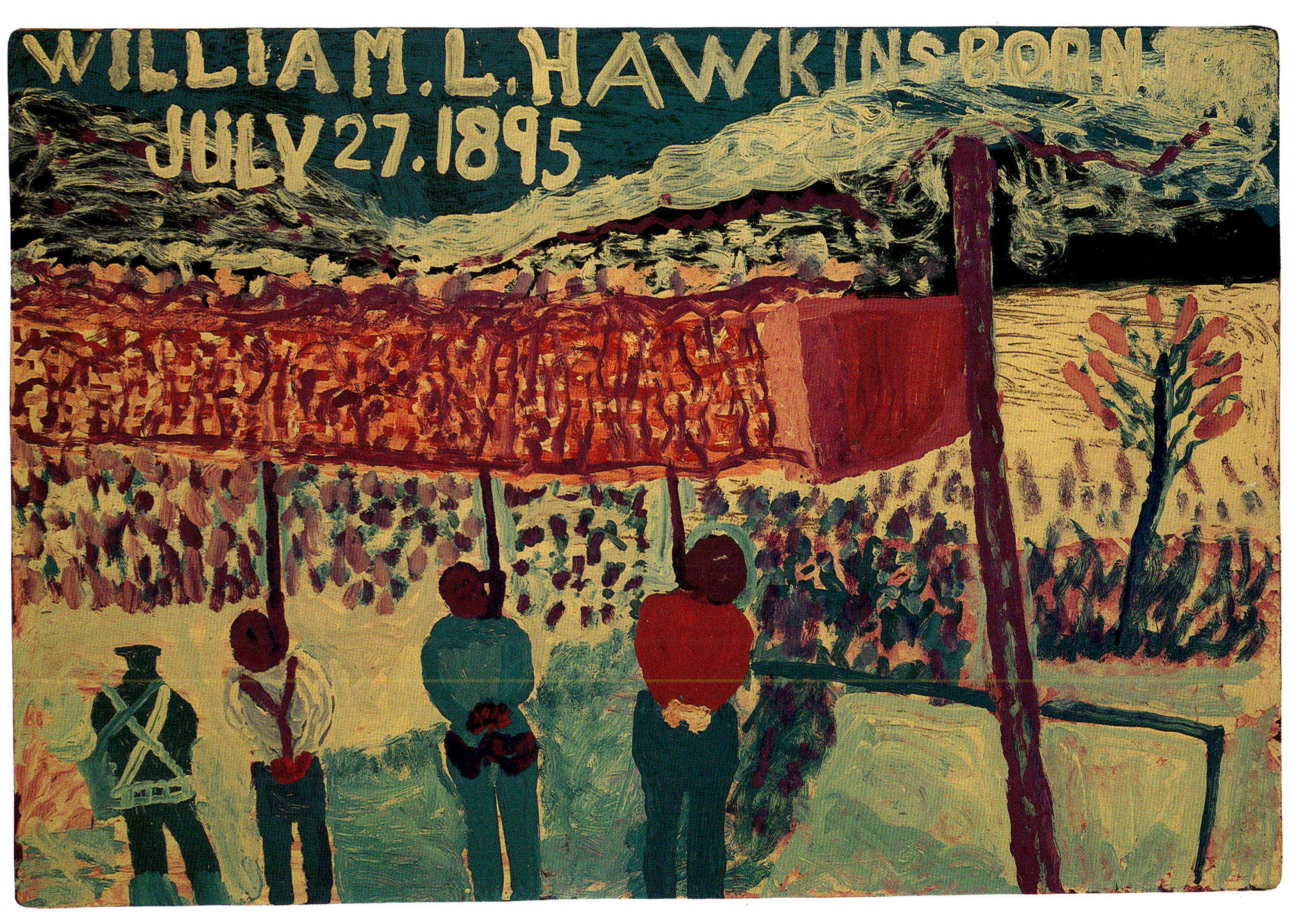

Three Hanging Men, 1985

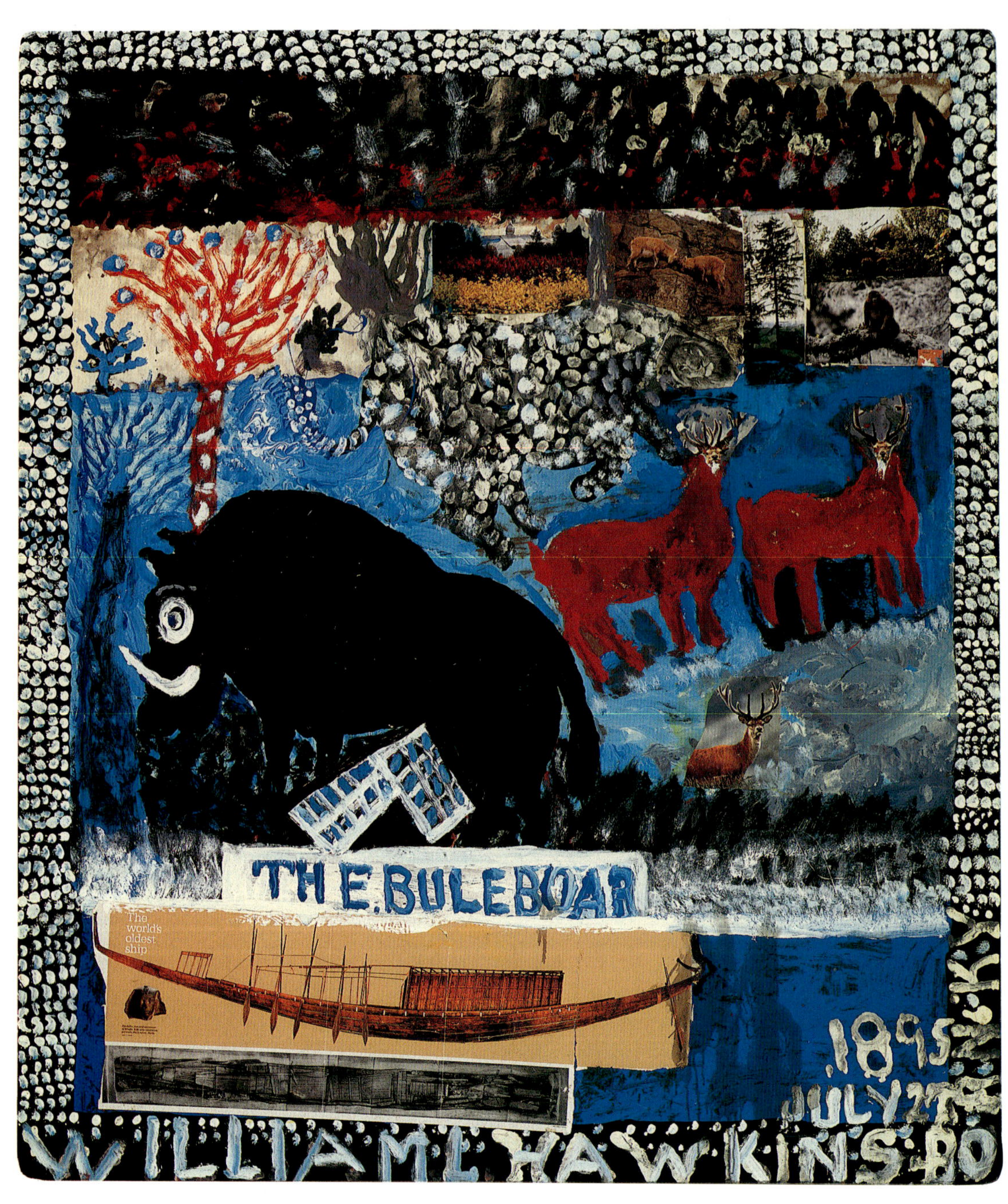

The Bule Boar, 1989

Enamel, collage, and mixed media on Masonite, 55″ x 48″

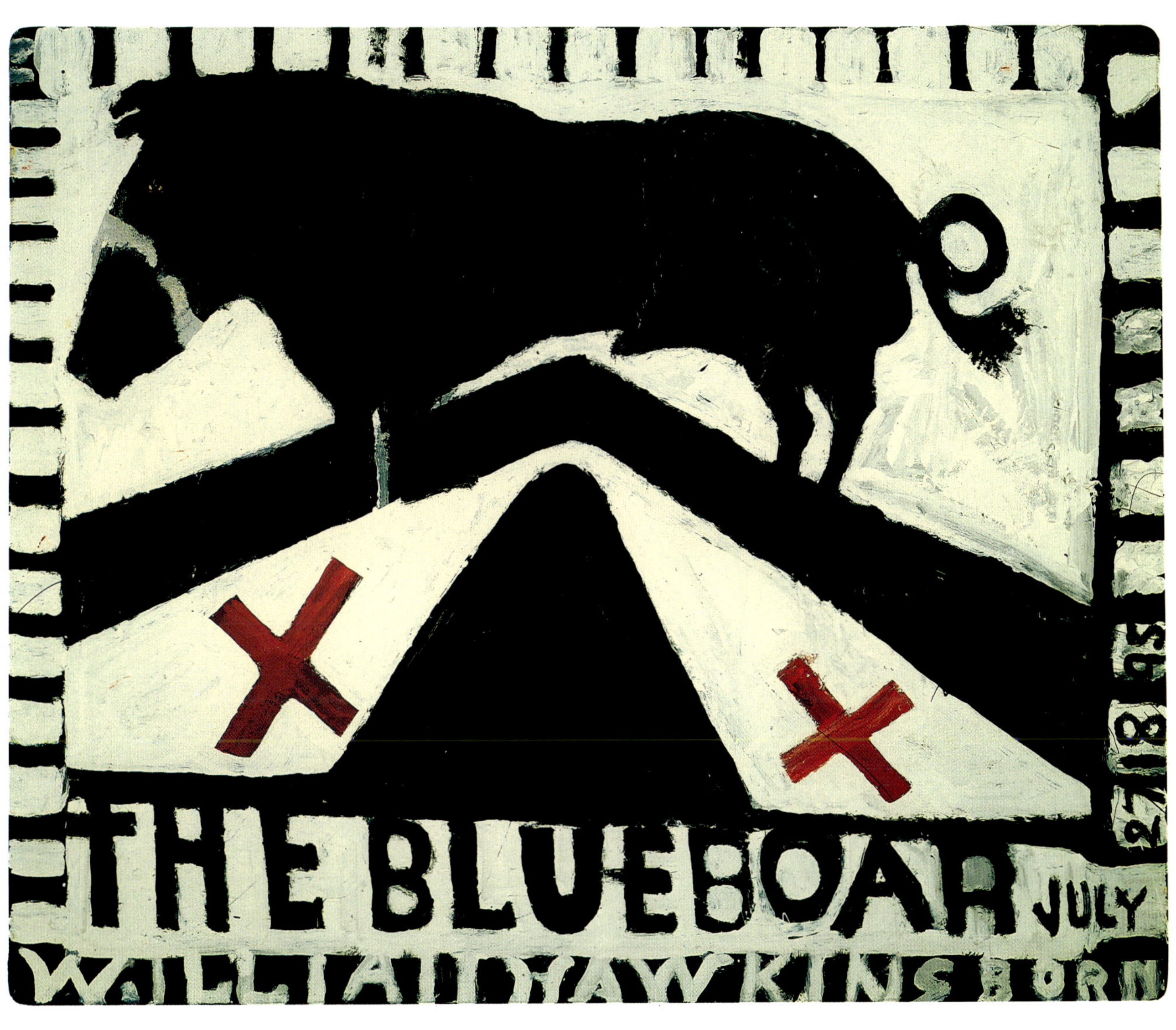

The Blue Boar #2, 1989

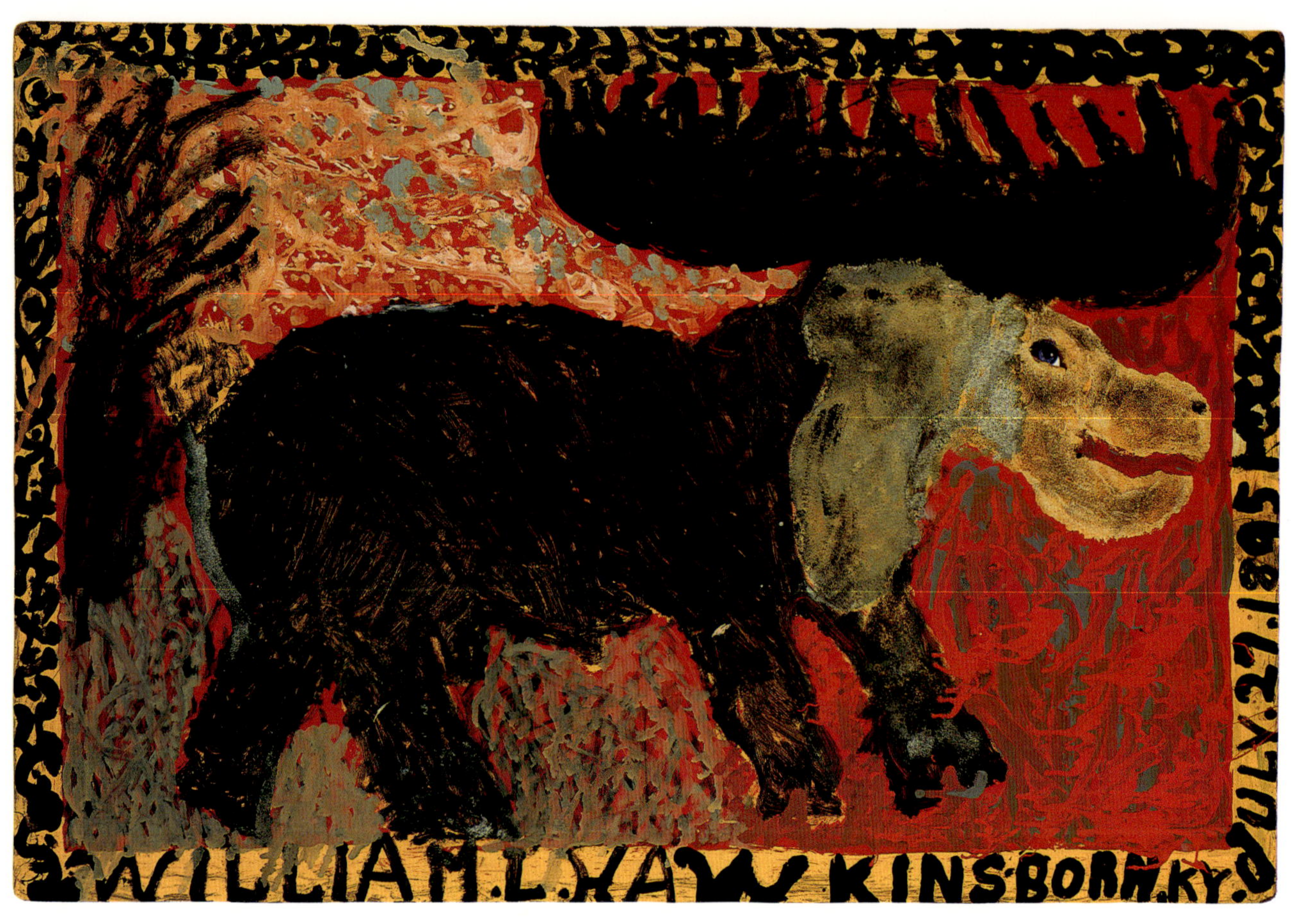

Bull Moose, 1988

Enamel, collage, and mixed media on Masonite, 48″ x 72″

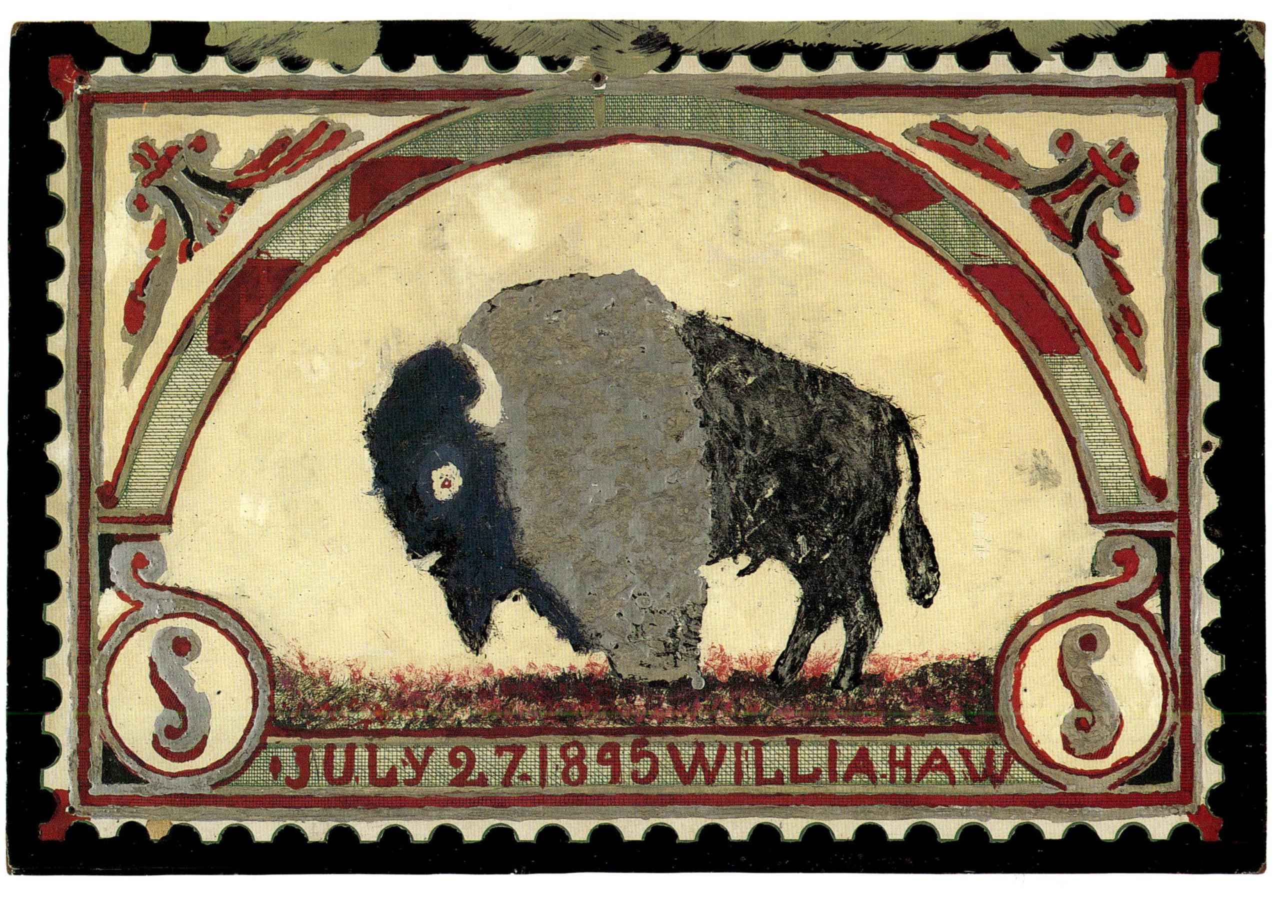

Small Buffalo Stamp, 1979

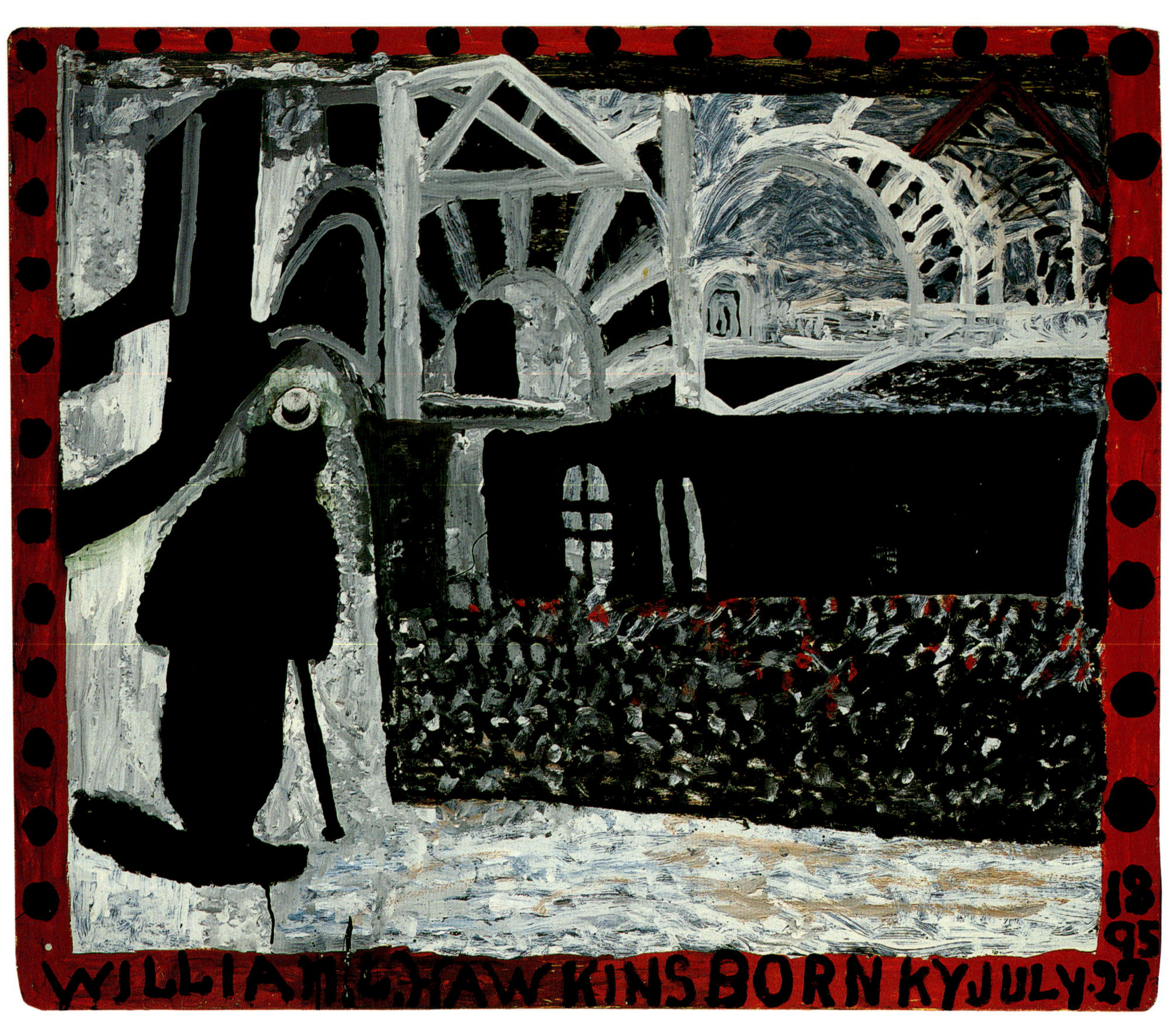

Demolition of St. Mary's, 1986

Enamel and collage on Masonite, 40″ x 48″

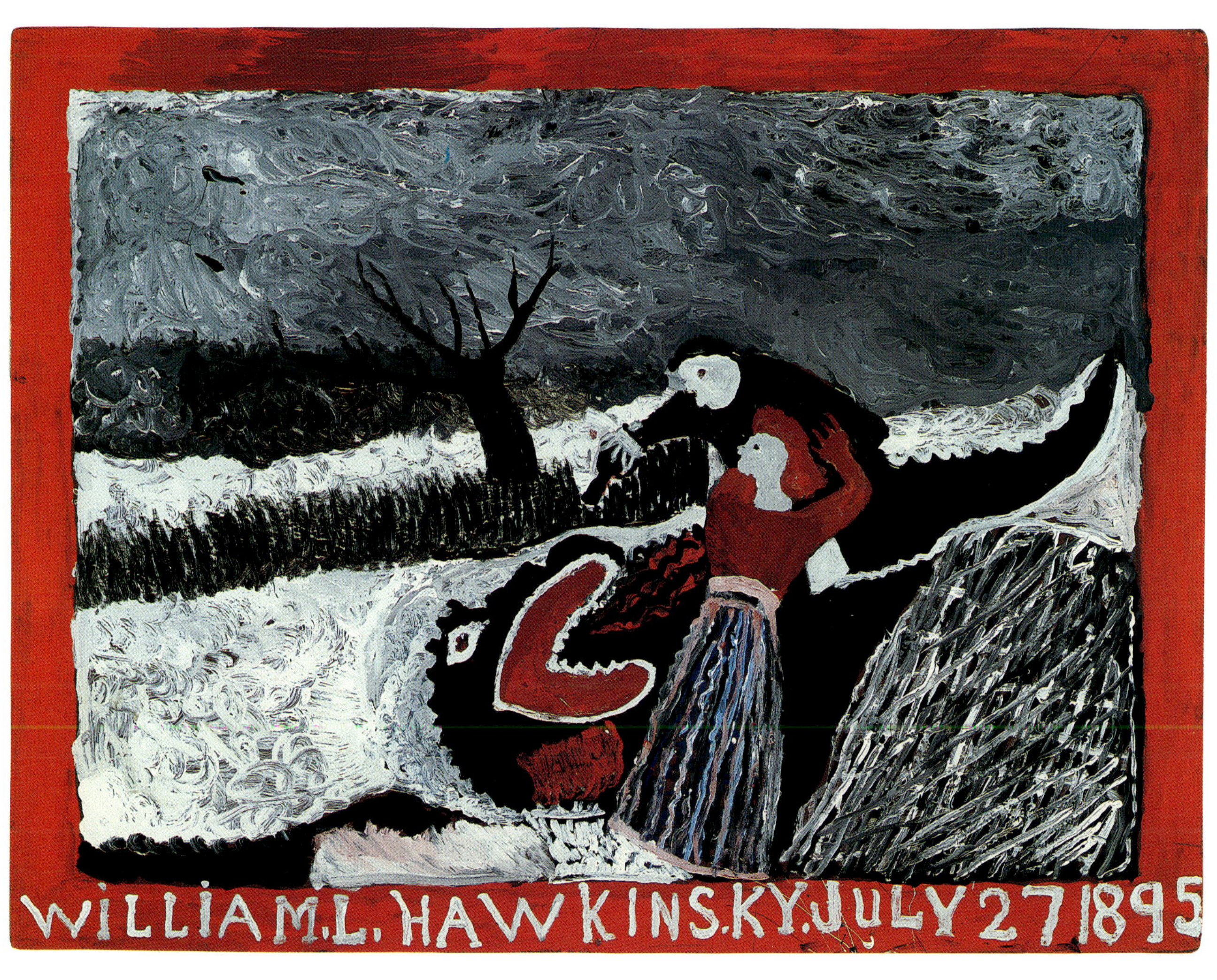

Alligator and Lovers, 1985

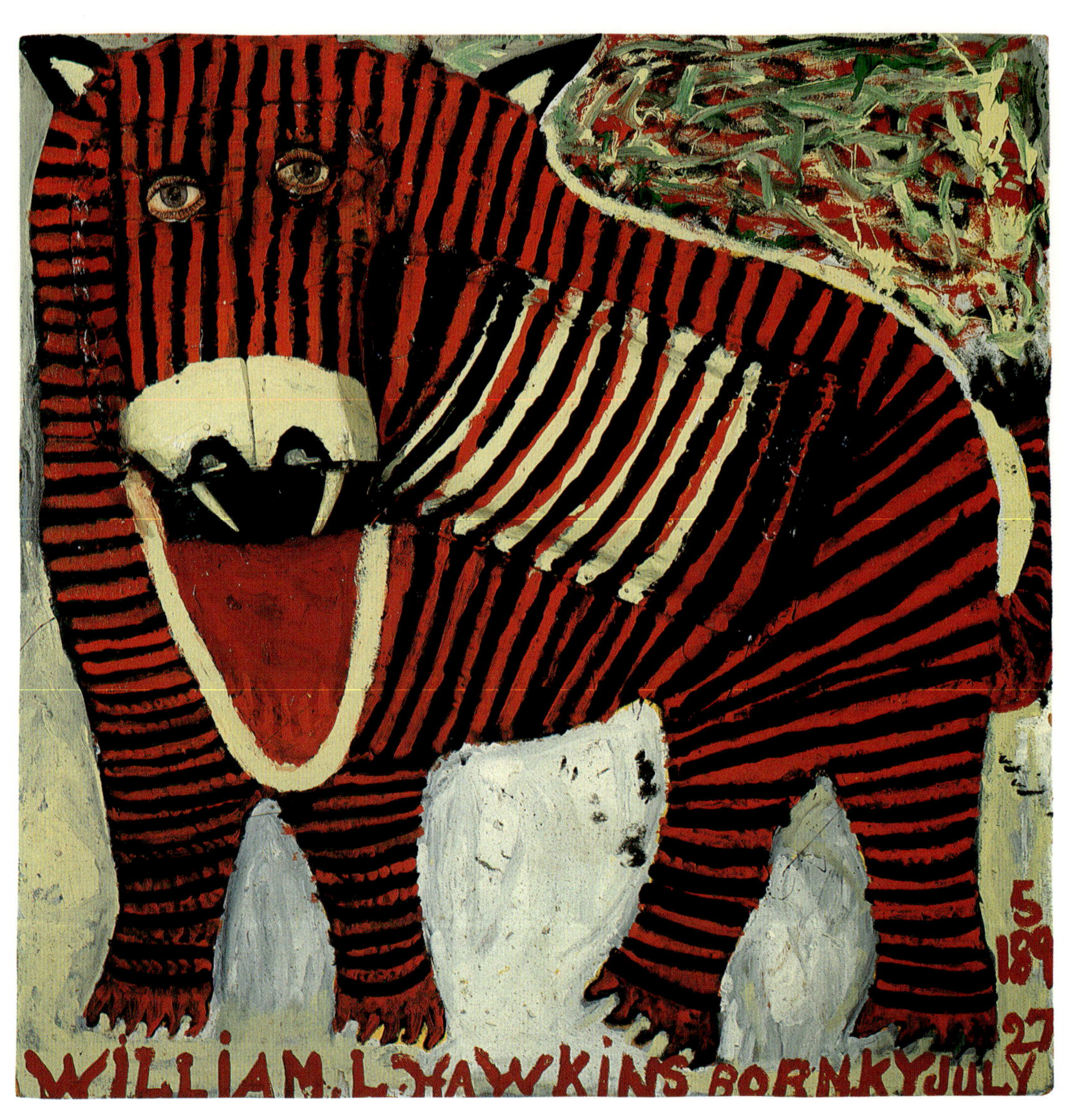

Tasmanian Tiger #3, 1989

Enamel and mixed-media construction on Masonite, 48″ x 48″ x 4″

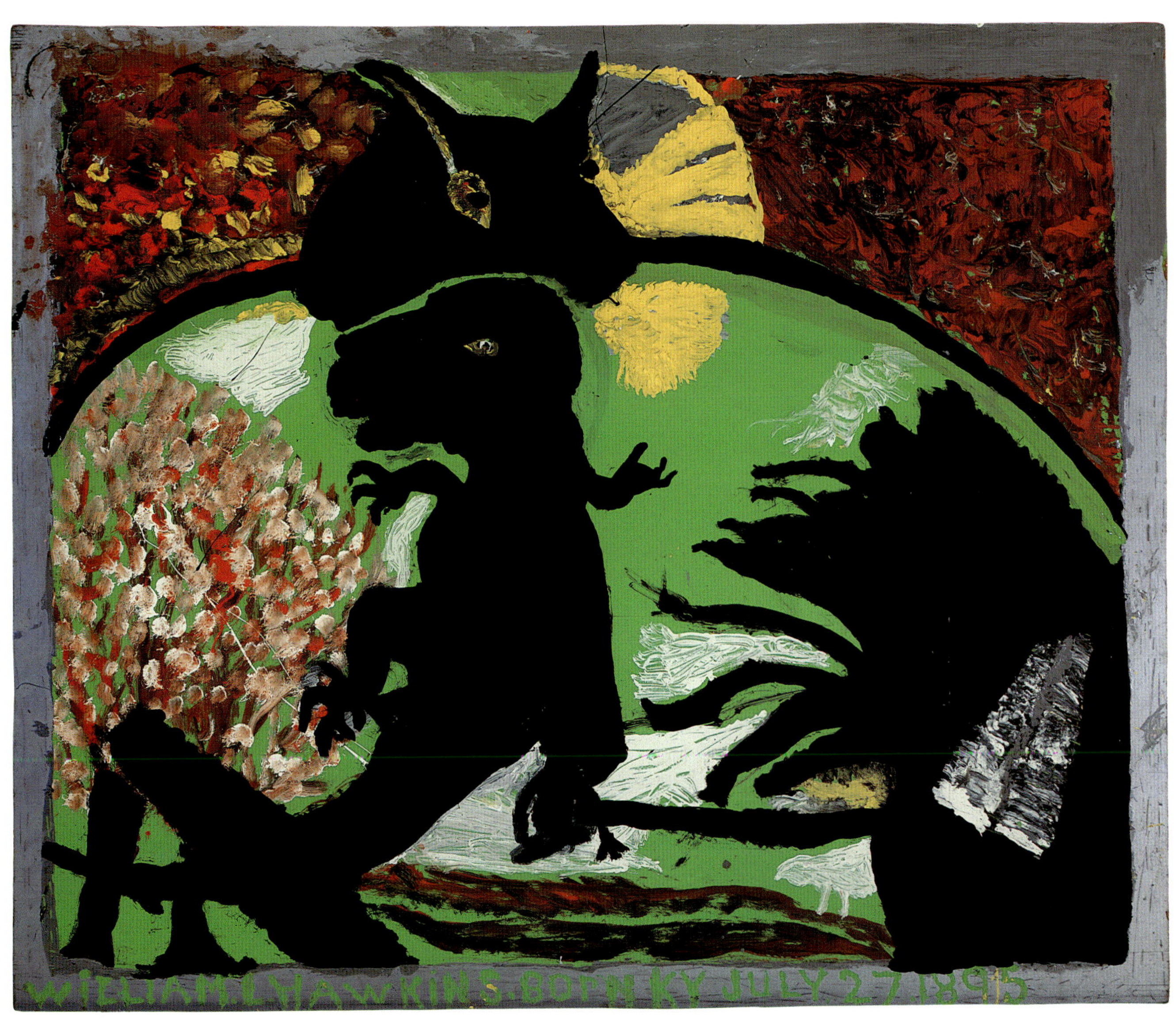

Man Eaters, 1985

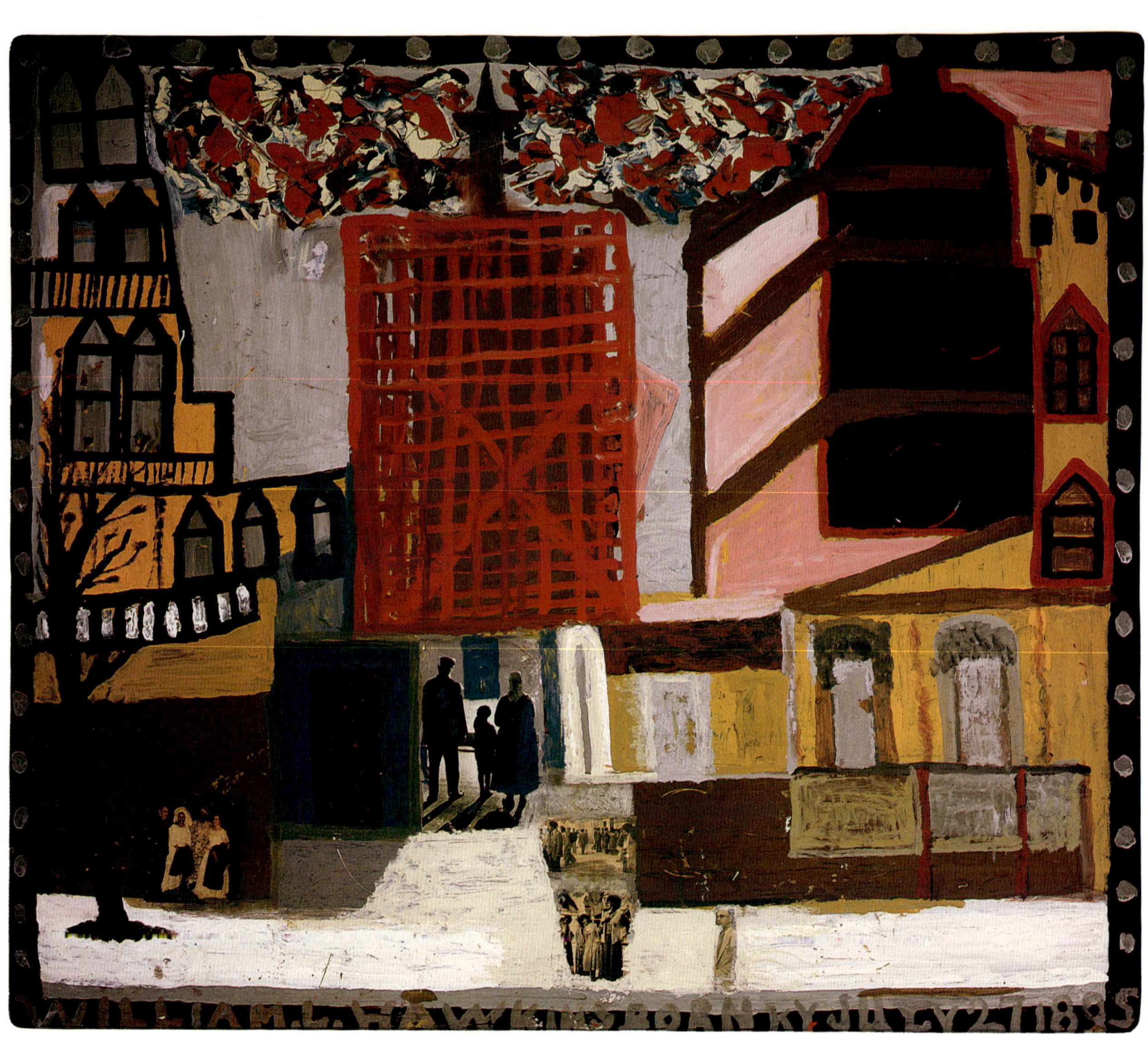

Building of the Statue of Liberty, 1987

Enamel and collage on Masonite, 48″ x 56½″

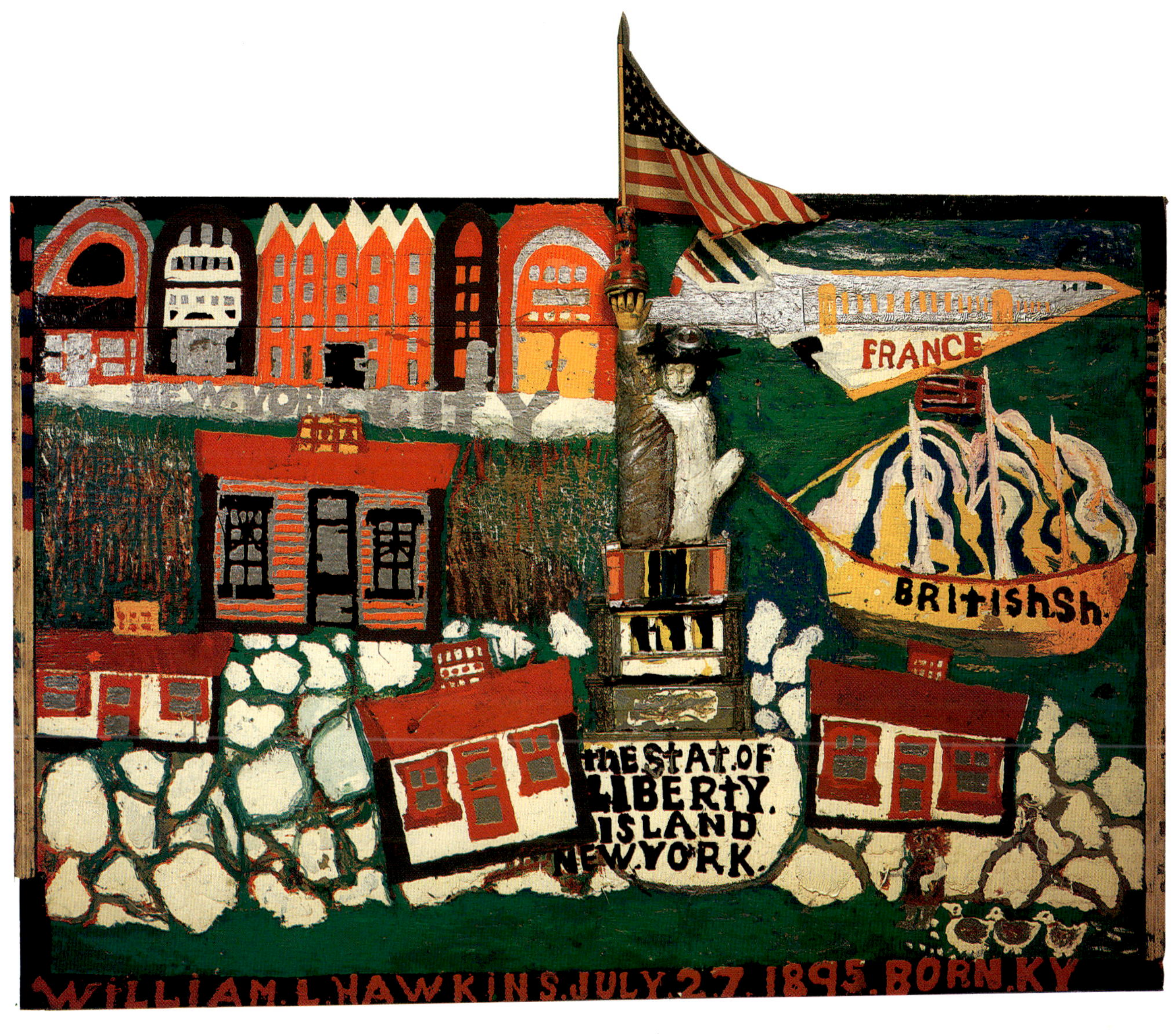

The Statue of Liberty, 1986

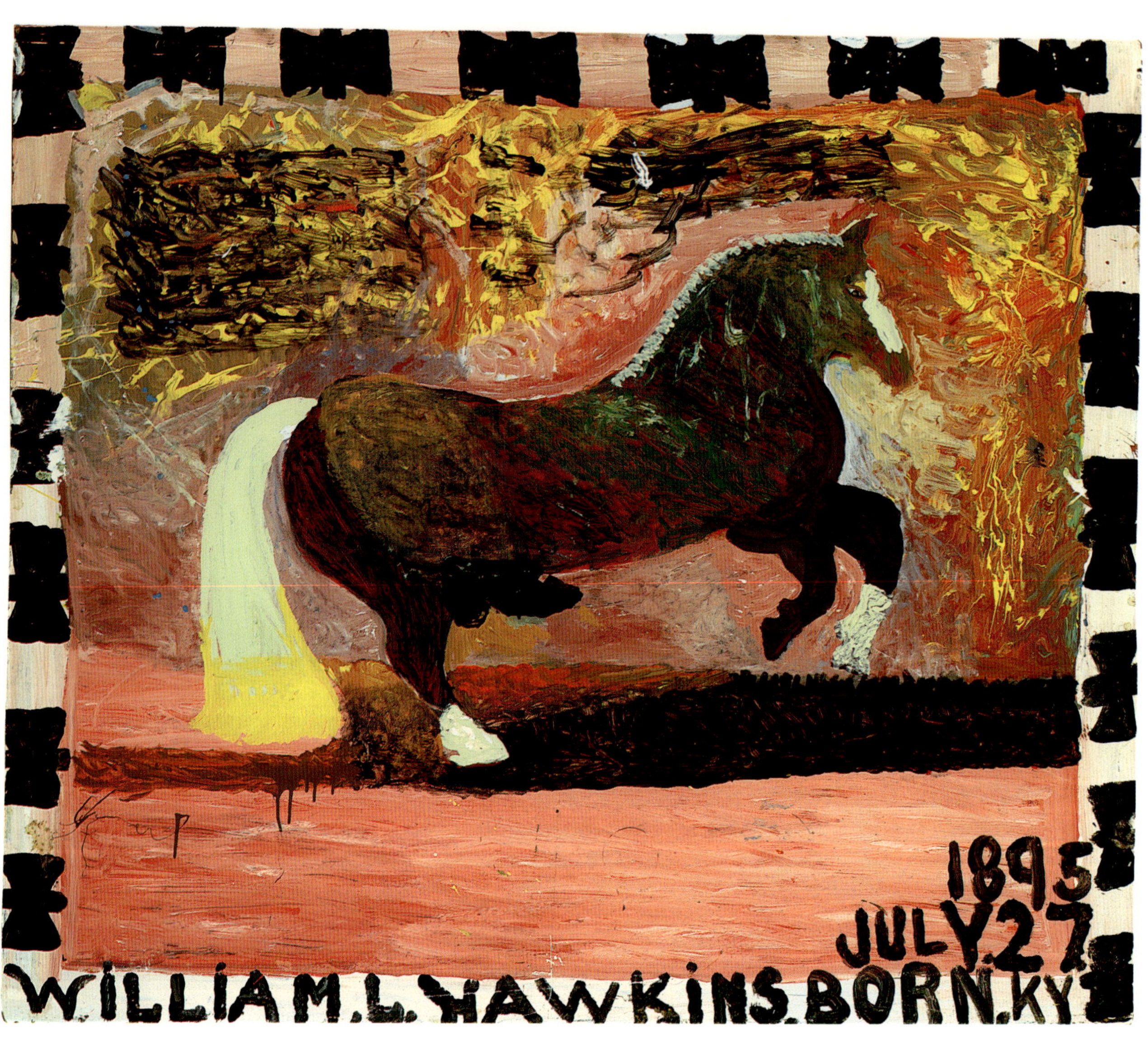

Rearing Stud Horse, 1987

Enamel on Masonite, 48″ x 56½″

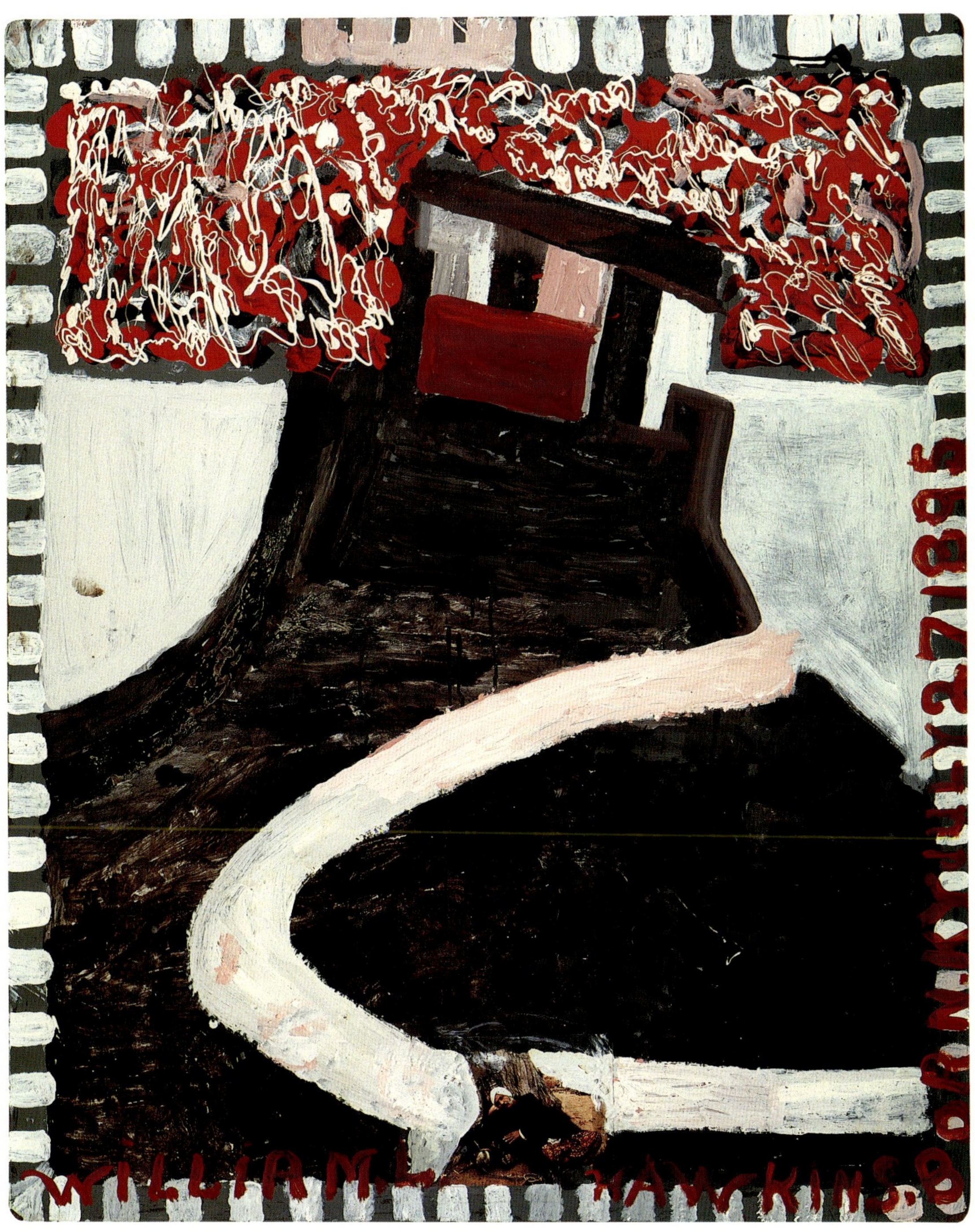

Resting Man with Castle, 1987

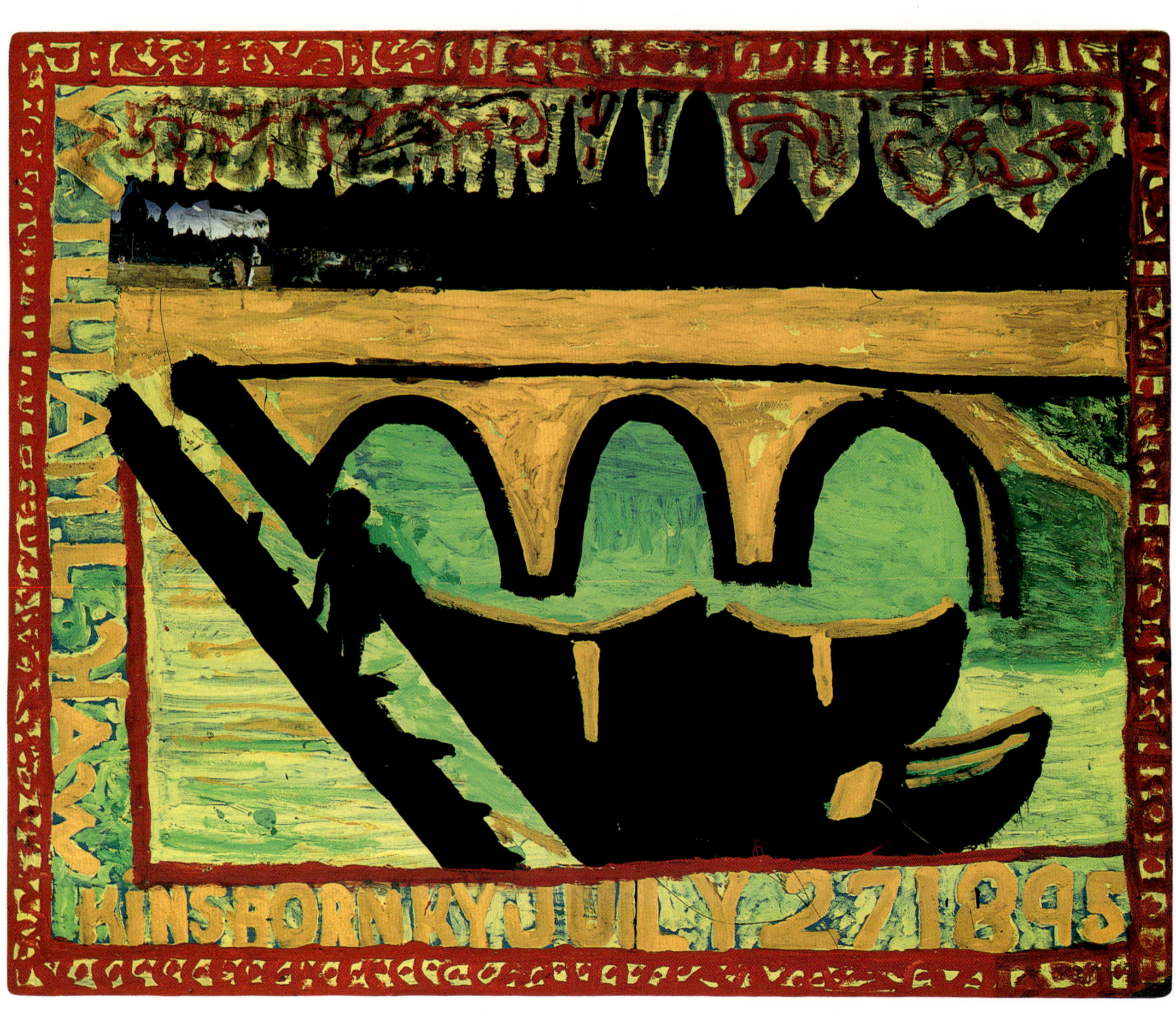

The Bridge #3, 1988

Enamel and collage on Masonite, 48″ x 60″

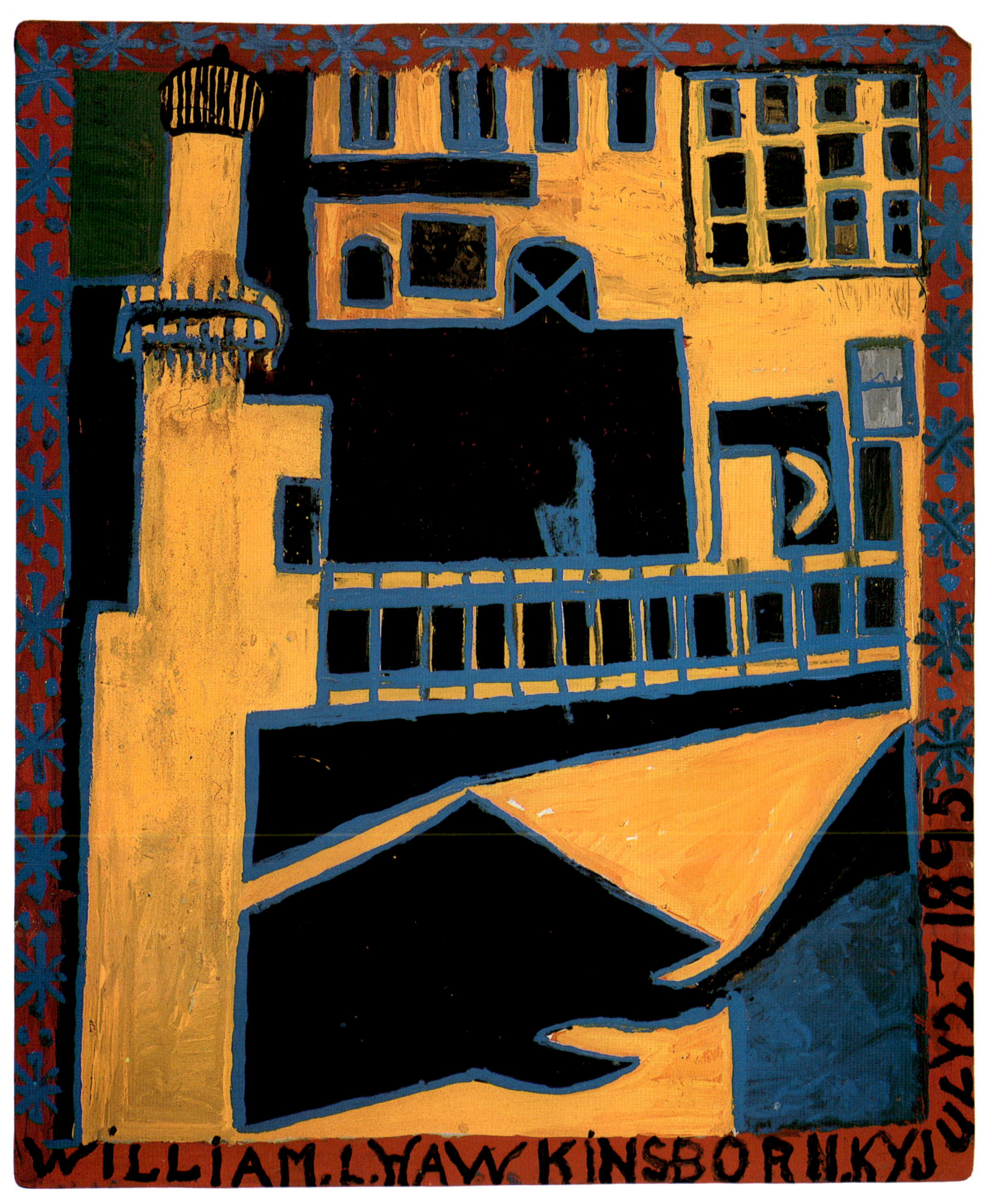

Yellow Buildings with Blue Trim, 1989

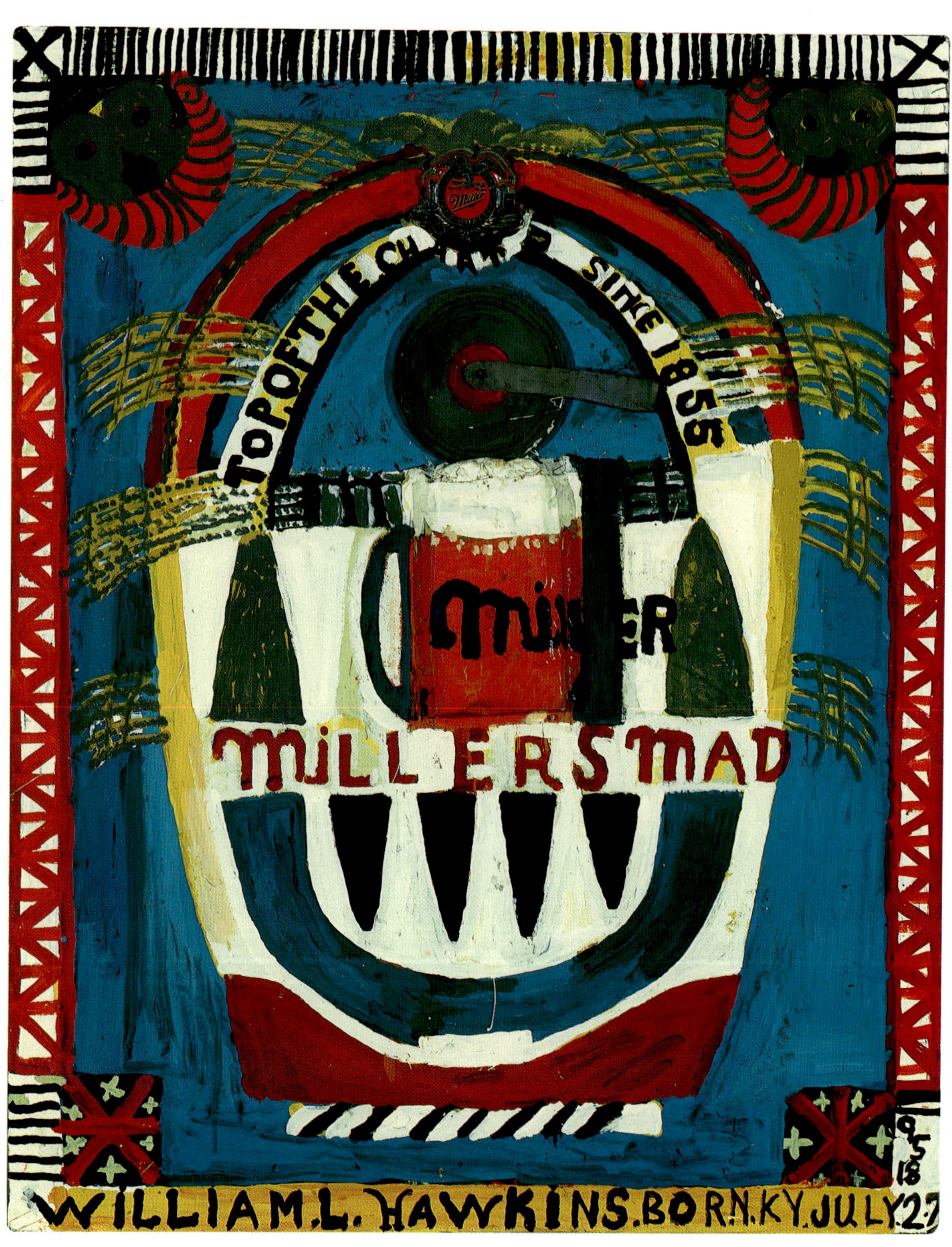

Juke Box, 1987

Enamel and mixed-media construction on Masonite, 60″ x 48″ x 5″

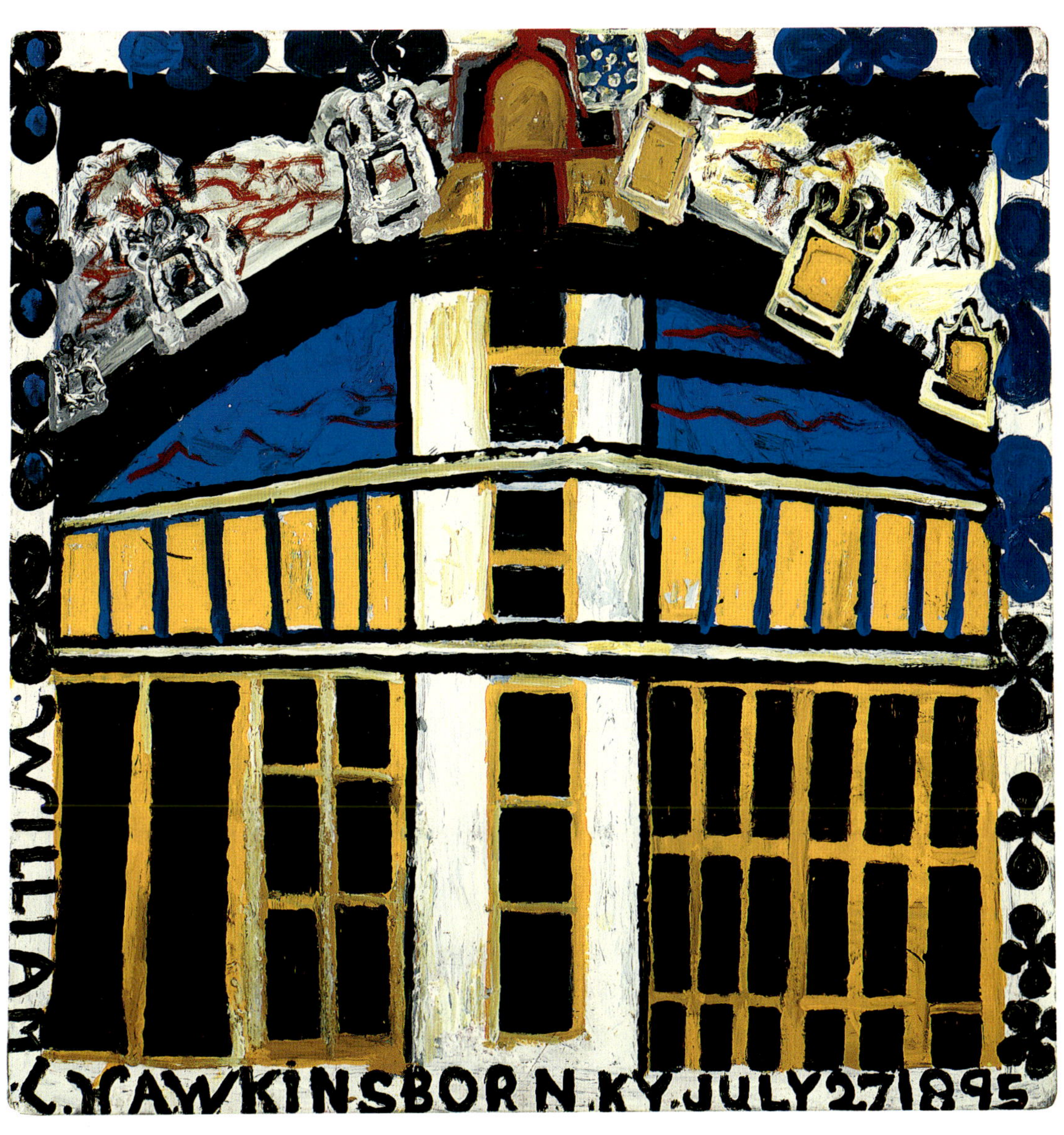

Willard Hotel #2, 1989

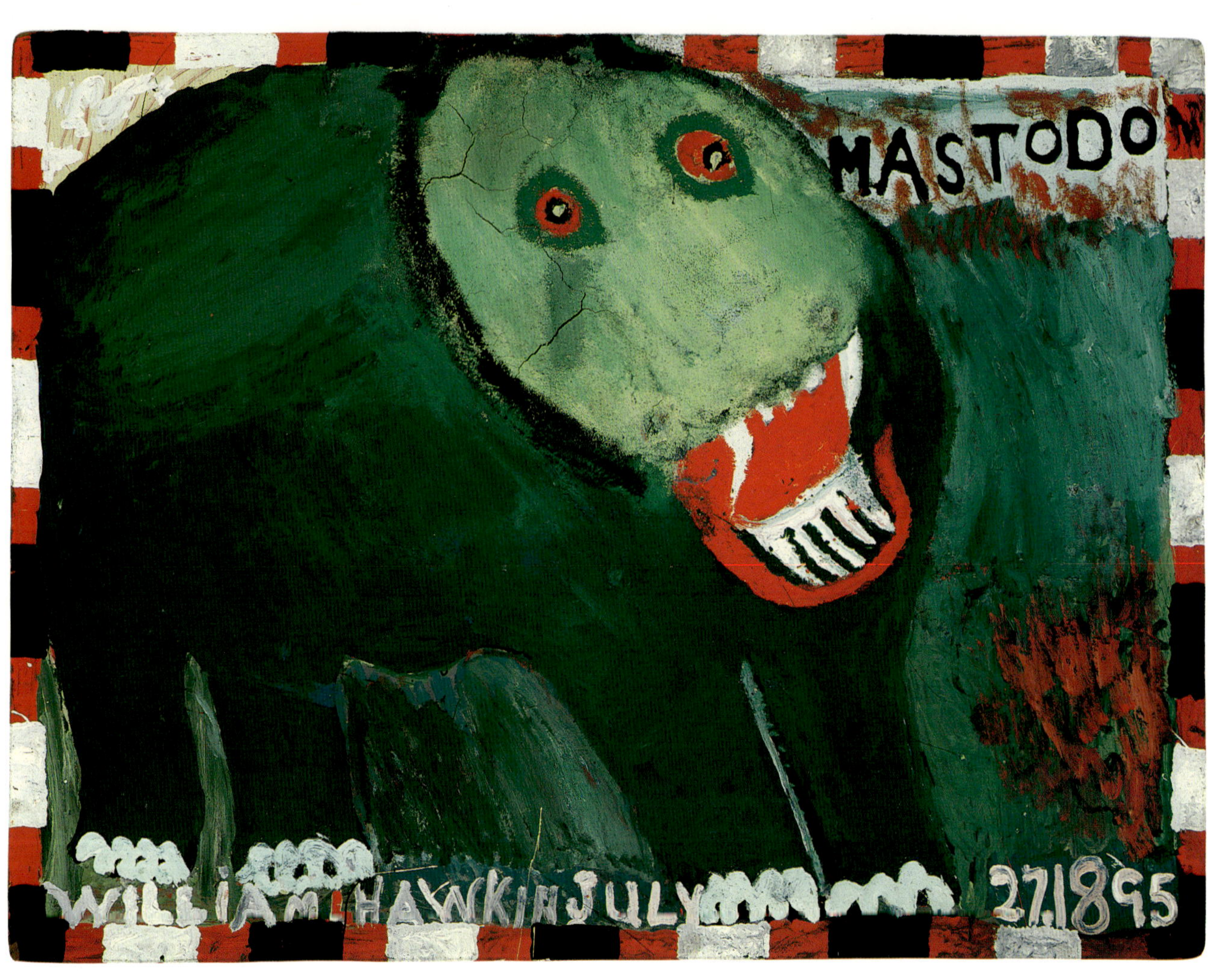

Mastodon, 1986

Enamel and mixed media on Masonite, 36″ x 48″

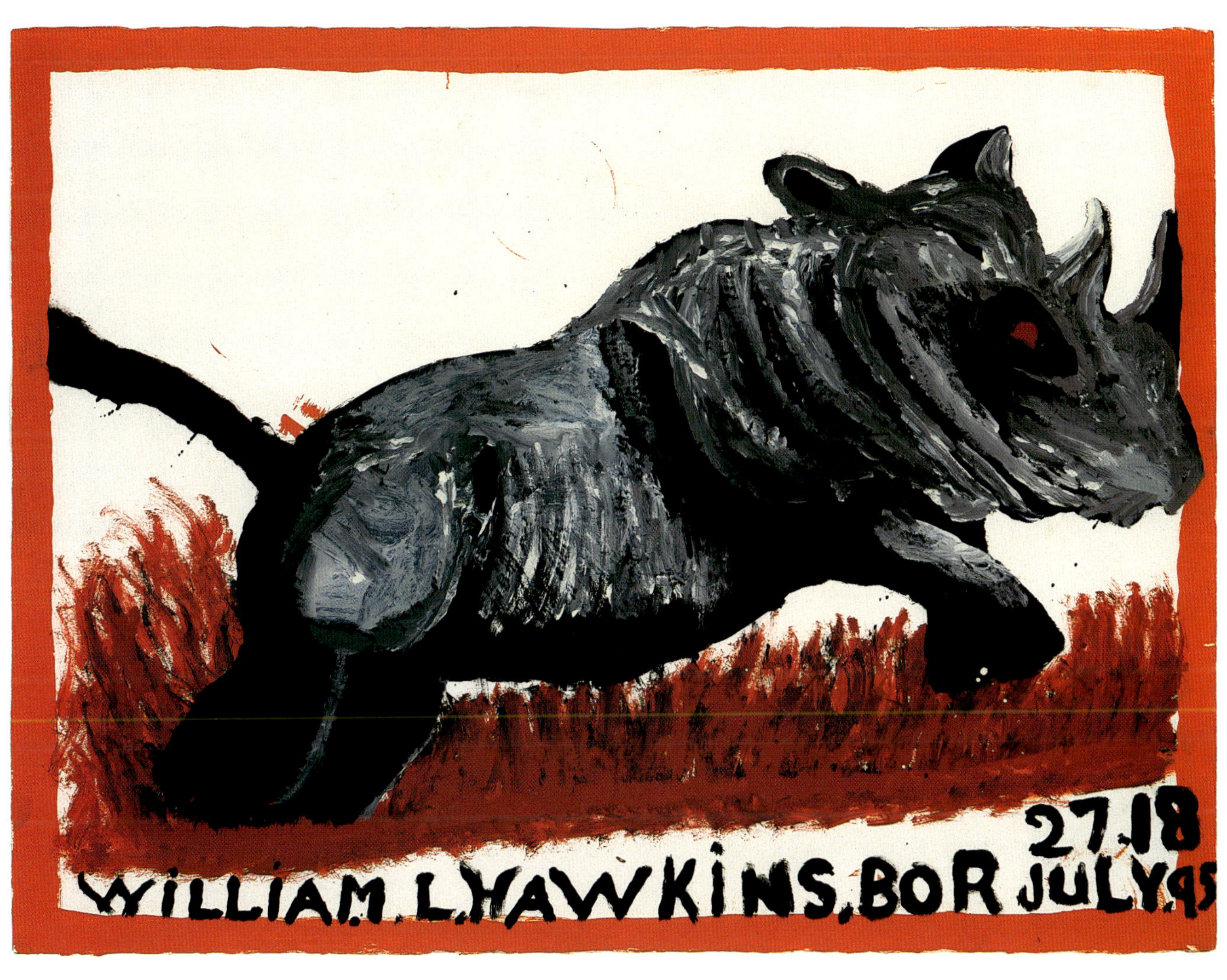

Rhino with Red Eye, 1985

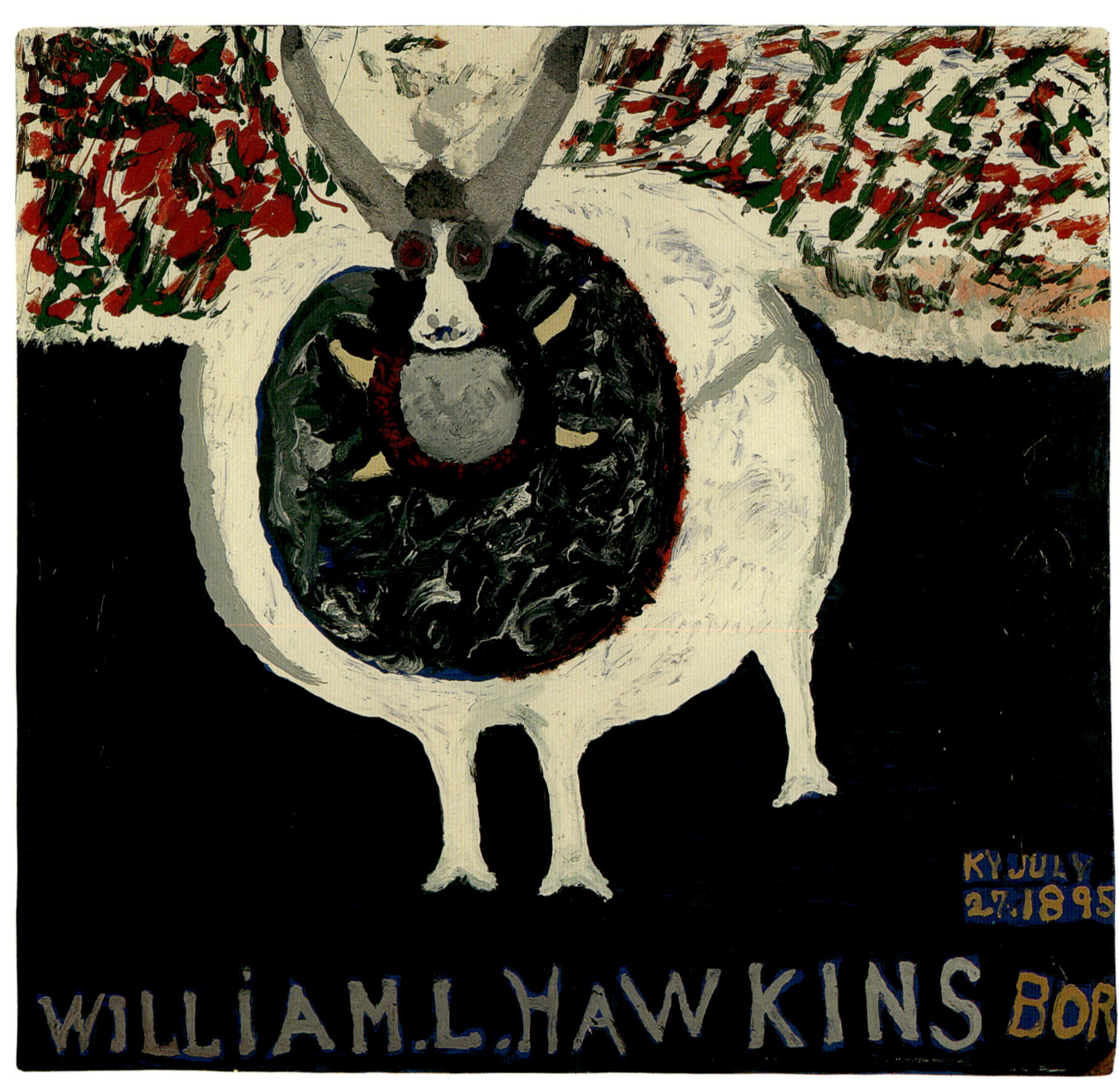

Jacob's Ram, 1985

Enamel on Masonite, 36″ x 46″

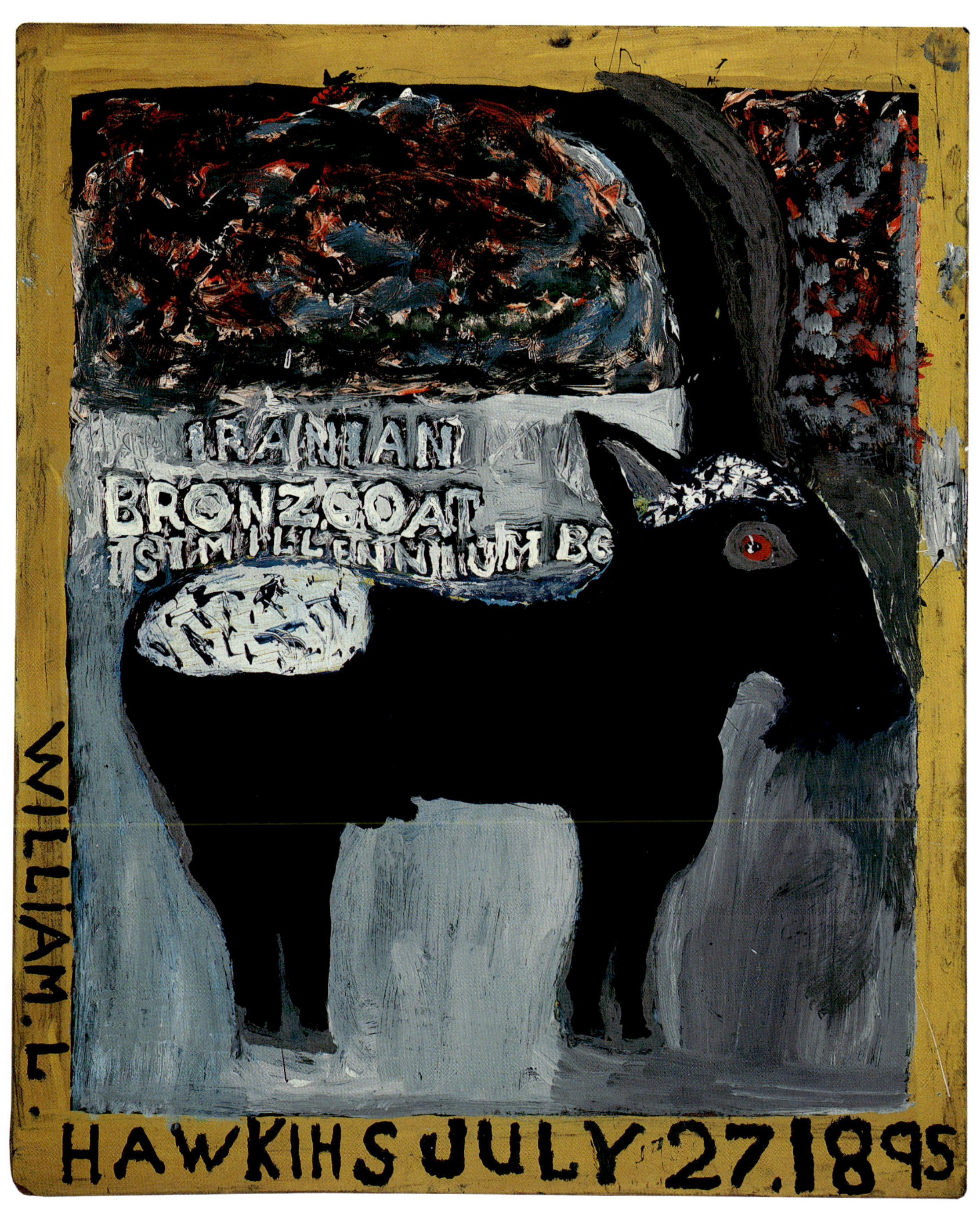

Iranian Bronze Goat, 1985

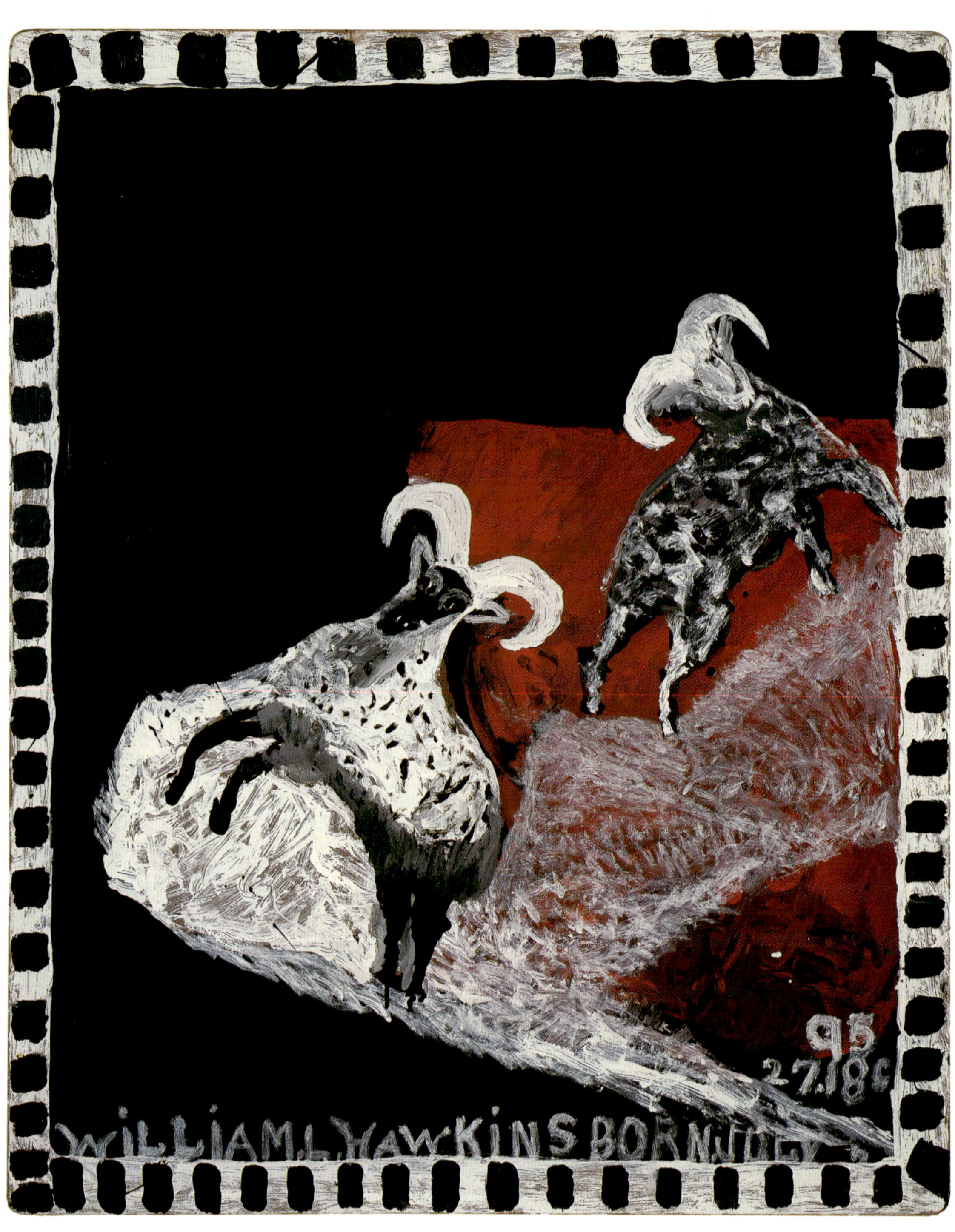

Two Mountain Goats, 1989

Enamel on Masonite, 48″ x 39½″

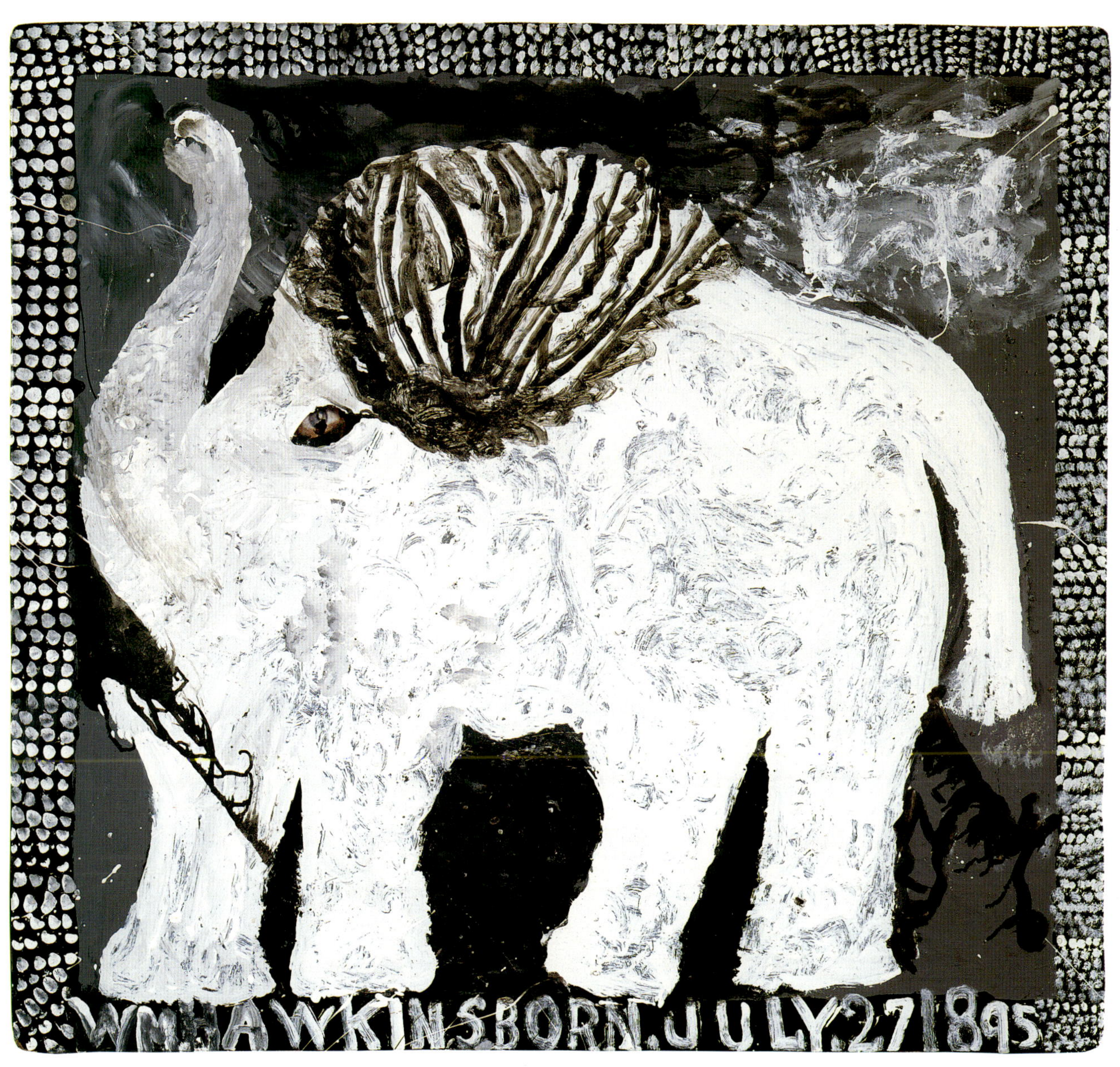

White Elephant, 1989

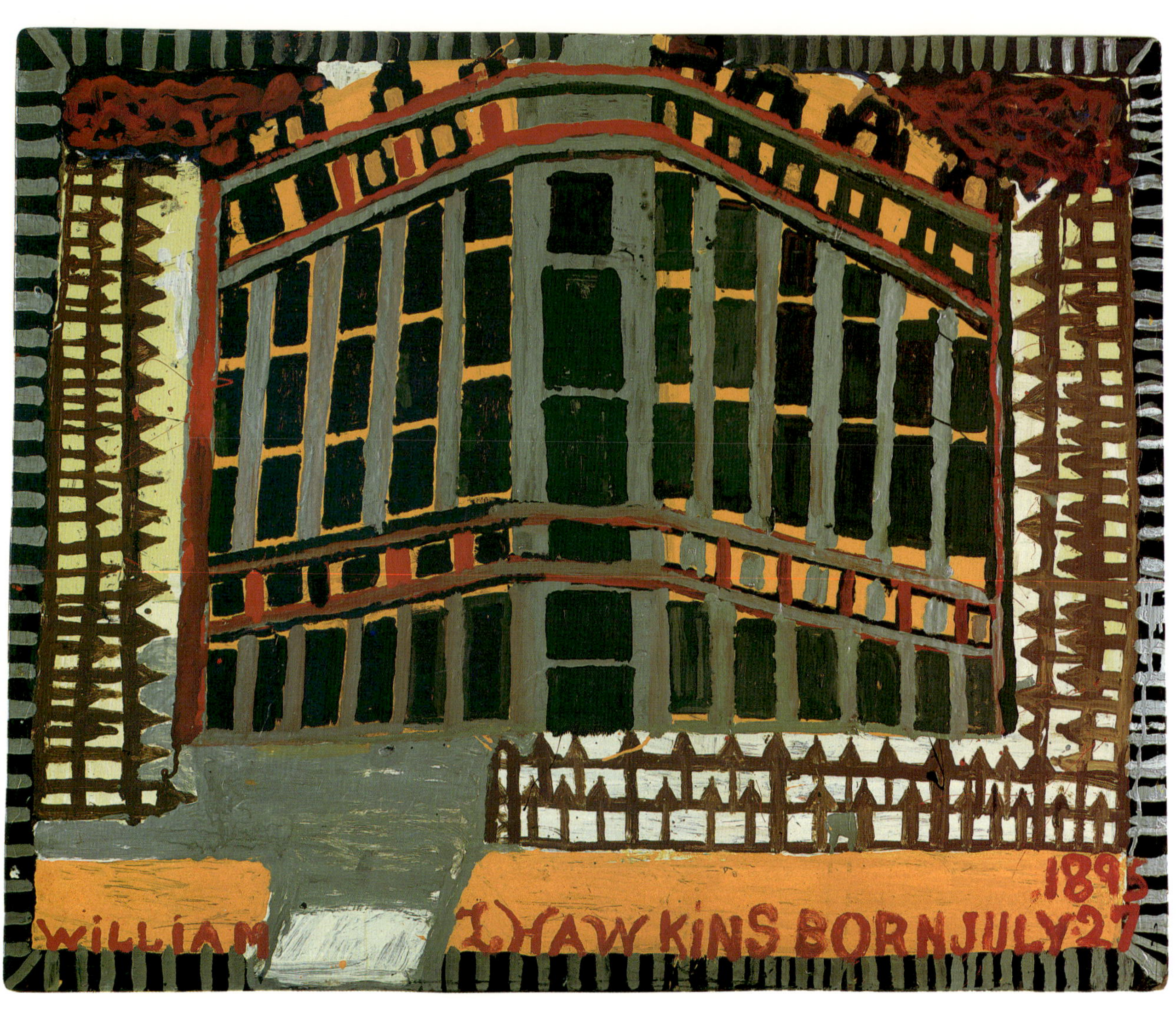

Willard Hotel, 1987

Enamel on Masonite, 48″ x 60″

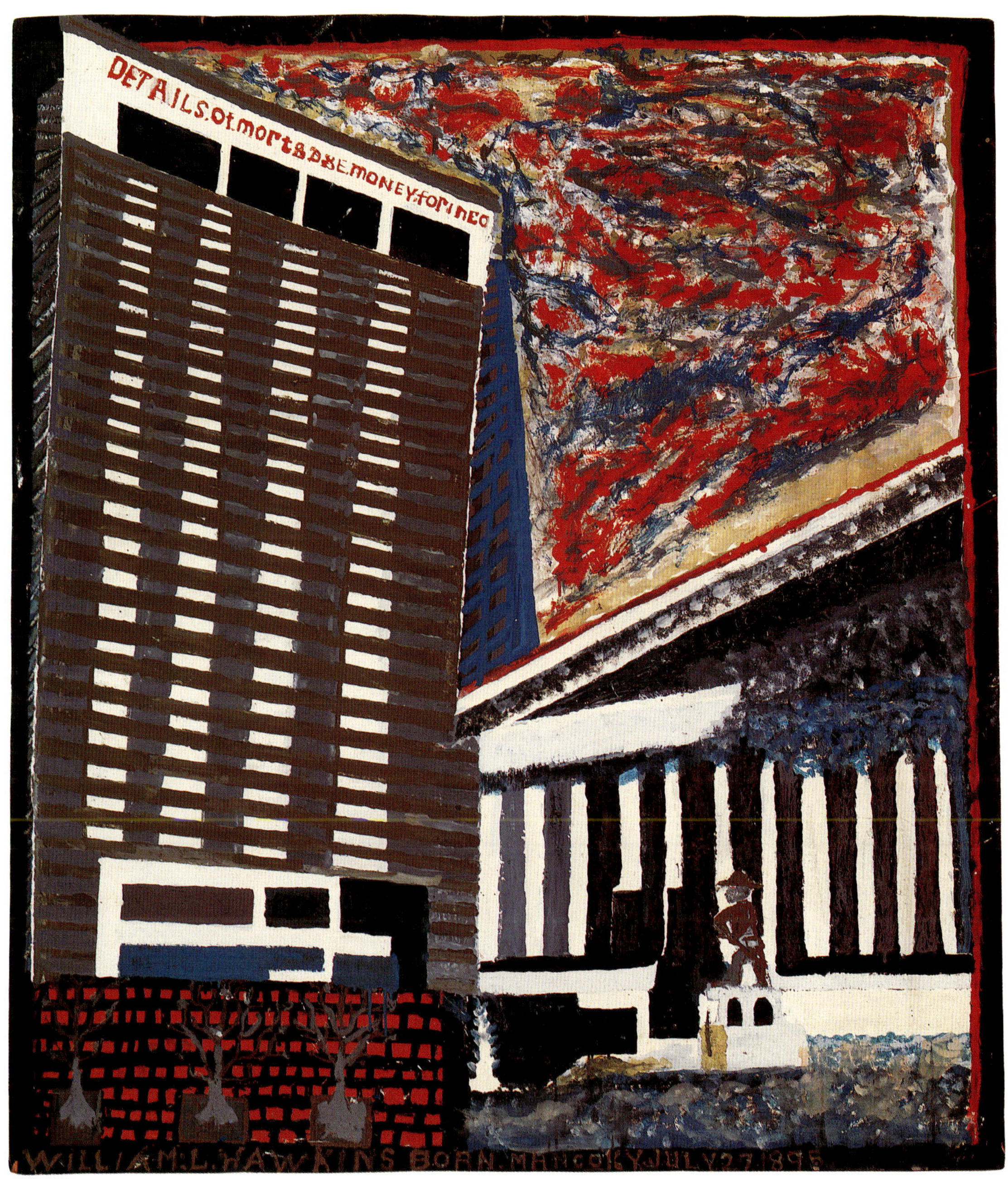

Northeast View from the State House Grounds, 1983

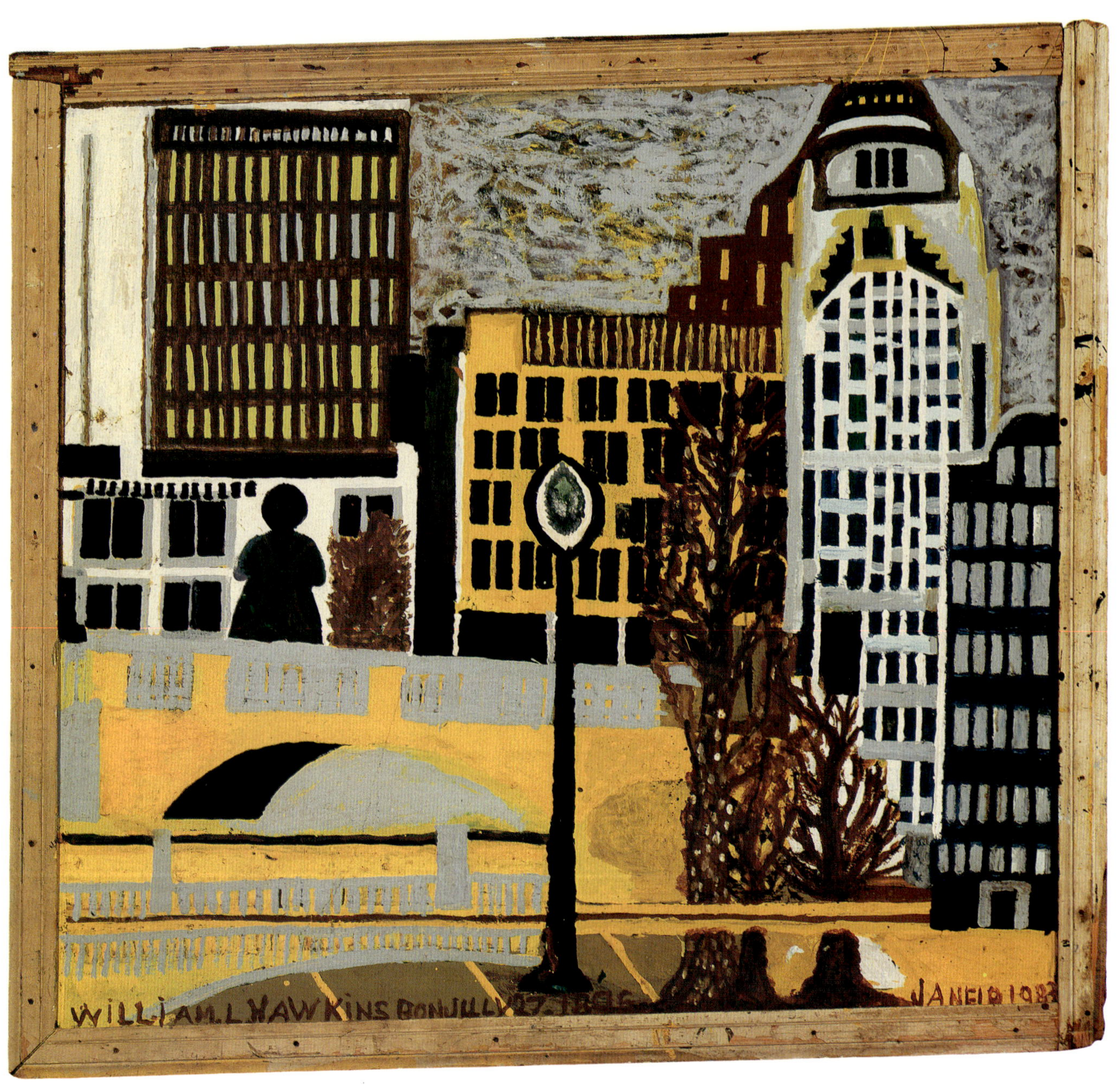

City Hall #1, 1983

Enamel on Masonite, 49″ x 53″

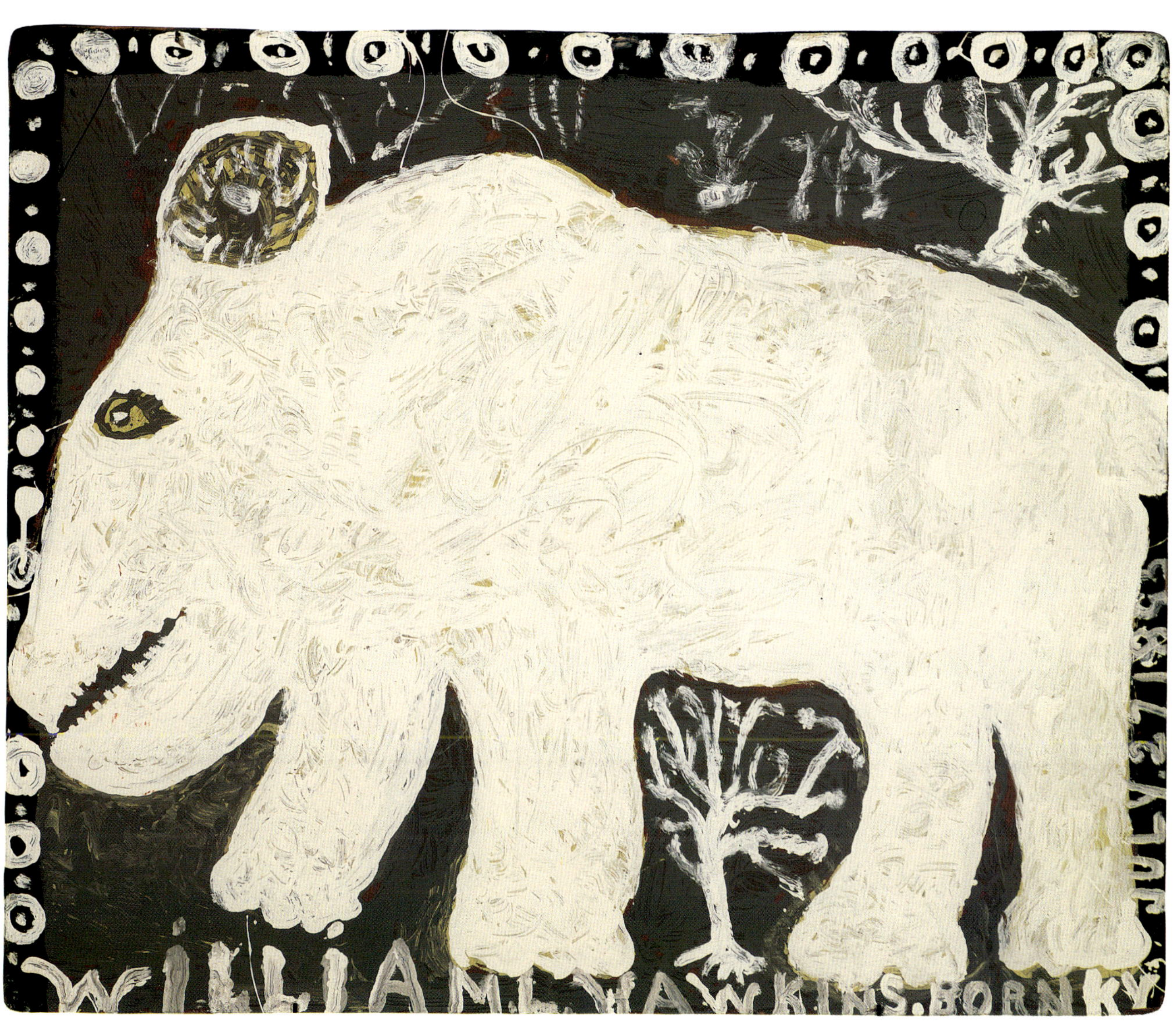

White Bear #2, 1989

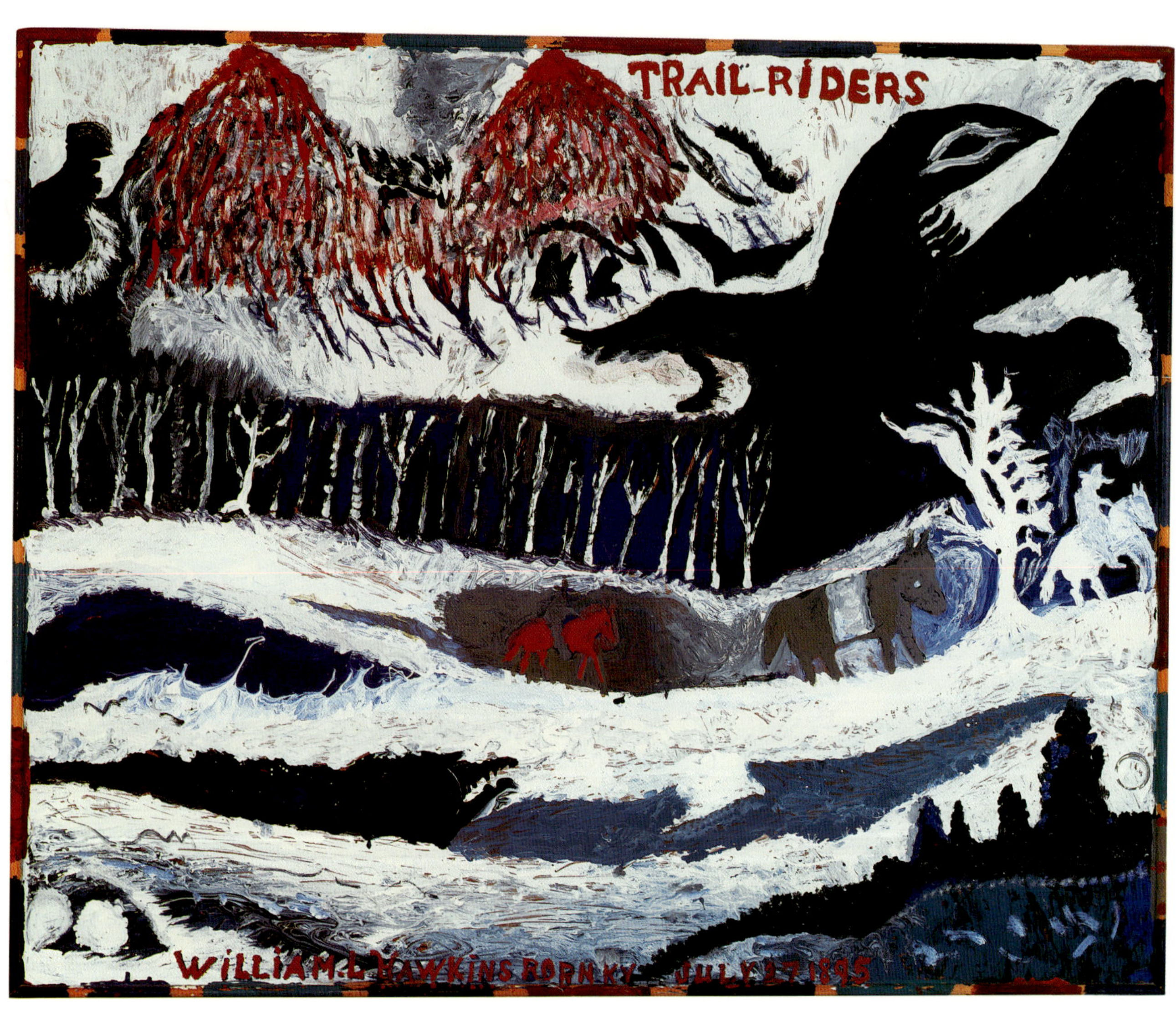

Trail Riders, 1986

Enamel on Masonite, 48″ x 60″

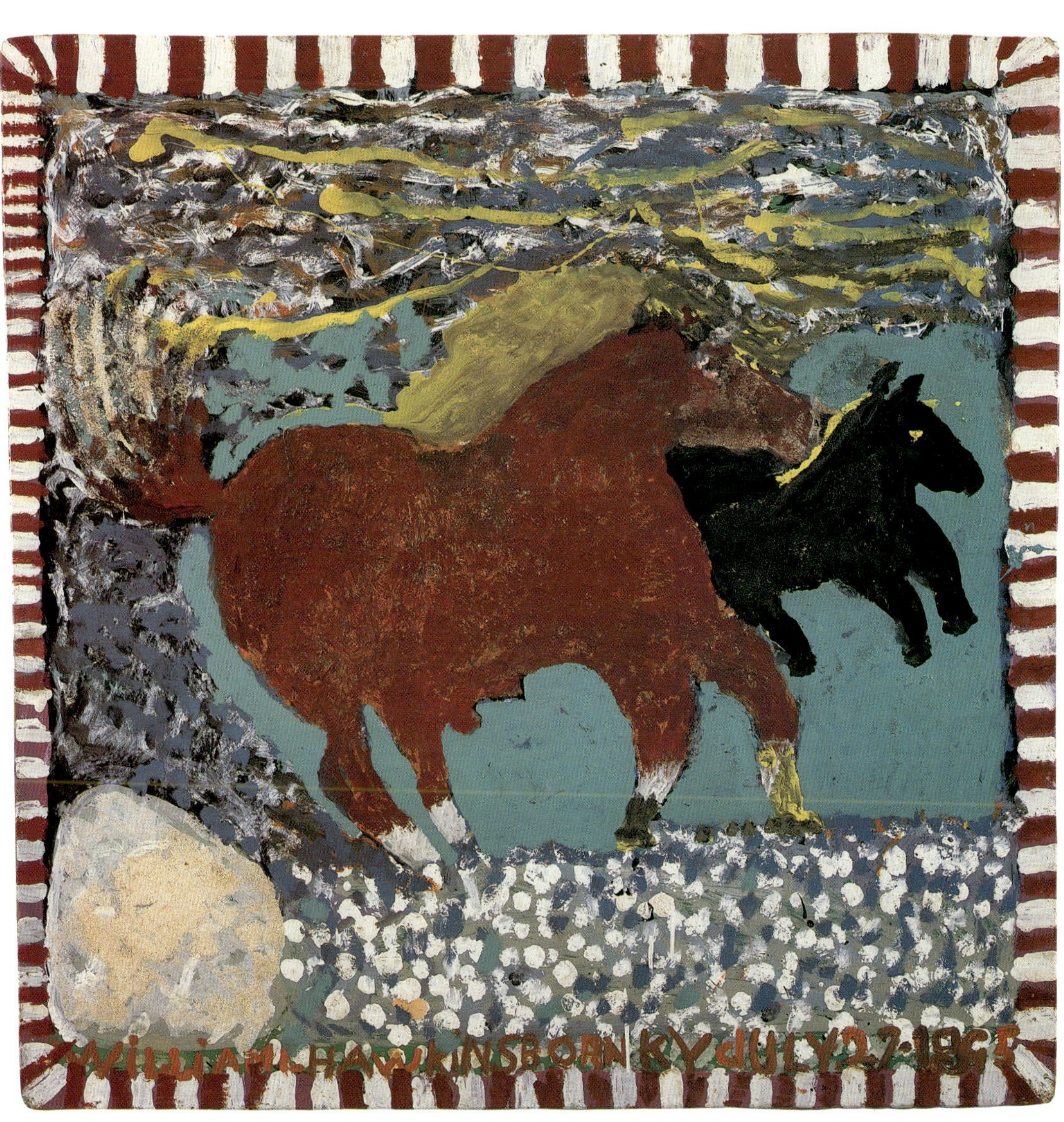
WILLIAM L. HAWKINS BORN KY JULY 27

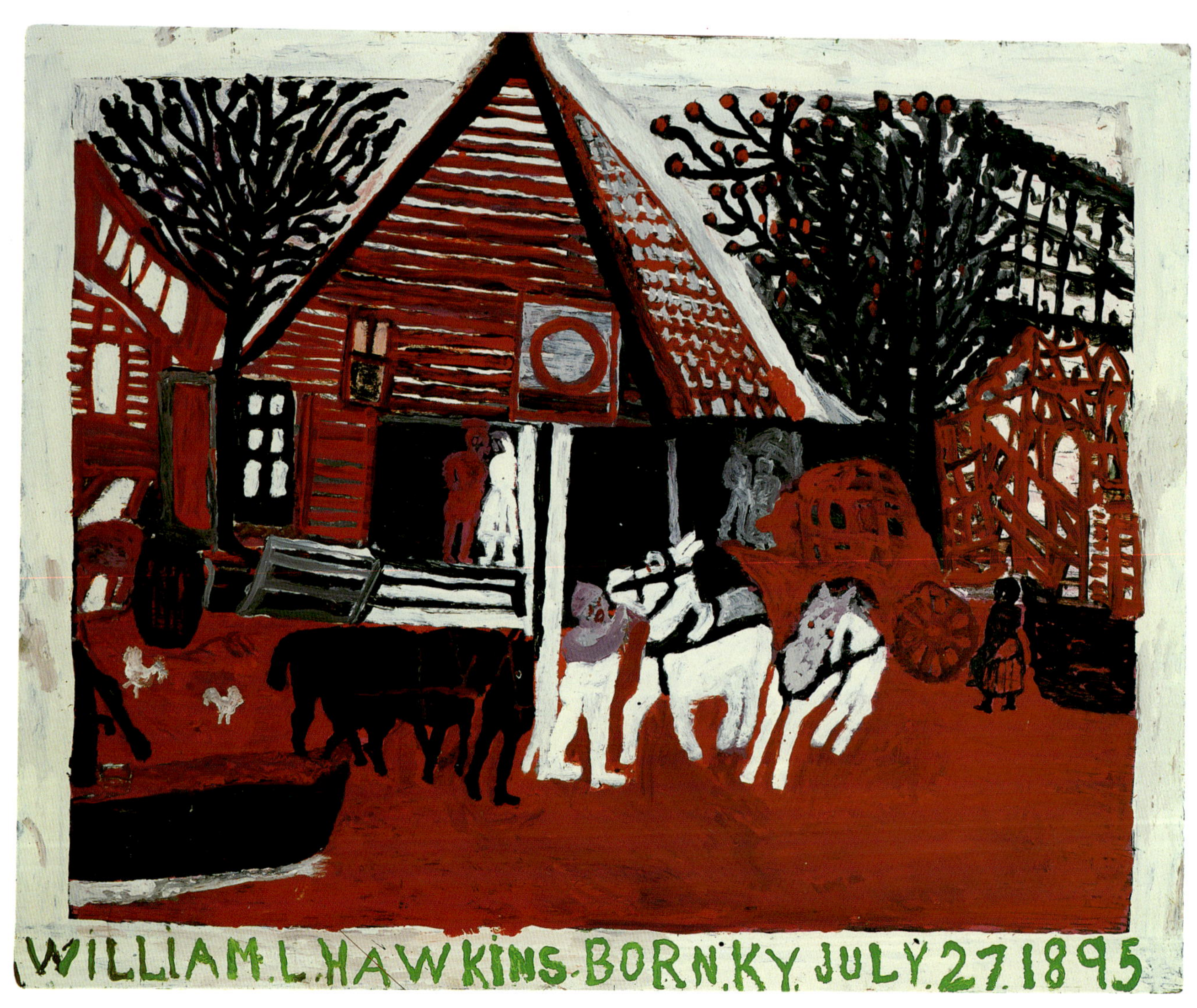

Thomas Jefferson's Birthplace #2, 1985

Enamel on Masonite, 45″ x 56½″

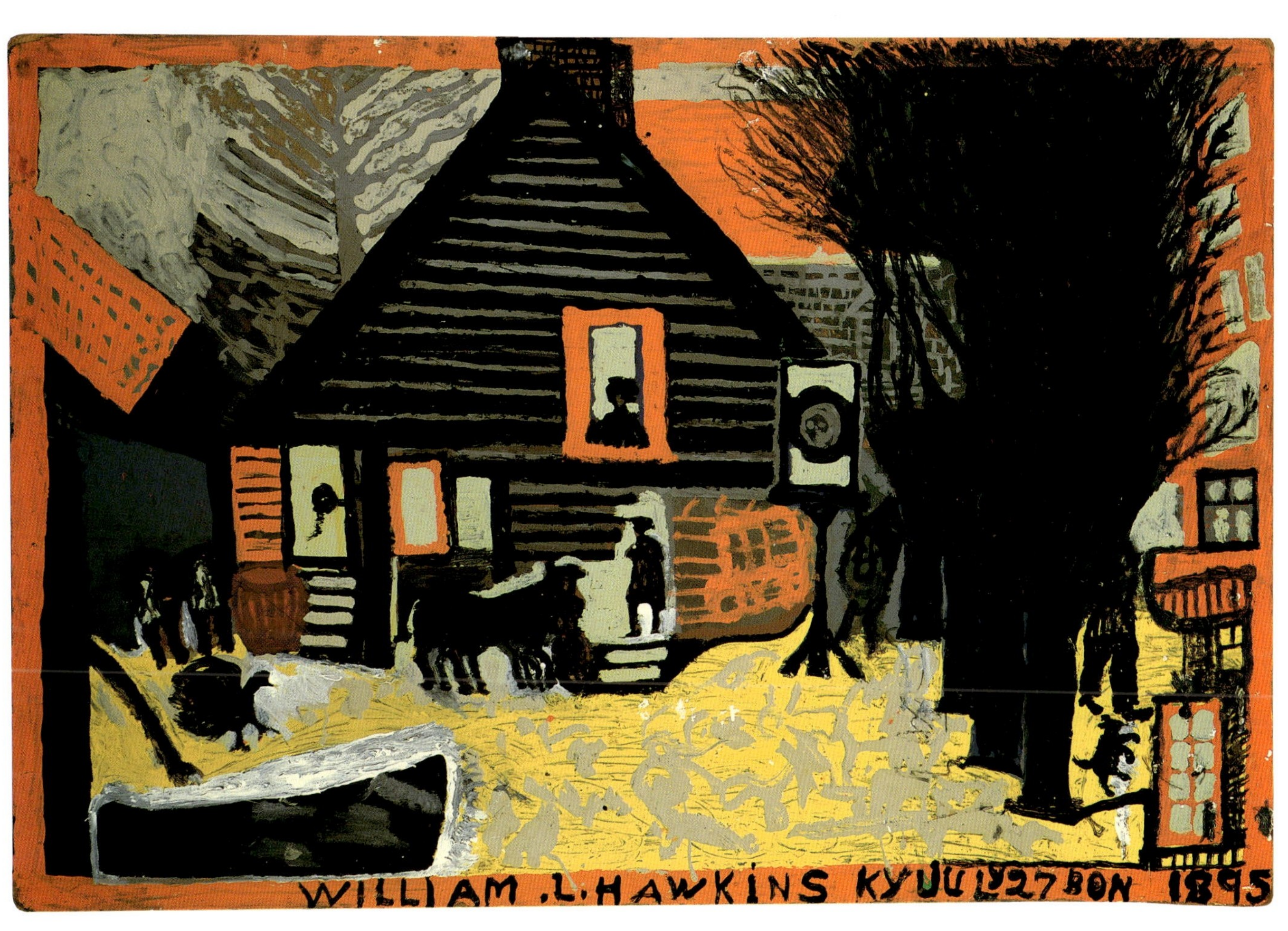

Thomas Jefferson's Birthplace #1, 1982

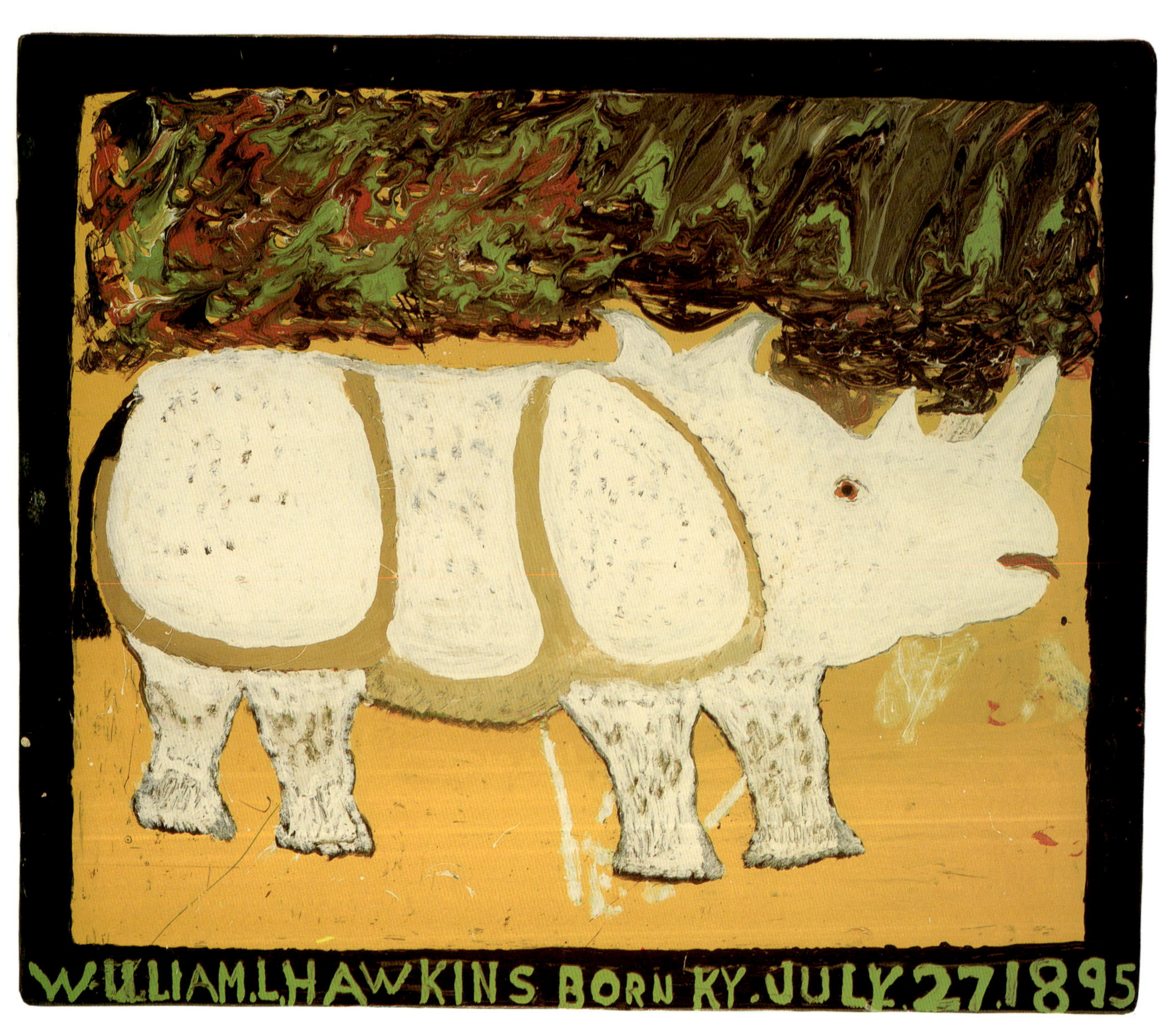

White Rhino with Yellow Ground, 1985

Enamel on composition board, 40″ x 48″

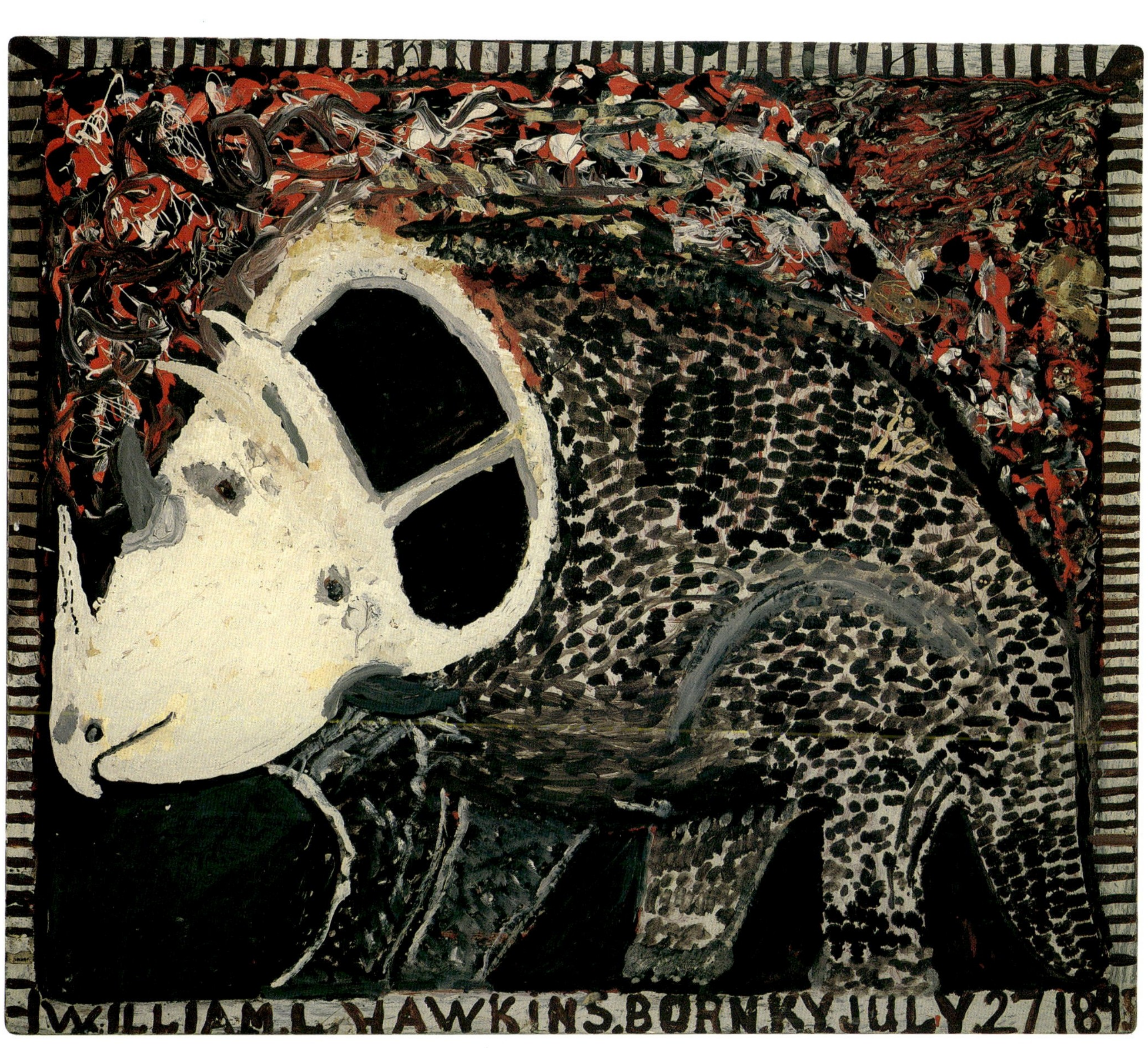
WILLIAM.L. HAWKINS.BORN.KY JULY 27 189

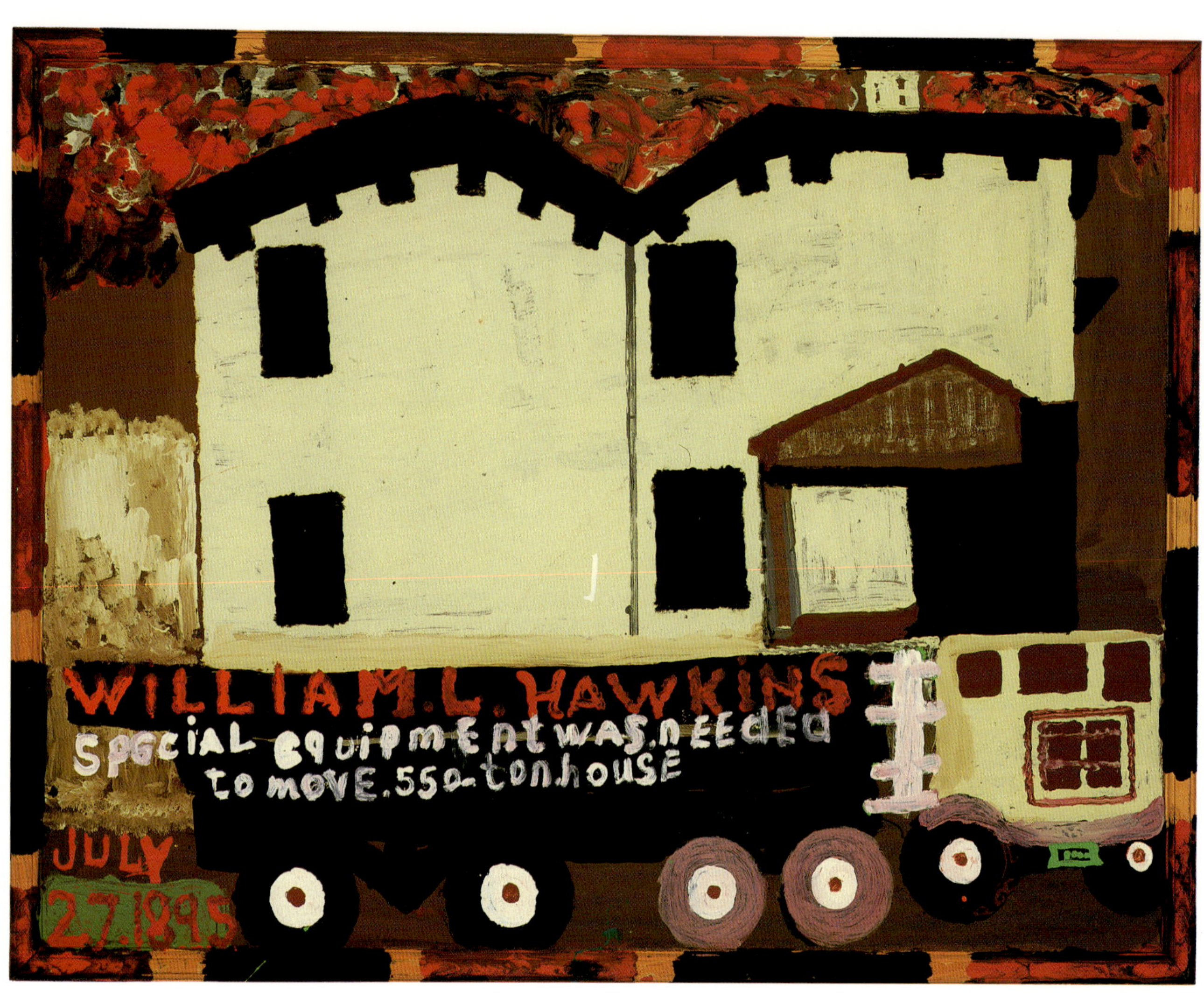

Trucking, 1984

Enamel on Masonite, 34″ x 43″

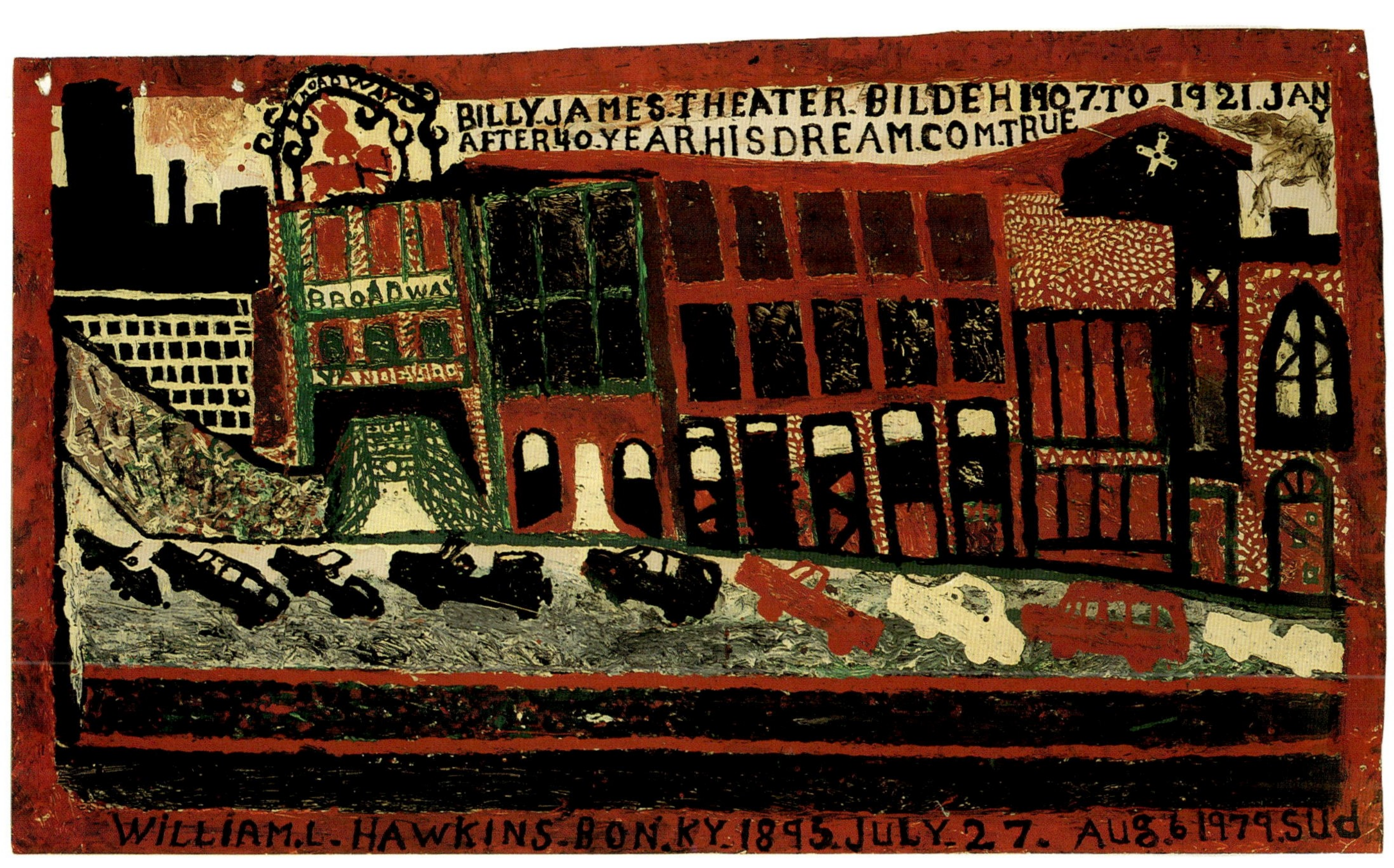

Billy James Theater, 1979

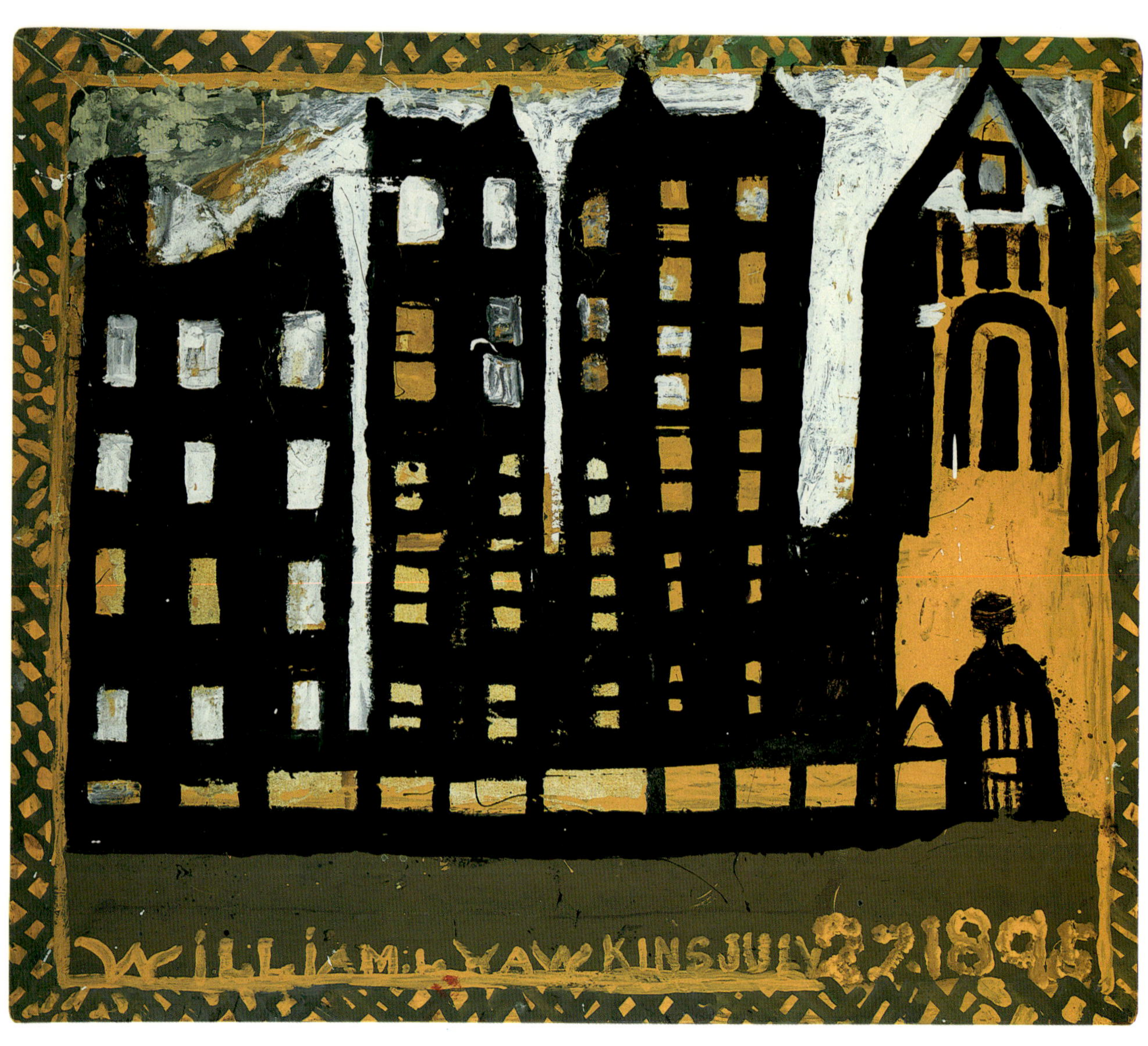

Columbus Buildings, 1988

Enamel on Masonite, 48″ x 56½″

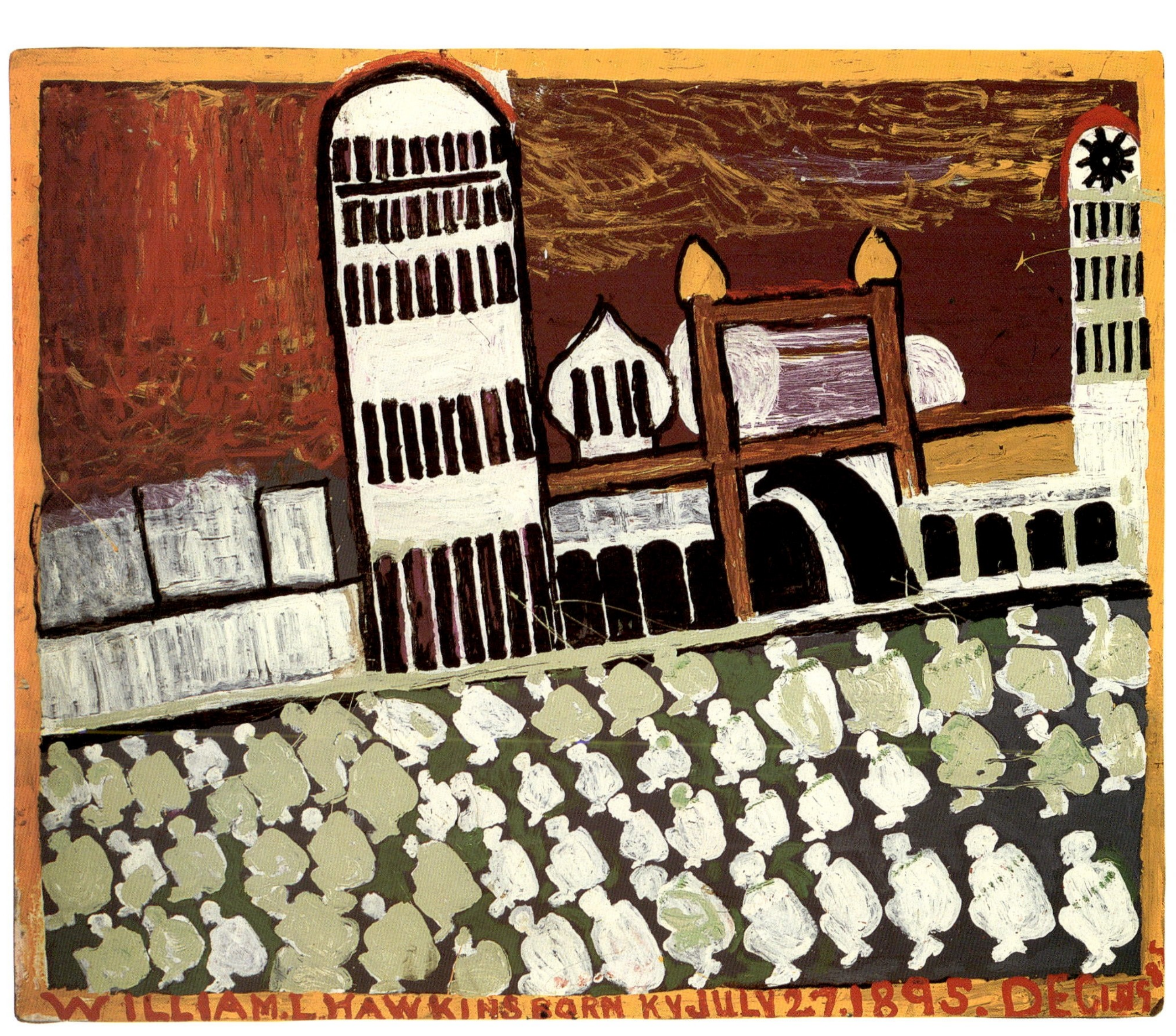
WILLIAM.L.HAWKINS BORN KY JULY 27.1895. DEC

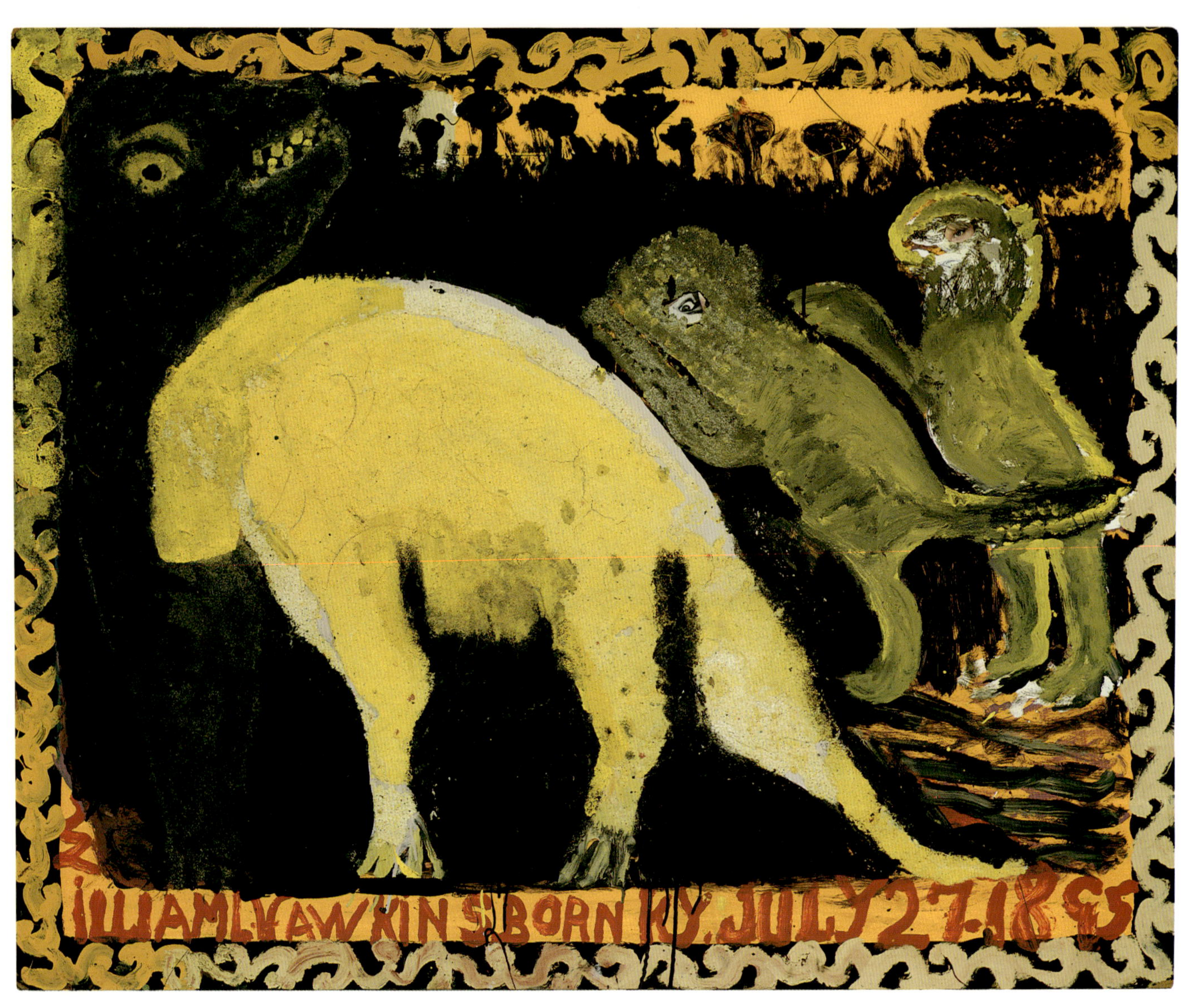

Three Dinosaurs #2, 1988

Enamel, collage, and mixed media on Masonite, 48″ x 60″

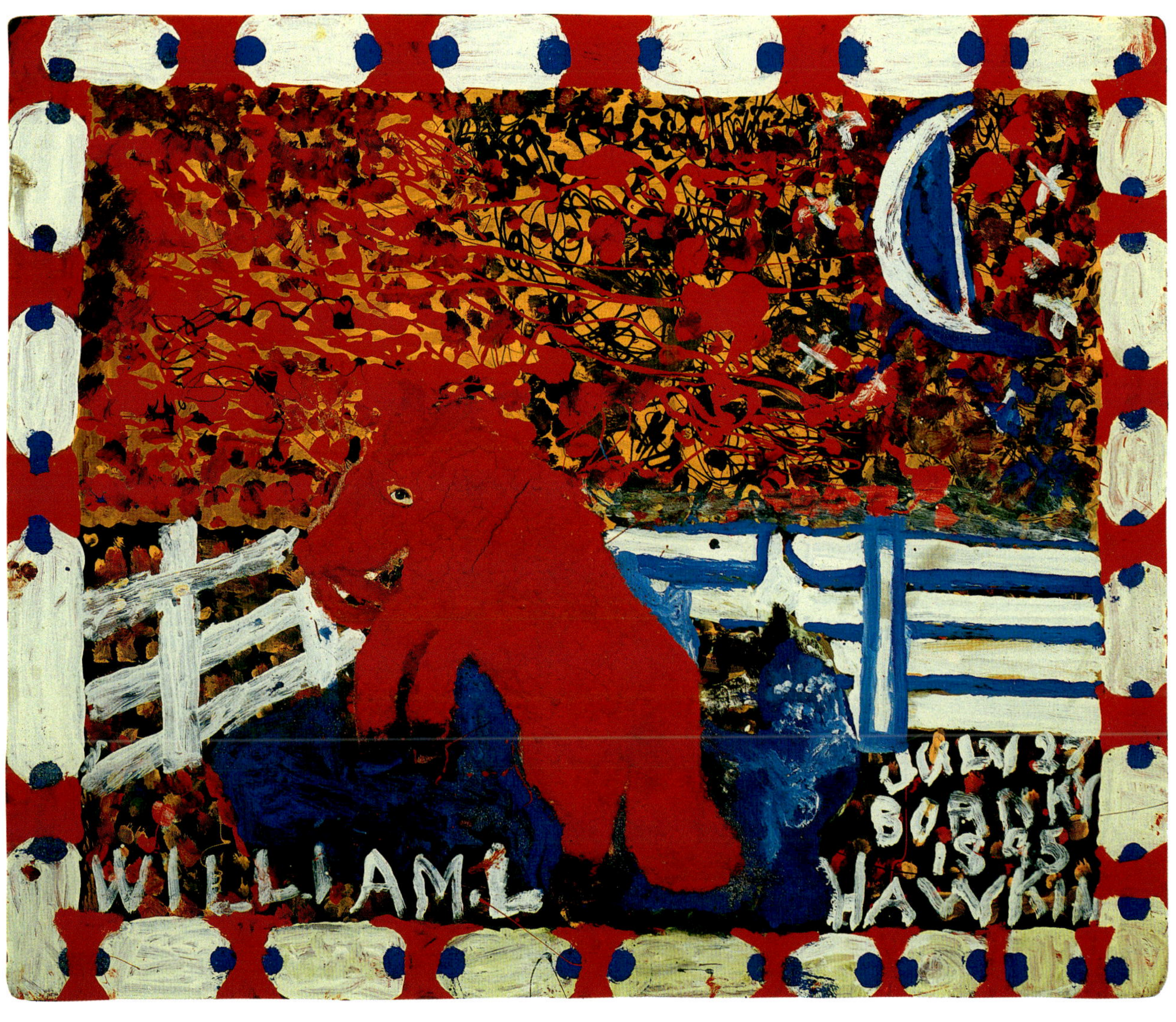

Bucking Horse, 1988

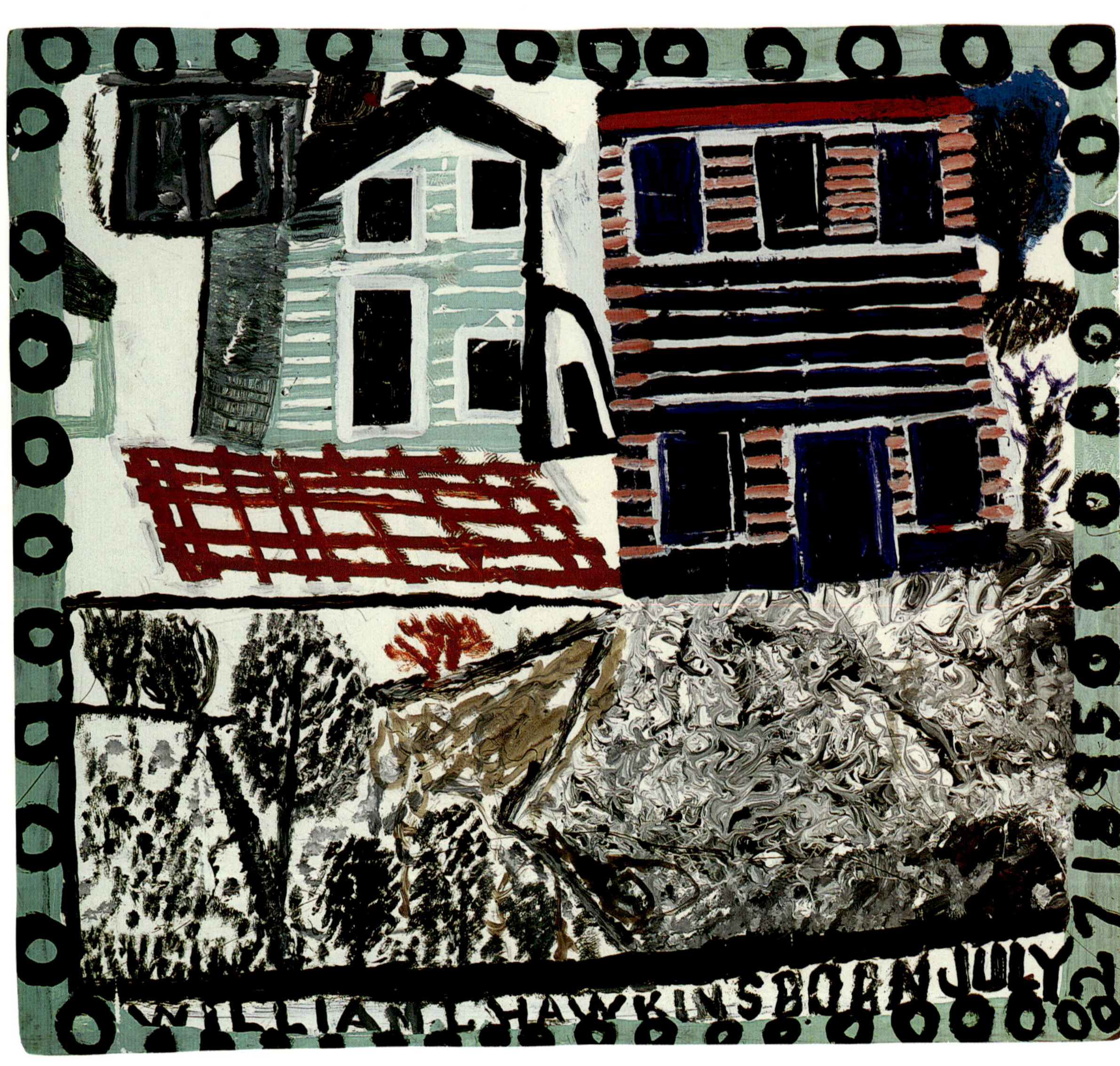

Green House and Blue House, 1989

Enamel on Masonite, 48″ x 54″

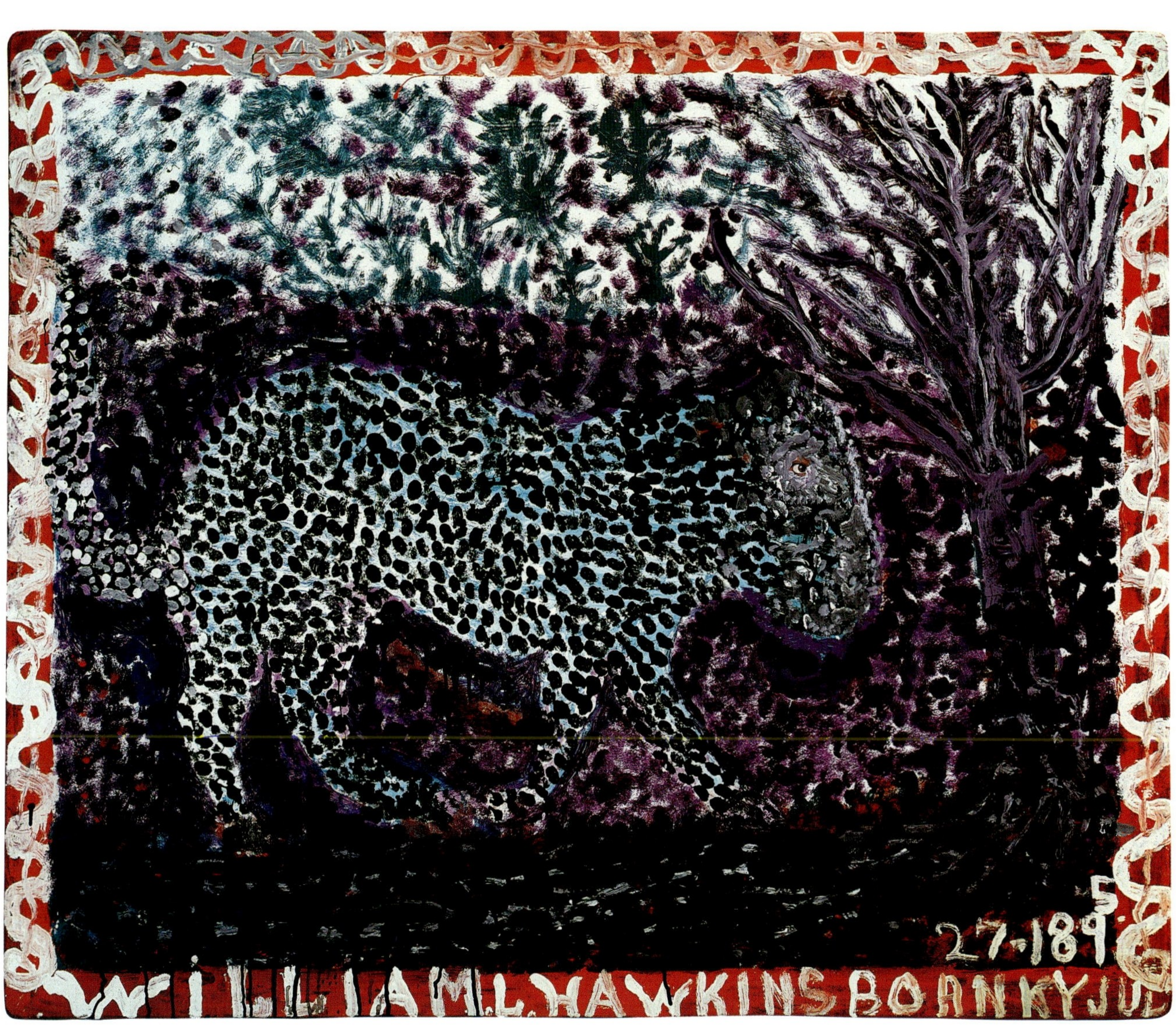

Turquoise Cheetah 1989

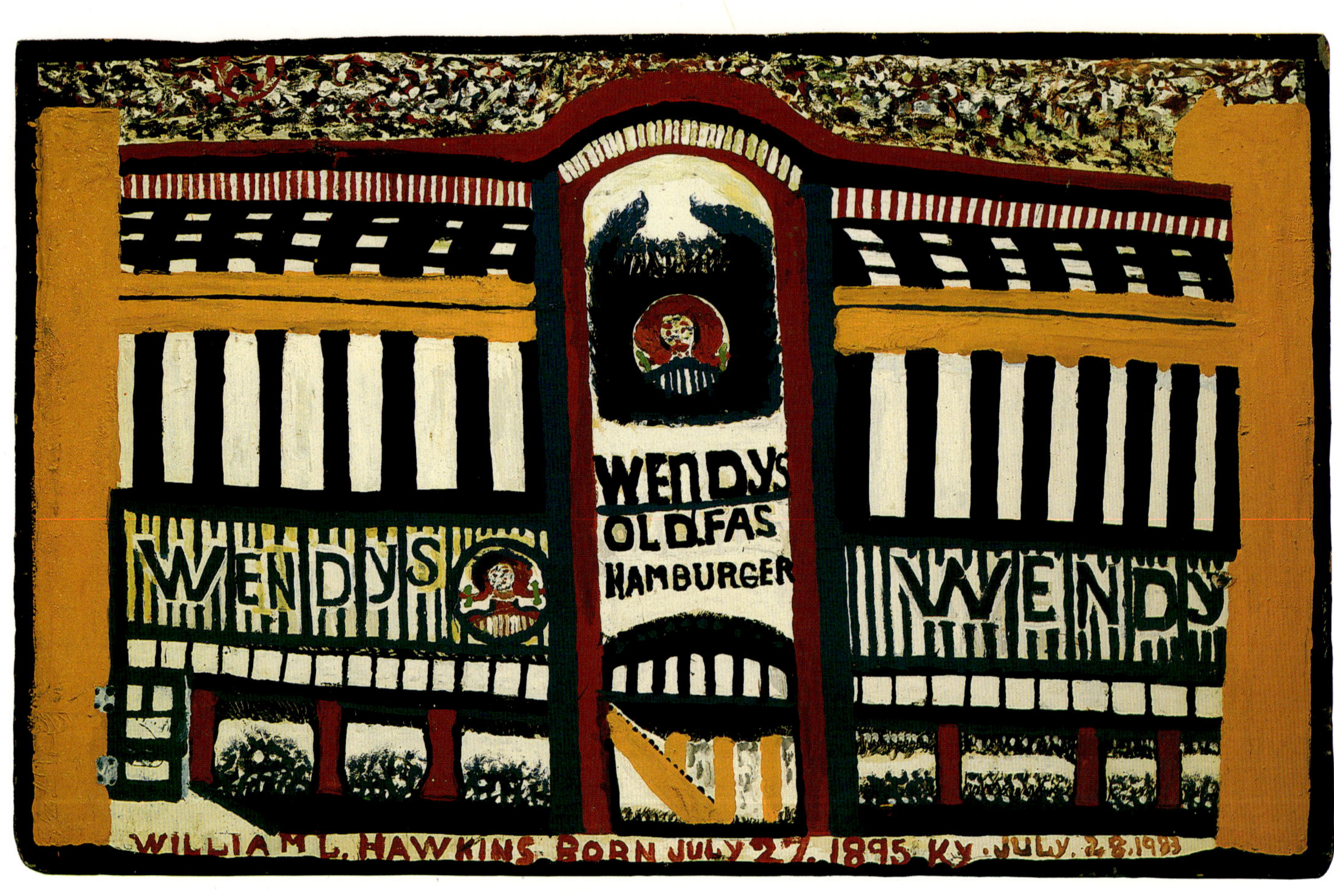

Wendy's Hot 'n Juicy, 1983

Enamel on particleboard, 37″ x 61″

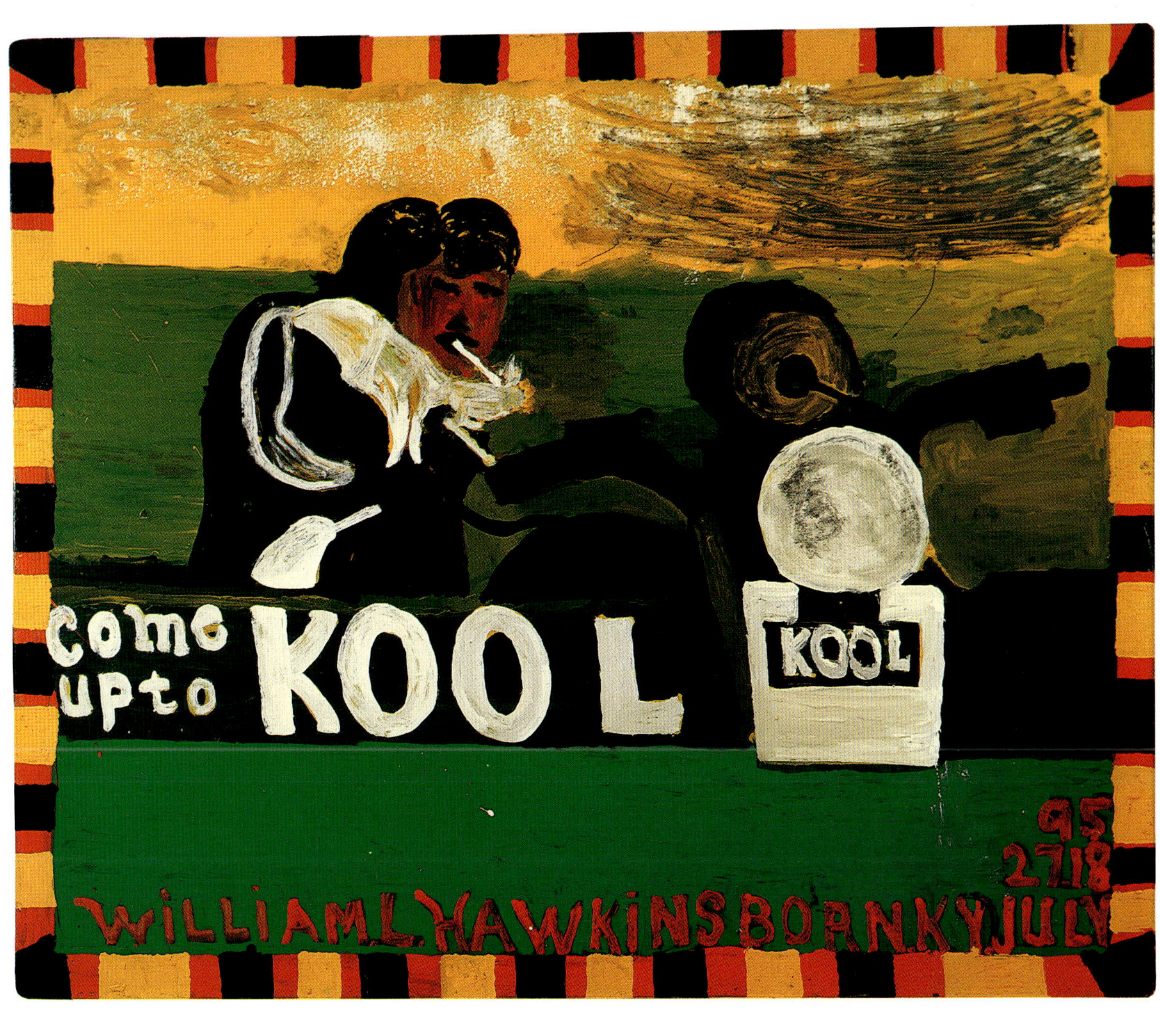

Come Up to Kool, 1995

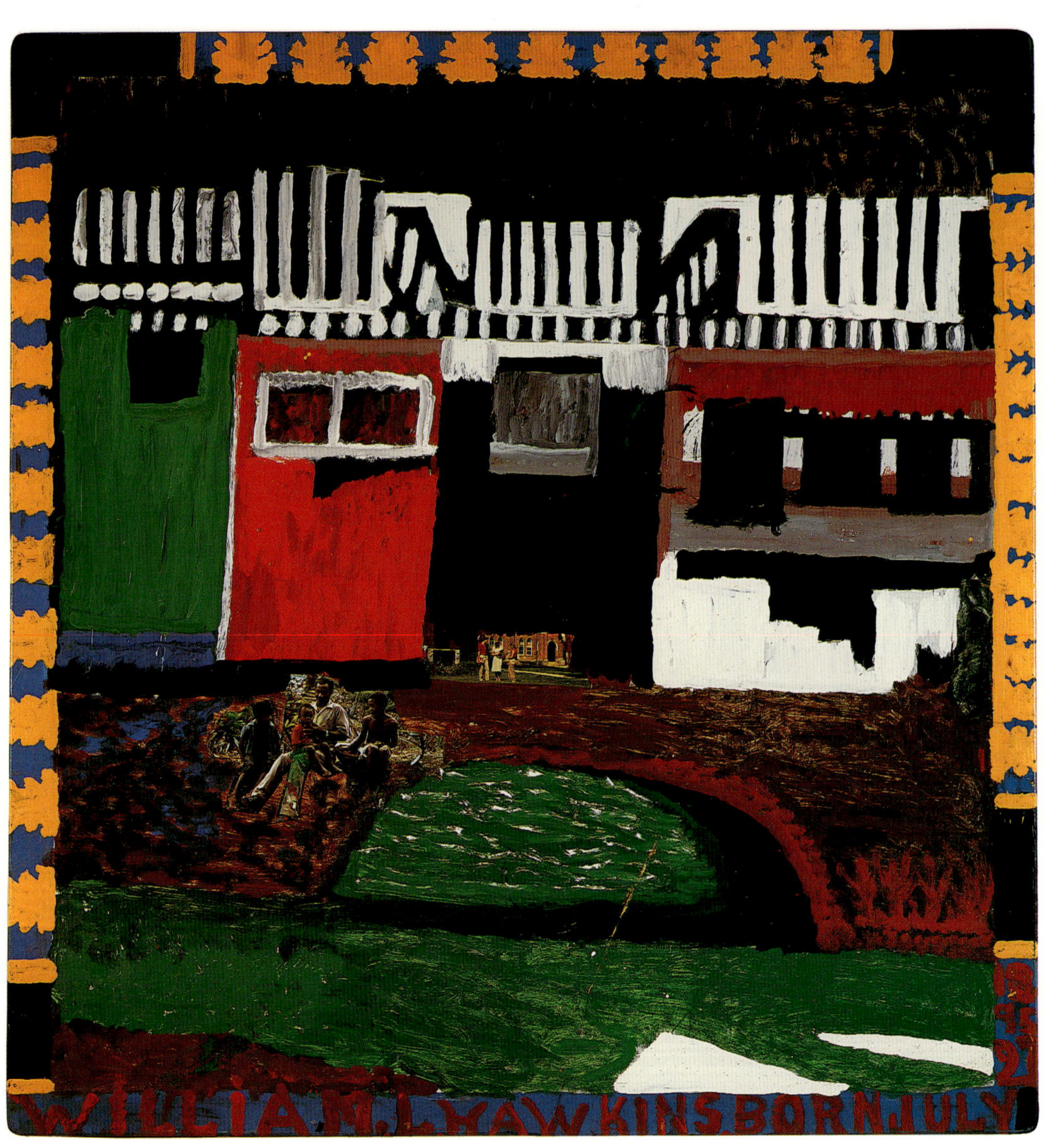

Jamaican House, 1986

Enamel and collage on Masonite, 45″ x 43″

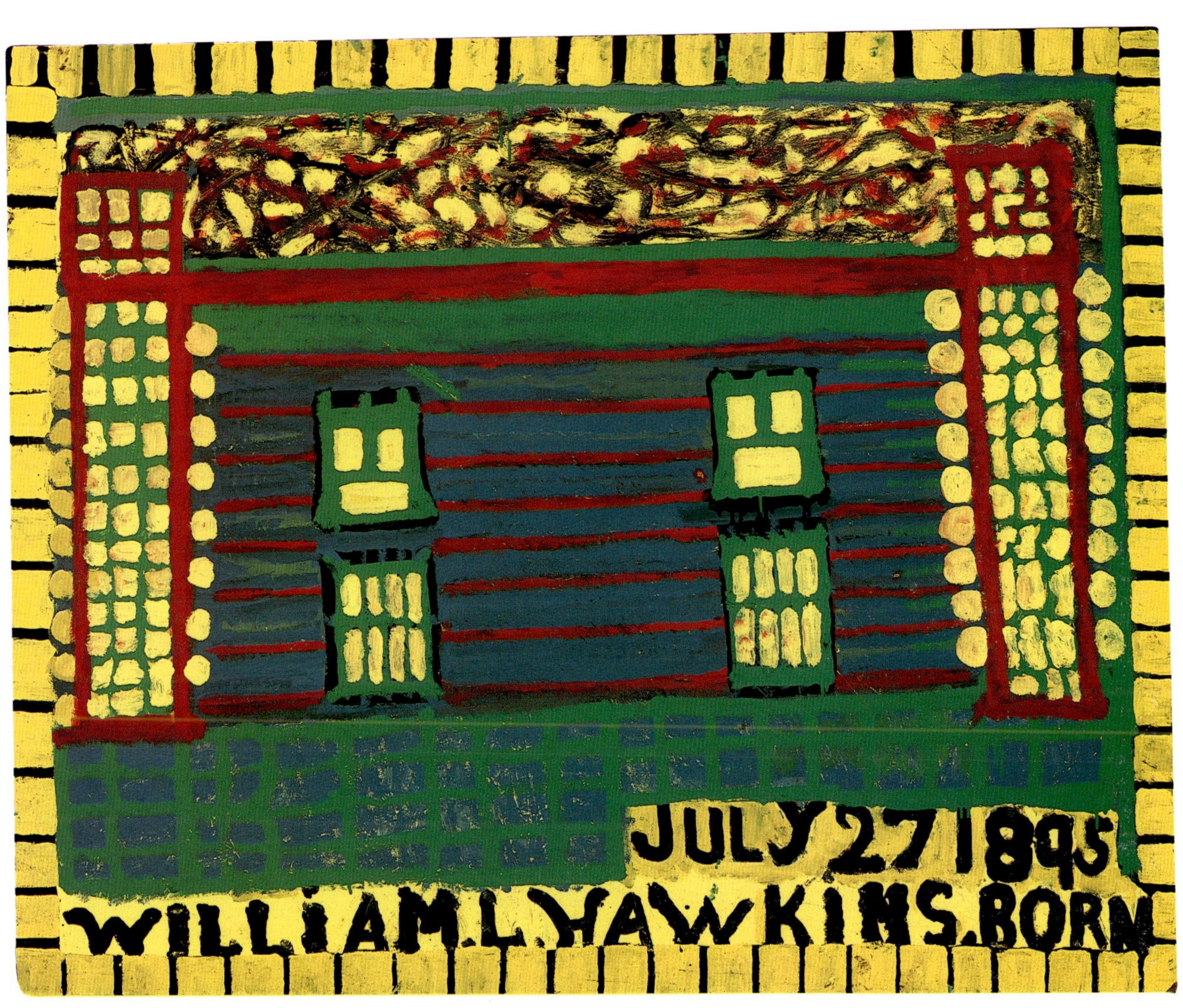
JULY 27 1895
WILLIAM.L.HAWKINS.BORN

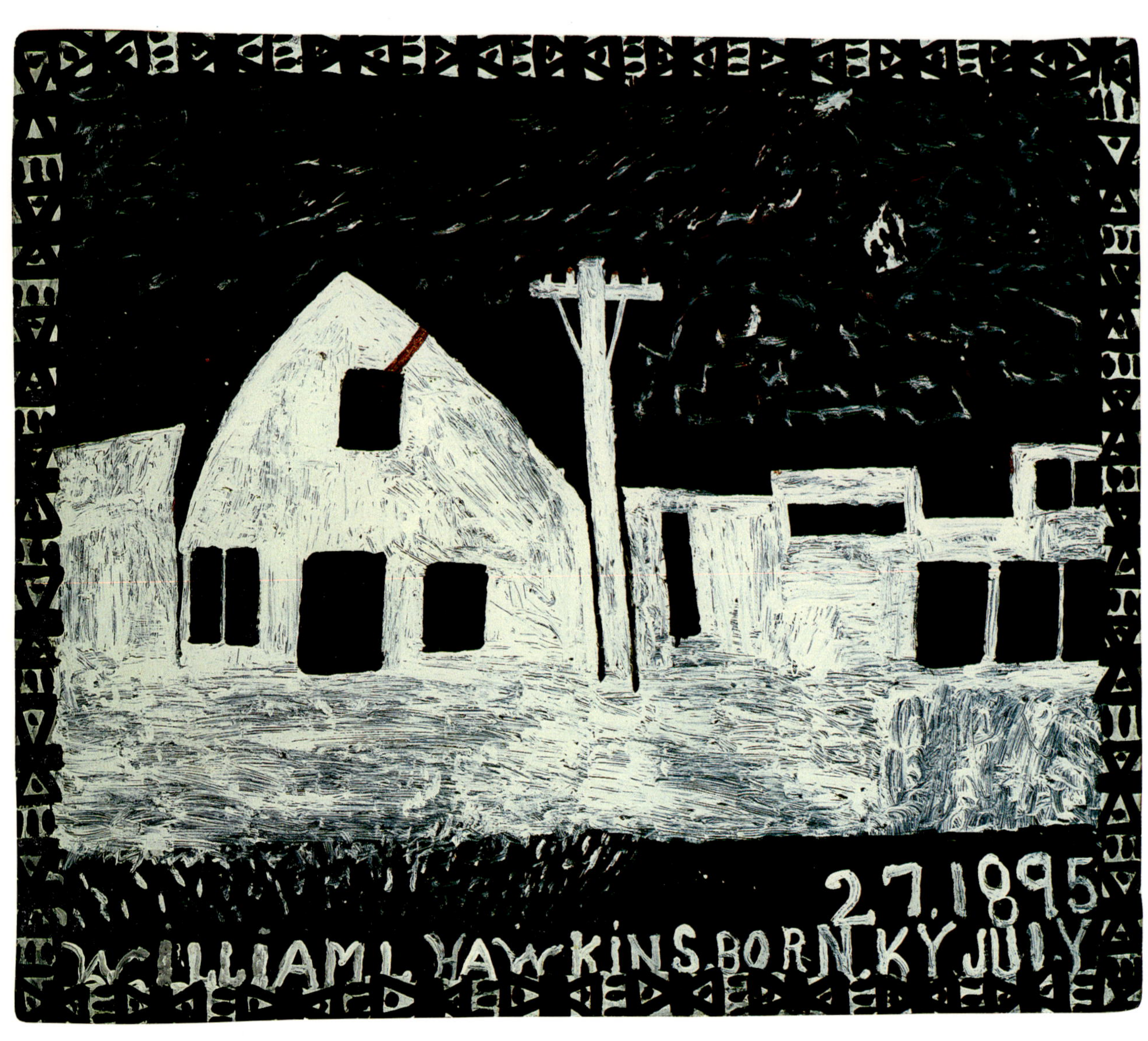

Coal Town, 1989

Enamel on Masonite, 48″ x 56½″

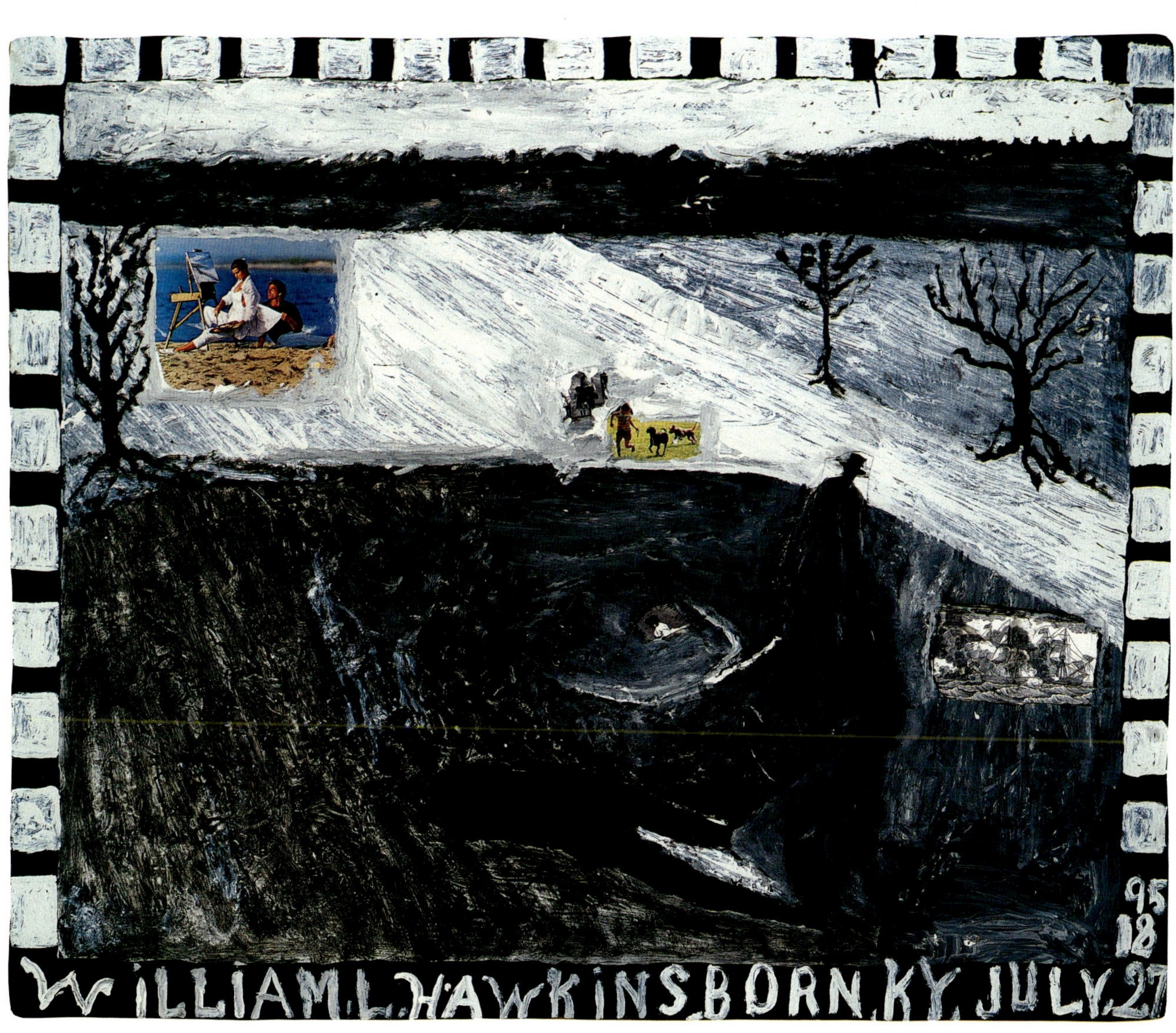
95
18
WILLIAM.L.HAWKINS.BORN.KY.JULY.27

William Hawkins' primary intention was to astound and entertain. His work packs a one-two punch—a quick initial jab followed by a far more formidable right. On the one hand, it entertains, as he intended, in the most direct, pleasurable way; yet it also offers a decidedly troubling allure, a more fundamental challenge to viewer and institution alike. The former quality has allowed his work to circulate for more than a decade in the folk-art milieu, but the latter has made its presence in that world an uneasy one. The black laborer become autodidactic phenomenon seems to fit the folk profile to a tee, but his oeuvre reveals a different story altogether.

In order to understand how and why Hawkins' work outstrips and inherently challenges the limits imposed on it by the context of folk art, it is necessary to consider the academically sanctioned and popularly accepted historical narrative that begins in earnest in ancient Greece, wanes during the Middle Ages, waxes again in the Renaissance, and continues through the twentieth century, only to dwindle again sadly with each passing Whitney Biennial. This mainstream of Western art is the measuring stick by which all other forms of expression are deemed inferior. It underlies the prevailing belief that a sculpture by Marcel Duchamp will be more significant than one by Lonnie Holley, and that a Salvador Dali painting will be more important than one by Henry Darger. This continues to affect curators, collectors, and critics of work by self-taught artists, but, thankfully, not the artists themselves. Each time a self-taught artist reinvents what are thought to be historically specific art-historical discoveries, the notion of measurable, mainstream aesthetic "progress" is rendered obsolete.

William Hawkins poses just such a threat to the arbitrary distinction between folk art and fine art. He hit upon a number of the key aesthetic and conceptual solutions thought to be exclusive to the modern and postmodern movements, from forays into abstraction and unapologetic celebrations of the flat picture plane, to the appropriation of found objects and pop-culture images. The results are uncanny.

From Paul Gauguin to Henri Matisse, early modern painters heralded the expressivity of pure, unmixed color, enjoying a novel freedom from inherited methods of classical shading and chiaroscuro, something that Hawkins achieved in the majority of his works. In *Mountain Lion Drinking Water* (1985; page 22), in which discrete fields of shocking color flow together to form a dynamic composition, Hawkins treads definitively on fauve territory. From Edouard Manet to Paul Cézanne, early moderns eschewed Renaissance perspective to explore the formal possibilities the flat surface had to offer—something Hawkins arrived at by following his own path. To be sure, self-taught genius is not simply the result of an inability to master Renaissance perspective, but instead emerges in the formal/alchemical magic enacted in its place. Hawkins was such an artist-alchemist. From his patterned buildings such as *Huntington Bank #2* (1985; page 58) to his landscapes, from his historical tableaux to his reworking of popular advertisements, Hawkins embraced pictorial flatness and engaged in a free play of abstract form and unorthodox materials.

Hawkins' accomplishments within the terrain of modernism extend to the expressionist moments that have punctuated the art of this century. His gleefully distorted human figures are relatives of those angst-ridden, European urban denizens of Otto Kirchner's paintings; Kirchner's figures, by virtue of a penchant for formal elegance, lack the frenetically built-up, energized rawness of Hawkins'. Hawkins worked on a horizontally oriented surface, often dripping and swirling his colors (especially in the "stormy" skies that top many of his tableaux). This method was self-consciously understood by Jackson Pollock to be revolutionary; for Hawkins, it was simply a convenient way to work. Hawkins' paintings are marked by an expressive freedom sought, but never truly achieved, by his mainstream counterparts.

In addition to inventing ways of building up painted surfaces with a paste concocted from a mixture of enamel and such materials as fish-tank gravel and cornmeal, he often fastened a range of objects to his surfaces. The beast in *Tasmanian Tiger #2* (1986; page 49) sports carved tusks, while the central figure in the artist's tour-de-force *All About Eve* (1989; page 24) explodes in high relief, fully clothed, entangled by a serpent made of junk tubing that emerges from a small tree. This and many other examples of Hawkins' work recall the work of Marcel Duchamp and Robert Rauschenberg, both of whom employed found objects and materials, even if Hawkins didn't share their avant-garde vision.

Perhaps most important of all are the ways in which Hawkins engages a postmodern anti-aesthetic. His working process—each piece began with a reaction to an image taken from pop culture—was essentially media-informed and thus inherently media-critical, although not part of any larger agenda. His use of collage, a strategy he employed after 1986, makes his engagement with popular culture more explicit. By appropriating images from a variety of pop-cultural sources—especially newspapers and magazines—he framed these images to suit his own purposes. Hawkins opened his collages up to quite unpredictable results, not the least of which is humor. This sense of play enabled him to simultaneously amuse and challenge his audience. This is especially true of his *Last Supper* series (pages 56 and 57), Hawkins' own versions of a mass-produced copy of Leonardo's well-known work in which Christ and his disciples are unmistakably black. Here Hawkins goes head to head with the savviest, most theory-driven identity politicians.

The work of William Hawkins invites a new sort of viewer—one willing to be an active participant, not a passive consumer—to replace critics and historians who have guarded the status quo. Hawkins' work offers a pleasurable experience even as it challenges Western art.

Jenifer P. Borum

Information concerning the biography and working process of William Hawkins was made possible through the unpublished video footage taken by Roger Ricco and Frank Maresca during visits with the artist, and through the published writings of Gary Schwindler, including *William L. Hawkins* (Ricco/Maresca Gallery, New York, 1990); "The Art of William Hawkins (1895–1990)," in *Popular Images, Personal Visions* (Columbus Museum of Art, Columbus, Ohio, 1990); and "William Hawkins, Master Storyteller" (*Raw Vision 4*, Spring 1991: 41–45).

A NOTE ON THE SOURCE MATERIAL

Every attempt has been made to secure proper credit information on the source material used by William Hawkins. However, due to the fact that he scavenged for materials in Dumpsters and on the streets of Columbus, it was not always possible to locate the original publication in which the images appeared.

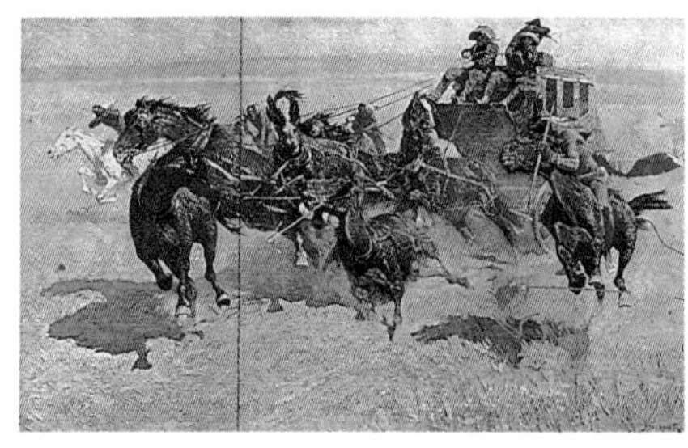

Overland Stage from *The Golden Book of America,* adapted by Irwin Shapiro, 1957, from *Frederick Remington* by Harold McCracken; courtesy J.B. Lippincott Company. Source material courtesy of Lee Garrett.

Most of Hawkins' artworks were inspired by printed images culled from a variety of media sources: local and national newspapers, magazines such as *Life* and *National Geographic,* postcards, calendars, and books. He would clip out pictures that interested him—especially images capturing current events, faraway places, exotic animals, and American history—and file them in an old suitcase for subsequent perusal and transformation into his own unique pictorial language. The Wild West was a favorite topic. The above image of a stagecoach is one of many he appropriated from a book titled *The Golden Book of America* (see frontispiece).

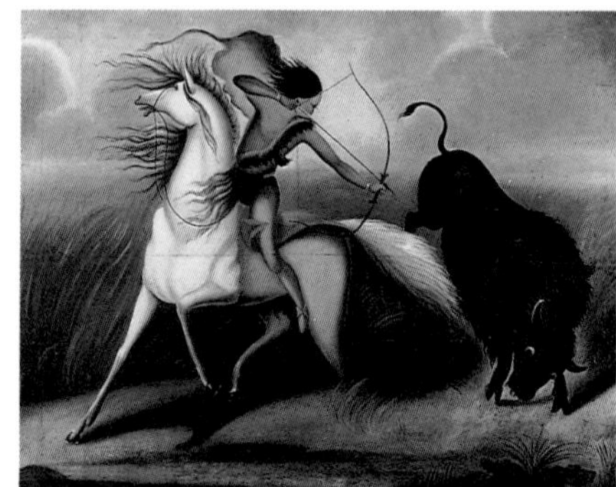

Buffalo Hunter, ca. 1844, Anonymous, from *The Golden Book of America,* adapted by Irwin Shapiro, 1957, courtesy of the Santa Barbara Museum of Art. Source material courtesy of Lee Garrett.

Animals, and especially horses, were one of Hawkins' favorite subjects to paint. This image was also taken from *The Golden Book of America* (see page 51).

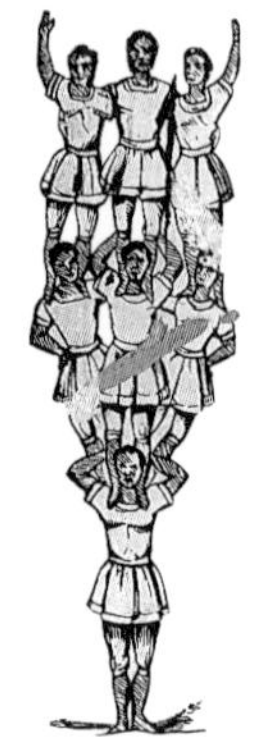

Circus Acrobats, publication unknown. Source material courtesy of Lee Garrett.

The unpredictable nature of Hawkins' work was due to his penchant for the bizarre and the fantastic. This image is of a gravity-defying stunt performed by circus acrobats. A comparison of this source and the painting it inspired (see page 7) illustrates how vital Hawkins' working process could be. Hawkins used collage elements primarily to save the time it would have taken to represent figural details such as hands, eyes, and faces, but the results, far surpassing this simple intention, reveal a rare, risk-taking formal wit.

EXHIBITION HISTORY

Selected Solo Exhibitions

1984
Janet Fleisher Gallery, Philadelphia

Carl Hammer Gallery, Chicago

Ricco/Johnson Gallery, New York

1985
Harris-Brown Gallery, Boston

Ricco/Johnson Gallery, New York

1986
Carl Hammer Gallery, Chicago

Janet Fleisher Gallery, Philadelphia

Keny-Johnson Gallery, Columbus, Ohio

1987
Carl Hammer Gallery, Chicago

Ricco/Maresca Gallery, New York

1989
Edward Thorp Gallery, New York

Ricco/Maresca Gallery, New York

William L. Hawkins: Transformations
Tarble Arts Center, Eastern Illinois University, Charleston, Illinois

1990
Popular Images, Personal Visions: The Art of William Hawkins, 1895–1990
Columbus Museum of Art, Columbus, Ohio

William L. Hawkins, 1895–1990
Ricco/Maresca Gallery, New York

1991
Ginza Art Space, Shiseido Corporation, Tokyo

1993
Ricco/Maresca Gallery, New York

1995
Centennial Exhibition: The 100th Anniversary of the Birth of William L. Hawkins
Ricco/Maresca Gallery, New York

1997
William L. Hawkins Born July 27 1895
Museum of American Folk Art, New York

Selected Group Exhibitions

1982
Two-Person Show
Ohio Gallery, Columbus, Ohio

1984
Beyond Tradition: Contemporary American Folk Art
The Katonah Gallery, Katonah, New York

Folk Art: Then and Now
Stamford Museum, Stamford, Connecticut

Since the Harlem Renaissance
Center Gallery of Bucknell University, Lewisburg, Pennsylvania
(Pennsylvania, New York, Maryland, and Virginia)

Soul Catchers
Stellweg-Seguy Gallery, New York

Webb & Parsons Gallery, Long Island, New York

1985
Masterpieces of Primitive Art
Janet Fleisher Gallery, Philadelphia

Out of Ohio—Two Visions
Janet Fleisher Gallery, Philadelphia

Rebuilding Liberty: Old and New Themes in American Folk Art
Stamford Plaza, Stamford, Connecticut

1986
Black American Folk Art
Robbeson Center Gallery, Rutgers University, Newark, New Jersey

Interface: Outsiders and Insiders
Lancaster Gallery for Visual Arts, Ohio University, Lancaster, Ohio
(Athens Trisolini Gallery, Ohio University, and the University of Akron)

Liberties with Liberty
The Museum of American Folk Art in cooperation with the Statue of Liberty Foundation, New York

Muffled Voices
The Museum of American Folk Art at the Paine-Webber Galleries, New York

1987
Acquisitions '87
Buscaglia-Castellani Art Gallery of Niagara University, Buffalo, New York

Making the Mainstream
SVC Fine Art Gallery, University of South Florida, Tampa

Paintings and Sculpture by Black American Self-Taught Artists
Janet Fleisher Gallery, Philadelphia

1988
Folk Heroes: 20th-Century American Self-Taught Artists
George Ciscel Gallery, Baltimore

1989
Expressions of a New Spirit: Highlights from the Permanent Collection of the Museum of American Folk Art
Museum of American Folk Art, New York

How the Eagle Flies: Patriotic Images in Twentieth-Century Folk Art
Meadow Farm Museum, General Sheppard Crump Memorial Park, Richmond, Virginia

New Traditions, Non-Traditions: Contemporary Folk Art in Ohio
The Riffle Gallery, Columbus, Ohio

Selections from the Collection: Contemporary Art
The John and Mable Ringling Museum of Art, Sarasota, Florida

1990

Into the Mainstream: Contemporary American Folk, Naive, and Outsider Art
Miami University Art Museum, Oxford, Ohio

1991

The Cutting Edge: Contemporary American Folk Art
Museum of American Folk Art / Eva and Morris Feld Gallery, New York

Different Drummer: Works by American Self-Taught Artists
MetLife Gallery, New York

Made with Passion: The Hemphill Folk Art Collection
National Museum of American Art, Washington, D.C.

Outsider USA
Malmö Kunsthalle, Malmö, Sweden
(Esbo Art Hall, Esbo/Helsinki, Finland, and Wälnö Altonens Konstmuseum, Åbo, Finland; Ronneby Cultural Centre, Ronneby, Sweden; Bergens Kunstforening, Bergen, Norway; Hafnarborg, Reykjavik, Iceland; Kunstmuseum Kartause Ittingen, Warth, Switzerland; Brandts Klædefabrik, Odense, Denmark)

Personal Intensity: Artists in Spite of the Mainstream
University of Wisconsin—Milwaukee Art Museum, Milwaukee

Personal Voices: Outsider Art and Signature Style
American Center for Design, Chicago

1992

19th- and 20th-Century Afro-American Artists
Philadelphia Museum of Art, Philadelphia

Contemporary American Folk Art: The Bales Collection
Haggerty Museum of Art / Marquette University, Milwaukee

Give Me a Louder Word Up: African American Art
Metropolitan State College of Denver / Center for Visual Arts, Denver, Colorado

Sam Doyle, William Hawkins, Purvis Young
Edward Thorp Gallery, New York

Works of Art . . . Worlds Apart
Fenimore House / New York State Historical Association, Cooperstown, New York

1993

Bob Bishop: A Life in American Folk Art
Museum of American Folk Art, New York

Driven to Create: The Anthony Petullo Collection of Self-Taught and Outsider Art
Museum of American Folk Art, New York

Passionate Visions of the American South: Self-Taught Artists, 1940–Present
New Orleans Museum of Art, New Orleans, Louisiana
(University Art Museum and Pacific Film Archive; University of California at Berkeley; San Diego Museum of Art; Corcoran Gallery of Art, Washington, D.C.; North Carolina Museum of Art, Raleigh)

Primitivism: A Historical Overview
Setagaya Art Museum, Tokyo

1996

Expressions of Trust: Recent Gifts to the Permanent Collection
Museum of American Folk Art, New York

Pictured in My Mind: Contemporary American Self-Taught Art from the Collection of Dr. Kurt Gitter and Alice Rae Yelen
Birmingham Museum of Art, Birmingham, Alabama
(DeCordova Museum, Lincoln, Massachusetts; Southeastern Center for Contemporary Art, Winston-Salem, North Carolina)

1997

A Place for Us: Vernacular Architecture in American Folk Art
Museum of American Folk Art, New York

Selected Public Collections

The Akron Museum, Akron, Ohio

ARA Services, Philadelphia

Castellani Art Gallery, Niagara University, Buffalo, New York

Columbus Museum of Art, Columbus, Ohio

High Museum of Art, Atlanta, Georgia

Museum of American Folk Art, New York

National Museum of American Art, Smithsonian Institution, Washington, D.C.

PepsiCo, Inc., Purchase, New York

Shearson–American Express, New York

Setagaya Art Museum, Tokyo

COLLECTIONS

Collections (listed by page number)

Photographs by Charles Bechtold, unless otherwise noted

Frontispiece Collection of Dr. and Mrs. Armand J. Castellani; photo courtesy Biff Henrich / Keystone Film Productions, Inc.
3 Darin Ricco
4 Robert M. Greenberg
5 The Anthony Petullo Collection of Self-Taught and Outsider Art
6 T. Marshall Hahn, Jr. Collection, High Museum of Art, Atlanta, Georgia
7–9 Private Collection
10 Ricco/Maresca Gallery
11 Private Collection, Chicago, courtesy Fleisher/Ollman Gallery
12 Private Collection
13 Robert M. Greenberg
14 Sandra and Gerald Fineberg; photo courtesy Edward Thorp Gallery, New York
15 Frank Maresca
16 Ricco/Maresca Gallery
17 Robert M. Greenberg
18 Ricco/Maresca Gallery
19 Private Collection
20 Frank Maresca
21(top) Christa Saffran; photo courtesy Jock Pottle/Esto
21(bottom) Roger and Cia Ricco
22 Joan and Charles Gross
23 Setagaya Art Museum, Tokyo; photo courtesy Setagaya Art Museum, Tokyo
24 Ricco/Maresca Gallery
25 Robert M. Greenberg
26 Private Collection
27–28 T. Marshall Hahn, Jr. Collection, High Museum of Art, Atlanta, Georgia
29 Collection of Marion Bolton Stroud, courtesy Fleisher/Ollman Gallery; photo by Joseph Painter, courtesy Fleisher/Ollman Gallery
30 Frank Maresca
31 Carla Emil and Rich Silverstein
32–33 Private Collection
34 Blumert-Fiore Collection
35 Alexander Figge
36 Alexander Figge; photo courtesy Edward Thorp Gallery, New York
37 Roger and Cia Ricco
38 Siri von Reis
39–42 Private Collection
43 Frank Maresca
44 Private Collection
45 Setagaya Art Museum, Tokyo
46 Marvill Collection
47 Private Collection
48 Joan and Michael Salke Collection
49 Blumert-Fiore Collection
50 Ricco/Maresca Gallery
51 Roger and Cia Ricco
52 Marvill Collection
53–54 Private Collection
55 Ricco/Maresca Gallery
56 Robert M. Greenberg
57 Robert A. Roth
58 Robert Bishop Collection, courtesy Gary Davenport; photo courtesy Bob DeGise
59 Private Collection
60 T. Marshall Hahn, Jr. Collection, High Museum of Art, Atlanta, Georgia
61 Selig D. Sacks
62 Siri von Reis
63 Blumert-Fiore Collection
64 Ricco/Maresca Gallery
65 Frank Maresca
66 Private Collection
67 Ricco/Maresca Gallery
68 Private Collection
69 James and Donna Pressman
70 Alexander Figge
71 Private Collection
72 Collection of the Museum of American Folk Art, New York. Gift of Warner Communications Inc. 1988.19.1. Photo courtesy John Parnell
73 Private Collection
74 Mark and Karen Hauser, photo courtesy Edward Thorp Gallery, New York
75–76 Private Collection
77 Robert M. Greenberg
78 Lael and Eugenie Johnson
79 Private Collection
80 John and Margaret Robson
81 Collection of Ann and John Ollman; photo by Joseph Painter, courtesy Fleisher/Ollman Gallery
82 Gael Mendelsohn Collection
83 Frank Maresca
84 Private Collection
85 Lael and Eugenie Johnson
86 Marvill Collection
87 Ricco/Maresca Gallery
88 Mark and Taryn Leavitt
89 Kathleen Worthington
90 Gael Mendelsohn Collection
91 Private Collection
92 Dann Gershon
93 Patricia L. and Maurice C. Thompson
94 Collection of the Museum of American Folk Art, New York. Gift of Dan and Jeanne Fauci/Outside-In Gallery, Los Angeles. 1991.20.1
95–96 Private Collection
97 Lael and Eugenie Johnson; photo courtesy James Prinz
98 Robert M. Greenberg
99 Ricco/Maresca Gallery
100 John and Margaret Robson
101 Nancy Green and Michael Donovan
102 Ilene Donin
103–104 Private Collection
105 Christopher Owles
106 The ARAMARK Corporation Art Collection at the ARAMARK Tower, Philadelphia
107 Frank Maresca
108 Roger and Cia Ricco
109 Elizabeth and Geoffrey Stern
110–114 Private Collection
115 Ricco/Maresca Gallery
116 Pria Harmon
117 Stephanie and Bob Tardell; photo courtesy Alan S. Brooker
118 Bill and Laraine Tomassi; photo courtesy Michael McKelvey
119 Ricco/Maresca Gallery
120 Roger and Cia Ricco
121 Collection of Edward V. Blanchard and M. Anne Hill, courtesy Fleisher/Ollman Gallery

ACKNOWLEDGMENTS

The conception and development of this book has been many years in the making, and many people have provided us with enthusiastic support along the way.

Our extended thanks go to our publisher, Vicky Wilson, who kept us in touch with reality by reminding us, "There are going to be tears!"; to Connie Sullivan, whose knowledge and expertise have touched virtually every page of this book; and to Iris Weinstein, Archie Ferguson, Debra Helfand, and Lee Buttala at Knopf.

Special thanks to Laura K. Wiley, who coordinated all aspects of this book, assisted in the development of our essay, and kept us on track throughout; and to Jenifer P. Borum, our friend and literary guide. To Gary Schwindler for his generous contribution of invaluable research and writings; to Lyle Rexer for his editorial talents; and to Charles Bechtold for his impeccable photography. A very deep-felt thank you to Joanne Cubbs and Gene Metcalf for their endless understanding and passionate involvement in this project.

Additional thanks go to all of those in the field who recognize the importance of the work of William L. Hawkins: at the Museum of American Folk Art, Gerard C. Wertkin, Director, Riccardo Salmona, Deputy Director, and Stacy C. Hollander, Curator, along with all of our other friends at the museum whose hard work and support have helped us to grow together; Joseph Jacobs, Curator of Painting and Sculpture at the Newark Museum; Carl Hammer and the Carl Hammer Gallery; John Ollman and the Fleisher/Ollman Gallery; and Ed Thorp and the Edward Thorp Gallery.

We are especially grateful to Lee Garrett, who was the first to recognize the genius of William L. Hawkins, and whose friendship and generosity throughout the past fifteen years have provided us with the invaluable information that made this book possible.

A NOTE ABOUT THE TYPE

The text of this book was set in a typeface called Bell. The original punches for this face were cut in 1788 by the engraver Richard Austin for the type foundry of John Bell (1745–1831), the most outstanding typographer of his day. They are the earliest English "modern" type design, and show the influence of French copperplate engraving and the work of the Fournier and Didot families. However, the Bell face has a distinct identity of its own, and might also be classified as a delicate and refined rendering of Scotch Roman.

Separations were made and printing realized in Hong Kong, through Palace Press International, New York

Design and composition by Iris Weinstein